CPL TECH NAUMAN
CSS
RESCUE
139
GLOBAL
7500
C-FXA
JF-17 Fighter
YINGS - III
YINGS-III

FIZA'YA II

PAKISTAN AIR FORCE

1990-2025

BASSEM

FIZA'YA II

PAKISTAN AIR FORCE 1990-2025

Ravi Rikhye

Pushpindar Singh Chopra

KW Publishers Pvt Ltd
New Delhi

Reprint 2025

ISBN 978-81-975190-4-8 Hardback
ISBN 978-81-982677-9-5 ebook

Published in India by Kalpana Shukla

KW Publishers Pvt Ltd
4676/21, First Floor, Ansari Road
Daryaganj, New Delhi 110 002
Phone : +91 11 43528107
Production : kw@kwpub.in
Marketing : sanjeev@kwpub.in
Website : www.kwpub.in

Special Acknowledgement

to

VIKRAMJIT SINGH CHOPRA

Editor/Publisher

VAYU

Aerospace & Defence Review

1797

Contents

BLACK
SPIDERS
10-117

Acknowledgements

This work is dedicated to my colleague and late friend of 50 years, Pushpindar Singh Chopra. The Indian Air Force (IAF) was his first consuming passion. He was close to senior officers, and respecting their confidence meant he could not write much about what he knew. He had an encyclopaedic knowledge of the IAF, so much so that often the IAF had to consult him about its own history!

Once, British Aerospace brought its BAe 146 to India for a sales tour. I accompanied him for a demonstration flight from Safdarjung Airport. The BAe official mentioned this was the first time a jet had operated from the airport. Pushpindar got the dreamy look he did when recalling facts as if he was reading from an internal screen. "4-engine, yes. But first jet? No." An IAF fighter jet had to make an emergency landing, he said, giving the date, aircraft type, the nature of the emergency, the aircraft serial number along with the name of the pilot.

As an Order of Battle analyst, I had little interest in writing history, though I was an avid reader of war history. Pushpindar, however, was full of entrancing tales of the past and got me interested in writing about the field. His second love was the Pakistan Air Force, and due to his access to people all the way to the top he was the most informed private person on the subject. He sponsored and co-wrote my first history work, on the Pakistan Air Force (PAF) 1947-1990.

The book was balanced in its observation on PAF. Indeed, for one thing, the still-prevalent myth of Squadron Leader M. M. Alam shooting down five Indian Hunters in 5 minutes. In fact, Alam's 1965 war record was highly distinguished: he downed two Vampires in one action, and two Hunters over Sargodha. There was no need to embellish his fine record. Pushpindar was not about to publicise anyone's propaganda, and as a scholar, I insisted on seeing conclusive proof, which he provided. The Pakistan Air Force even has a large photo of him at Risalpur, from his 2004 visit. They appreciated his scrupulous fairness.

This fairness is to me the most important part of his legacy. He taught me to ditch my learned anti-Pakistan narratives on the India-Pakistan Wars. He never thought of the Pakistan armed forces as the enemy. To him, Pakistanis and Indians were brothers split by politics. I have written a series of three books on the India-Pakistan 1971 War and am working on a fourth. You will be hard put to find bias in *Fizaya,* our first book together. And there is none in this follow up, because this book is simply about Pakistan, not fraternal quarrels between the two sides.

Unfortunately, Pushpindar's belief that India and Pakistan were not enemies started eroding in India in the late 1980s. I have no intention of condemning anyone for this or playing *tu quoque,* so I will stop here.

Nonetheless, though rivers with bad blood have flowed since 1987, I still think Pushpindar was right. Few today accept his values. But they are the right ones.

I also wish to thank Pushpindar's sons, Vikramjit and Karanjit, and his grandnephew Angad, for carrying out his work and continuing to sponsor me. Many thanks to Kalpana Shukla of KW Publishers New Delhi for her endless patience with my idiosyncrasies! And my gratitude to Tom Cooper for permission to use his drawings.

When Pushpindar and I wrote the first volume of this work, covering the PAF 1947-90, detailed information was difficult to come by. The PAF, while more open than the IAF, still operated under the restrictive information rules of the British Raj. In 1990s more information became steadily available, not just on the internet, but from Pakistan itself. For example, in this book, we list PAF aircraft losses over several decades directly from Pakistan sources.

Equally important is that both India and Pakistan are more relaxed about talking to the press, and less prone to take offence if officially unapproved material gets published. In the IAF, at least, insiders are much more willing to talk in the background. Sometimes the talk is intended to trash a rival, but from the viewpoint of the air enthusiast, more information, no matter how obtained, is all for the greater good!

Figure: The classic Sabre on display. 1797 was at last in Faisal (Karachi). It was a Luftwaffe CL-13B transferred via Iran in 1967 and belonged to No. 5 Squadron at Masroor (Falcons). It is the second oldest PAF squadron. It flew the Tempest II, Hawker Sea Fury, F-86, CL-13B, F-104, Mirage III (four versions including photo-recon), and since 2010 has the F-16C/D Block 52+ and now at Shahbaz AB. S/L Sarfraz Rafique, who belonged to this squadron, in 1965 shot down two Indian Vampires over Chaamb and a Hunter over Halwara. His guns jammed, but he continued to cover his colleague Cecil Chaudhary and was shot down and killed at the age of 30. Photograph by Pushpindar Singh Chopra.

In 1990 the first volume was published without change, regardless of the sensitivities of the IAF. Twenty-plus years later the current IAF high command would likely be astonished at being told a previous generation had objected, quite vehemently, to the first volume. Indians are more confident today. The bogeyman is not Pakistan, but China. And given how small and short of resources Pakistan is compared to India, this is only sensible. I anticipate the second volume will ruffle no IAF feathers. Perhaps the IAF might even thank Pushpindar for what is a handy guide to today's PAF!

One last thing. Obviously, any mistakes in this book are mine, but I want to emphasise the difficulty for an amateur historian in obtaining material. Books and magazines cost money which s/he may not have. I no longer have access to intelligence sources. And—most frustrating—many Pakistani web sources don't work. So, this book has many limitations.

Introduction

The PAF reached its zenith in 1965. It was a small air force with about 150 combat aircraft, but carefully nurtured by the US. It was tightly geared to holding off China or Russia for the two weeks required for US reinforcements, but not to fight India. The PAF fought India anyway, and immediately suffered a cut-off of US aid until limited assistance was restored in the 1980s when the Soviets invaded Afghanistan.

The story of how Pakistan continued trying to get more US aircraft is a lengthy one, Pakistan remained frustrated till 1984, when a mere 40 F-16s started to come into service. Otherwise, the PAF had to make do with Mirage 3/5s, mostly second hand. In the 1990s the US insisted on cash. Even then the US embargoed 71 aircraft already paid including many already built. This was to pressure Pakistan to put its nuclear weapons program under US/IAEA control. Eventually in the 2000s the US agreed to sell Pakistan 36 F-16C for cash because it was Pakistan's insistent demand for its continued support of US forces in Afghanistan, of which Pakistan could afford only 18. It allowed the PAF to buy 14 Royal Jordanian F-16s, and update kits to bring all F-16s to Block 50 standards. In the 2010s it allowed Pakistan to obtain 28 of its own aircraft, returned from US storage. For the rest Pakistan bought the Chinese F-6 (MiG-19) and the F-7 (MiG-21).

The persistent blockades led Pakistan to design and build the JF-17 in cooperation with China. It entered PAF service in 2008 to become the PAF's mainstay. Meanwhile Pakistan continued rebuilding Mirage even as they fell out of sky due to wearing out. Then in 2022 it began procuring the Chinese JF-10 and went on to the upgrade the JF-17. Then it placed an early delivery order for the Chinese JF-31 in 2024. As of mid-2024, the PAF had eight JF-17 squadrons (including one in the Combat Commanders School); five F-16 (understrength); and three J-10 (two equipping or due to reequip). That leaves three with F-7/Mirage squadrons, towards its planned strength of 20 squadrons.

The problem for India is that it while it once had a 3-1 superiority in aircraft, now the Indian Air Force is dropping to 26 squadrons from about 42 at its peak (all figures approximated). In addition, China is building up the capacity of 8 airbases in the Tibet/Sinkiang region opposite India, each with 24 fighters, after arrival of fly-units. We don't know how many aircraft will go to PAF stations in wartime. This decline is due to delays in the Tejas light fighter program, purchase of only 36 Rafales. The ratio is now 1.5 – 1, but whereas earlier China was a nominal air enemy, it's now a real threat.

Meanwhile Pakistan is adding SAM batteries, a modest Search and Rescue element of 2-4 helicopters per main base, a tight multilayer radar network, and at least six UAV squadrons more including navy and army resources. PAF also has the advantage of a joint air defence network with navy, army, and air force fighter and missile networks.

Last, and perhaps most important, the PAF has only to focus on defence of one sector, the West. Aside from its alliance with China, Pakistan is building an offensive capability. Where is the Tejas? Just three squadrons to Pakistan's eight!

Tables and Figures

Tables

Figures

1

The PAF Versus the Afghan and Soviet Air Forces

At the time of finishing the first volume in 1989, little was known of the air engagements between the PAF and the Afghan and Soviet Air Forces. Today two excellent sources are available. The first is the PAF's own history, 'The Pakistan Air Force 1988-98: Against All Odds.'[1] The second is a multi-source account of the air war written by Cooper and Ali.[2] Their account is not, of course, as detailed as the official history, but it has the advantage of information from the Afghan and Soviet sides, including the air units involved.

The Pakistan Air Force faced five serious problems during the Afghan War:

- Lack of resources. When the First Afghan War began, the PAF lacked a single modern fighter. It was equipped with F-6s and had just one Mirage air superiority squadron (No. 18, which transitioned to F-7s before the end of the war). Taking on a superpower must have constituted a nerve-wracking experience for the PAF. And even when the US provided aircraft, it gave only 40 F-16s, just adequate for two squadrons.
- The air defence network was oriented toward the Indian frontier. Moreover, the mountainous Afghan border with its extensive radar-dead-zone was a challenge to cover in the absence of AEWs/AWACS. And PAF had only a handful of Crotale launchers, used to protect its main bases. The Crotale 2000 was a pedestrian SAM, likely purchased solely because it was cheaply available.
- Because of fears of escalation, the government imposed very tight and quite absurd Rules of Engagement on the PAF. The PAF fighters were not to open fire unless an elaborate chain-of-command gave permission.

Among other things, PAF was not to respond to incursions of less than 15 nm, where it was outnumbered more than 2:1, and when the debris could not be guaranteed to fall within Pakistan. The rules were relaxed during the end stages of the war.

- To meet these issues, the PAF developed the 'slash attack.' If a target was proceeding west-east, the attack was made on the vertical axis (north-south or vice versa), along the length of the border, to give interceptors maximum time to keep the target in view and to avoid inadvertently crossing into Afghanistan. This is a sub-optimal way to engage intruders.
- Because of extreme paranoia of India, particularly fears of an attack against its nuclear weapons facilities at Kahuta, the PAF believed it could not reduce its 'Eastcap'—Eastern Combat Air Patrols. It maintained a full alert posture against India. Even the squadrons assigned to 'Westcap'—Western Combat Air Patrols—were required to continue contributing to the defence of Kahuta. Readers familiar with India may be astonished at Pakistan's fears. Rumours of India permitting Israel to launch were based on complete fantasy, as was the hypothetical possibility India might attack Pakistan by itself. Nonetheless, the fears generated by India's Operations Brasstacks and Trident were evidence-based. Still, the possibility of a war with India surely did not require hyper-alertness because mobilization takes several weeks, and Pakistan would have had ample warning time.

Air-to-air Victories

PAF Part I gave the PAF six air-to-air victories with one own-goal loss. Later information says there were ten confirmed kills. Of these, in fairness to the adversary, three were transports, said to be on ELINT missions.[3] A more reasonable counting might be 7-1, an impressive total but with two qualifications.

- Six of the fighter kills were Afghan Air Force aircraft. There is little comparison between the highly trained PAF pilots and the Afghans. Cooper and Ali (2008) say:

  The few available reports from Russian sources indicate that Afghanis were excellent fliers, but terrible and undisciplined pilots and officers that would not care very much about tactics or weapons parameters. Certain is that after a series of coups and purges of the DRAAF during the 1970s the air force was weakened to a degree where it needed serious Soviet support to properly function. Nevertheless, the DRAAF apparently never lacked qualified fast-jet pilots.

- Second, the Pakistan side the aircraft were F-16s, a top-of-the-line air-to-air fighter, much superior to Afghanistan's MiG-23s and Su-22. These qualifications are not intended to diminish the PAF's achievement, only to put it in perspective.

One kill was a Soviet Air Force Su-25 *Frogfoot*, an inelegant NATO name surpassed only by the inelegance of the Soviets' own name, *Gvatch*. The pilot, a colonel, went on to become the then vice-president of Russia and was detained during the anti-Yeltsin coup. Released, he became a governor of a Russian province. He might have a good claim to being the 'future highest ranking' pilot shot down in the history of air warfare, behind President George H.W. Bush of the US[4] (President Bush lied about his age to join the Navy at age 17 and was shot down when he was 20).

An important point made clear by several sources is that while PAF pilots were forbidden to cross the border—as were Soviet pilots—on a number of occasions these orders were relaxed, or ignored, resulting in several PAF kills inside Afghanistan. This also included shot-down fighters that crashed inside Afghanistan, which the PAF did not claim for political reasons. It is likely, for example, that several more transport aircraft and helicopters were downed in Afghan airspace.

Westcap

PAF operations in the West were strictly defensive and designed to avoid inadvertent escalation. They were conducted under the general rubric of Westcap, Western CAP. The official history makes clear the tight restrictions imposed by the air defence controllers on the CAPs, in accordance with higher order. Naturally, the history says nothing about pilots who may have disregarded the orders deliberately or mistakenly. This is only to be expected.

For six years after the Soviet invasion of Afghanistan, the PAF exclusively used its second-line fighter the F-6 (MiG-19) to conduct CAPs along the Afghanistan border. Even to the end, the F-6 bore the brunt of Westcap efforts. The patrols were begun by the No. 15 Squadron (Peshawar), and later joined by the No. 23 Squadron (Samungli/Quetta). By May 1983 No. 17 Squadron took over from No. 23, and by October 1984 the No. 26 Squadron (Samungli/Quetta) arrived apparently to take over from the No. 23 Squadron. For almost four years the PAF was unable to attain control even of its own airspace on the Pakistan side of the border, but by 1984 had a good grip. Engagements with Soviet/Afghan fighters took place. Nonetheless, the F-6 was unable to attain any kills, in part due to the limitations of the aircraft, and in part because of restrictive Rules of Engagement. Until 1986 the PAF was required to follow civilian rules. Aircraft had to be identified, and permission was asked to engage, going all the way to the Deputy Air Chief of Staff! Usually, the intruders were well back in their own airspace by the time a decision was taken. Often the interceptors were told to escort the intruders back to their own airspace.

In 1986, Mirages from Nos. 5 to 18 Squadrons (Kamra) were deployed, but only for a short period. The No. 18 Squadron flew only 20 sorties, and the No. 5 only 108 sorties. Soviet/Afghan air attacks on refugee camps and Pakistani posts had become so numerous that the public demanded action. Why the Mirages were not sent in the first place and flown more is unclear to us. It is likely that these squadrons were reserved for the Eastcap, the defence of Lahore-Islamabad-Kahuta, which, presumably, had to be continually maintained because in the worst case, the PAF would get only a 3-minute warning of an impending attack. While the PAF did not claim any kills by Mirages, Cooper and Ali make clear engagements did take place, resulting in kills that crashed inside Afghanistan. Pakistan bloggers have claimed as many as 7 Mirage kills, which appears unlikely given the few CAPs mounted. Also, several additional claims by F-16s were disallowed by the PAF.

Now that the Soviet Union no longer exists, there seems to be no reason why the PAF should not declassify its records. Particularly as its total record is much higher than the official claims.

With the arrival of the F-16 to take over border CAPs, the balance shifted in Pakistan's favour. Eventually, Nos. 9 and 14 Squadrons were to fly 4000 sorties in three-and-a-half years and score all the acknowledged kills. This averaged 8 sorties a day, a considerable long-term burden for a force of just 28 fighters. No. 11 OCU also assisted. Some accounts say this squadron had one kill, but others dispute the matter. It is perhaps remarkable that just a handful of F-16s made such a large impact on operations, and this is a credit both to the PAF and the aircraft's designers.

Nos. 15 and 26 Squadrons flew 5000 sorties while Nos. 17 and 23 Squadrons flew 1350 sorties. The total given by the PAF historian was 10, 939 sorties and 13, 275 hours for Westcap. Naturally, with so few aircraft the PAF could nowhere near assure the integrity of the air frontier that continued to be systematically violated.

The air distance from Quetta to Peshawar is 600 km, indicating that a distance of 1200 km needed protection. Because the warning time was only minutes, it would seem that maintaining two continuous 2-ship CAPs 24 hours/day would require 35, 000 flying hours/year. Assuming that a limit of 300 hours/year per aircraft, 120 aircraft and about eight squadrons would have been required for Westcap alone. This is clearly impossible, given that the PAF had available 15 fighter squadrons, (5, 7, 8, 9, 11, 14, 15, 16, 17, 18, 19, 20, 22, 23, 25, 26). Of these No. 20 was a reconnaissance unit, No. 22 a training unit available as a combat squadron for short wars, and Nos. 11 and 25 were OCUs. Nos. 7, 8, 18, and 26 Squadrons were attack units (Mirage: Nos. 8 and 18; and A-5: Nos. 7 and 18). With just seven squadrons to cover both the Eastern and Western frontiers, Pakistan had to limit CAP coverage in the West.

Rather unusually, the PAF historian lists four engagements where kills were missed, and history has no hesitation in naming the pilots to blame. For example, one F-16 pilot forgot to adequately prepare his guns to fire and missed a kill. His Number 1's guns jammed due to an electrical fault. In another case, the pilot fired his Sidewinders at the absolute periphery of the missile's acquisition range and both missed. In writing histories, it is always productive to list what went wrong as much as what went right, providing learning opportunities for future generations. Though doubtless there were many more mess-ups than just four, the PAF is to be commended for its honesty.

Democratic Republic of Afghanistan Air Force 1988[5]

This was the peak strength of the Afghan Air Force, prior to the Soviet withdrawal.

232. OBVP 20 Mi-4, Mi-6, Mi-8 (Kabul IAP)

321. BAP 60 Su-22M-3K, Su-22M-4K, Su-17UM-2K (Bagram AB)

322. IAP 60 MiG-21MF/bis (four squadrons) stationed (Bagram AB), detachments elsewhere

332. OBVP Mi-8 helicopters stationed at Jurum

355. BAP 30 Il-28 and MiG-17 (Shindand) most Il-28s unrepairable

375. OBVP 25 Mi-24D/Mi-35V and Mi-8/17 (main base Mazar-e Sharif)

377. OBVP 25 Mi-35V, Mi-8, Mi-17 (Kabul IAP)

393. IAP 50 MiG-21MF/bis (Mazar-e Sharif)

377. OBVP 25 Mi-35V, Mi-8, Mi-17 (mainly at Kabul IAP) TAP with 40 An-2, Il-14, An-26/30/32 transports, (mainly Kabul IAP)

Soviet Air Force in the Afghanistan War, circa 1985

Initially, units were under the Air Force HQ 34th Corps. Then the corps was disbanded and units were put directly under the 40th Army (Temrez, then Kabul), making it the sole Soviet Army with integral air units.

Entering 1979-1980[6]

115. Guards Fighter Regiment

136. Regiment (fighter-bomber)

217. Regiment (fighter-bomber)

181. Regiment (helicopters)

280. Regiment (helicopters)

302. Separate Helicopter Squadron (attached to 5th Guards Division)

Mid-1980s[7]

378 Independent Attack Air Regiment with Su-25

3 fighter squadrons—until 1984 MiG-21bis of 927 Fighter Regiment, then MiG- 23ML of 905 FR

2 Fighter-Bomber squadrons with Su-17M3

263 Independent Recce squadron with Su-17M3R

Also:

190. IAP MiG-21 (stationed during the mid-1980s)

Fixed wing aircraft (1984)[8]

45 FLOGGER
90 FISHBED
90 Su-17
30 Su-25s
6 - 12 MiG-25s (FOXBAT B and D)

Departing (October 15, 1988)[9]

120th Aviation Regiment
134th Fighter Regiment
378th Separate Composite Aviation Regiment
263rd Separate Aerial Reconnaissance Squadron
254th, 262nd, 302nd Separate Helicopter Squadrons

This lineup excludes Tu-16 units that were frequently engaged in Afghanistan but flew from the Soviet Union:[10]

200th Heavy Bomber Regiment
251st Heavy Bomber Regiment

The above represents 450 reasonably modern Soviet and Afghanistan aircraft combined.

Evaluation

Pakistan versus a superpower

An evaluation of how a war was fought depends on three types of accounts: neutral, and from participants on either side. For the PAF's Afghanistan air war, we have only the official history. There is no significant material from the Afghans or the Soviets, nor is there sufficient interest for a neutral person to research the war. While the official history is surprisingly frank about pilot errors that enabled otherwise certain kills to escape, it must be assumed that it is cosmetically enhanced, with mistakes played down or washed from the picture, and with a focus on success. Nonetheless, some conclusions can be drawn.

On its western border, Pakistan faced a superpower. It may be agreed that the superpower was seriously preoccupied with the Afghan War and had little time to concern itself about Pakistan. Yet, from Pakistan's side, the overriding reality was that it was a willing base to support the insurgents in Afghanistan. As such, it was an active participant, providing money, logistic support, training, and leadership, both tactical and strategic, to the insurgents. For example, several thousand Pakistan army regulars operated with the insurgents inside Afghanistan.

Perhaps two decades after the end of the war—and of the Soviet Union, to us in India the possibility of a major Soviet invasion of Pakistan seems remote, from the Pakistan viewpoint it was an ever-present possibility. As an analogy, let us assume that Tibet revolts against China, and India is the primary supporter of the rebels, backed by the US. Sitting in New Delhi would anyone be nonchalant about the possibility of major Chinese retaliation? This seems unlikely. Even if the US provides assurances to India that it will come to our help, it is impossible to imagine India taking on the Chinese in the manner Pakistan took on the Soviet Union.

Like it or not, Pakistan should be given credit for facing down, in its small way, the Soviet Union. Perhaps long decades of facing India as a much larger adversary gave Pakistan some confidence in the matter.

Making do

The PAF's readiness to do what it could with what it had was impressive. The PAF accepted its limitations and spent its time showing the Soviet/Afghan air forces that the latter could not violate Pakistan air space with impunity. But it also lay low until the F-16s arrived, and only then became more aggressive in defending its space.

Careful planning and training

The official history underlines a constantly recurring theme: the PAF may have lacked resources, but the hallmark of its operations was careful planning and training. An example is that though the F-16 started arriving in Pakistan in 1983, it was not committed to combat until 1986 despite the dire need.

A second example is Pakistan's rejection of the US attempts to give it F-5s and A-10s in place of the F-16s. Even though the aircraft were almost free, PAF refused because the lower-capability aircraft were not within the parameters of its long-range planes. Also offered was the A-7, which the

US had agreed to sell in the 1970s and then backed down because Pakistan refused to accept limitations on its nuclear program. The F-20 Tigershark was also suggested by the US and ultimately refused by the PAF. It wanted the F-16, nothing less. Then the US tried to push the F-16 with a reduced-power engine and older radar. Pakistan again refused. Bargaining rigorously with a superpower especially when Pakistan was in severe need took a lot of determination. Pakistan's stand may be contrasted with the casual manner in which the Indian Government and IAF obtained the Su-7 from the Soviet Union.[11] The IAF had no requirement for this aircraft, but it was offered at the throwaway price of US$ 1 million, flyaway to an arms purchase mission that had come to buy other equipment. As if by magic, the Su-7 appeared in the IAF with everyone scratching their heads as to the how and the why.[12] Pakistan has always been concerned with the system cost vs capability gained, rather than the price of the aircraft.

A third example of careful planning and training is the MiG-29/BVR scare. Pakistan received information leading it to believe that the Soviets were about to introduce the MiG-29/Beyond-Visual-Range Missile combination into the Afghanistan theatre. The PAF pilots initiated research into tactics to counter this threat. Though not specified by the official history, and therefore leaving open the suspicion the PAF has engaged in hyperbole, the tactics were introduced. Later, the Combat Commander School validated the tactics and began teaching them to other squadrons.

In the event, the Soviets did not introduce the MiG-29/BVR into Afghanistan. One is forced to wonder if Pakistan overreacted, as was the case when it believed it had hard information that India and Israel were about to strike its nuclear infrastructure, where in reality there was only much speculation in the press, itself fired by the Israeli 1981 strike against Iraq's Osirak nuclear reactor. India's position on nuclear weapons has been quite different from that of the West, particularly of the US. India believes everyone has a legitimate right to nuclear weapons, including Pakistan. India has never been in the business of hypocritically deciding that some N-powers were acceptable because they were 'good' such as Israel and South Africa, and others were 'bad.' To imagine India would just lash out without warning in a preemptive attack is so unrealistic it does not merit serious discussion. To imagine further that India would collaborate with Israel, the Arab world's prime enemy, and simply abandon its long-standing and deep ties with the latter is even more fantastic.

Nevertheless, the intent here is to show that the PAF does not waste time when it feels a threat is developing. The Indian Air Force, along with the rest of the government is, in this respect, the polar opposite of the PAF. The IAF waits until—metaphorically—its airfield is under attack before mooting the idea to think about forming a committee to recommend proposing a study about what needs to be done about the threat. The classic example of this is that it has taken *fifty years*—half-a-century—to start hardening aircraft against China in the Northeast!

In conclusion, it is of interest to note that the US Stingers were not the first shoulder-fired SAMs in service with the Afghan rebels. Cooper and Ali (1988) mention a Pakistan Army unit in Afghanistan that used the UK Blowpipe in a futile attempt to down Soviet/Afghan aircraft and helicopters. Cooper is a meticulous researcher who has wide access to Pakistan, Afghanistan and Russian sources and should be taken seriously.

Entirely on another note, the PAF is at least as bad as the IAF when it comes to studying other countries' air wars. The PAF official historian asserts that "The air effort rates generated by the Russo-Afghan Air Forces must not have been less than those generated by the Americans in Vietnam." To those unfamiliar with South Asia, this may seem a peculiar thing to say, but it is quite typical of our people to pull figures out of the air. The US air war in Second Indochina is well known as the largest in world history after 1939-1945. At the peak of the air war in 1969, the US/Vietnam probably had 8000 aircraft and helicopters committed to the theatre.

Table 1.1: US/RVN aircraft in Indochina Theatre at peak

USAF (including Thailand and Guam)	1900[13]
Marines	500[14]
Navy	500[15]
Army	3900[16]
Long range transports	400
RVN	900[17]
Total	**8100**

The total figure is not entirely accurate because it represents the peak for each service and the peaks were at different times. Still, taking 7500 aircraft, this is 17 times the Soviet/Afghan air total.

There is no intent to diminish the PAF's Afghanistan War effort, but the reality is that the Soviets fought the Afghan War with shocking casualness. For example, they committed a peak of just 6 divisions to the theater at a time the Soviet Army likely had 210 active and reserve divisions, excluding artillery divisions. The Soviets had over 9000 aircraft excluding trainers;[18] sending 300 to a country just across from its borders again shows a complete lack of interest in the war.

Notes

1. A. Rashid Shaikh, Air Marshal. (2000). The Story of the Pakistan Air Force, 1988-1998: A Battle Against Odds. Shaheen Foundation (Islamabad: Pakistan). 414 pages
2. (Ali) Cooper, A. Rashid Tom and Ali, K. Shaiz. Afghanistan 1979-2001 Part 1. Warwick, UK: Helion and Company, 2008.
   Cooper, Tom and Ali, K. Shaiz. 2008. *Afghanistan, 1979-2001*; *Part 1.* Also available online at www.acig.info
3. "Pakistan Border Battles", n.d. Pakistan Military Consortium. http://www.pakdef.info/pakmilitary/airforce/war/indexafghanwar.html (This URL currently does not point to the right page, though the Consortium is active.)
4. President G.H.W. Bush was commissioned in 1943 as probably the youngest aviator in the US Navy. https://www.history.navy.mil/content/history/nhhc/research/histories/biographies-list/bios-b/bush-george-h-w.html. His biographer, James Meechum, speculates Bush might have been the youngest flying officer in the US Navy Siegel, Rachel. 2018. "For George H.W. Bush, Pearl Harbor Changed Everything, and World War II Made Him a Hero." Washington Post, December 1, 2018. https://www.washingtonpost.com/history/2018/12/01/george-hw-bush-pearl-harbor-changed-everything-world-war-ii-made-him-hero/?noredirect=on. Aug 29 16:23:24 EDT 2019
5. Cooper, Tom. 2008. Afghanistan, 1978-2001 Part II. Air Combat Information Group. Downloaded August 18, 2012. http://www.acig.info/CMS/index.php?option=com_content&task=view&id=158&Itemid=47.
6. Contributors. 2011. "армия в составе Туркестанского военного округа СССР (1979-1989). основа Ограниченного контингента советских войск в Афганистане." Translate.goog. Фонд Викимедиа. February 6, 2011. https://ru-m-wikipedia-org.translate.goog/wiki/40-%D1%8F_%D0%BE%D0%B1%D

1%89%D0%B5%D0%B2%D0%BE%D0%B9%D1%81%D0%BA%D0%BE%D0%B2%D0%B0%D1%8F_%D0%B0%D1%80%D0%BC%D0%B8%D1%8F?_x_tr_sl=ru&_x_tr_tl=en&_x_tr_hl=en&_x_tr_pto=sc.

7. Hist2004 (2004, 02-06) Afghanistan/Chechnya Order of Battle
8. Stadler, K. (1985) Air War in Afghanistan. *Marine Corps Staff and Command College* http://www.globalsecurity.org/military/library/report/1985/SKJ.htm
9. Grau, Lester W. 2007. "Breaking Contact without Leaving Chaos: The Soviet Withdrawal from Afghanistan." The Journal of Slavic Military Studies 20 (2): 235–61. https://doi.org/10.1080/13518040701373080.
10. Unknown. 2012. "✈ OKBTupolev ✈: Aircraft Tu-16." ✈ OKBTupolev ✈. May 24, 2012. http://okbtupolev.blogspot.com/2012/05/aircraft-tu-16.html.
11. Chopra, P. *A Whale of a Fighter*. 1983. The source reference is Bharat-Rakshak, which used information from the book to write an extensive article. https://www.bharat-rakshak.com/IAF/aircraft/past/sukhoi-7.html You might be unable to reach this URL, in which case go to forum.
12. Peripherally, Chopra, who was the closest the IAF has to an official historian, contests figures that were given to many people (including one of us, Ravi), of 34-36 losses. Chopra says losses were 14. Oddly, the Soviet air attaché in Delhi, in a conversation with Ravi, did not contest the higher number. He attributed the high losses to the IAF habit of making repeated passes over target from the same direction, permitting Pakistan flak to acquire and kill the attackers. Nonetheless, as Chopra notes, a 14 aircraft loss in a war where the IAF flew 500 sorties a day and the Su-7 was used extensively, is quite modest.
13. Correll, J. (2004, December). The Air Force in the Vietnam War. The Air Force Association. Original URL downloaded April 17, 2012 http://www.afa.org/mitchell/reports*/1204vietnam.pdf.* New URL http://higherlogicdownload.s3.amazonaws.com/AFA/6379b747-7730-4f82-9b45-a1c80d6c8fdb/UploadedImages/Mitchell%20Publications/The%20Air%20Force%20and%20the%20Vietnam%20War.pdf
14. Estimated
15. US Navy committed five aircraft carriers, each with 100 aircraft, to Yankee station in the South China Sea. Three carriers were continuously on station, two on rotation between Yankee station and Japan/Philippines for replenishment and rest.
16. Texas Tech University (n.d.) The Vietnam War Archive. Chapter 6: "Air Operations". [The information is from a declassified US *Marine Corps document]* http://www.virtual.vietnam.ttu.edu/cgi-bin/starfetch.exe?5mju6E.goHR01.v3PwY3e7uyVHOQSPX.FnipLAqtzYafvnn4bKGmVGY6QDInkvwg9yX92EQO0@n1gnscmDwCK6uBq19PjJ3Iu4LYoKc51KFUgjdWfGontQ/1201067181.pdf
17. South Vietnamese Air Force had 500 helicopters, 300 fighter aircraft, 100 transports.

18. Global Security (2011, September 7) Air Forces. The tally of Soviet aircraft can be found by clicking on Home-> Military -> World -> Russia -> Aircraft -> Agencies -> Air Force. Downloaded June 9, 2012. Agencies :: Air Force :: http://www.globalsecurity.org/military/world/russia/av-main.htm

2

1990-2000

The official PAF historian calls the years 1988-98 "the chequered decade." In 1988, President General Zia-ul-Haq was killed when his C-130 was sabotaged and it crashed. He was returning to Islamabad with several US and Pakistan officials after witnessing trials of the US M-1 tank in Multan—the President was an armored corps officer commissioned into the 6th Lancers shortly before independence. The suspicion in that the bomb was hidden in a crate of mangos loaded at the last minute. His death created major political instability in Pakistan, which continued through several years and was seen as big blow to the Pakistan military.

At the other end of the chequered decade came 1998 when Pakistan allegedly staged five nuclear tests and became an official nuclear weapon power. The word 'allegedly' is necessary because there was considerable debate in the Indian scientific community as to if these were successful tests. But that need not detain us because the Government of India immediately accepted Pakistan's nuclear status. Pakistan considered this as a major triumph and saw it as neutralizing an increasingly militarily strong India determined to be acknowledged as the predominant Indian Ocean power.

(Conversely, an Indian nuclear scientist who supervised the preparations of the 1998 Indian tests expressed doubts regarding the Indian thermonuclear, saying that the yield was much below expectation.[1] He was supported by Western and a leading Indian scientist who says the yield was 20-KT and not 45-KT as was announced by India. The government of India denied this which is akin to denying that the sun rises and sets every day. Dr K. Santhanam had been deeply involved in developing Indian nuclear weapons and was a man of impeccable integrity and patriotism. He was no dove; he wanted MORE tests since the thermo-nuclear one did not work).

From any realistic angle, however, the period 1990-2000 was disastrous for the Pakistan Air Force. An air force exists to fly. To fly it needs aircraft. And Pakistan's fighter aircraft procurement plans were thrown into disarray because of US embargoes imposed subsequent to the N-tests. Before going into this story in detail, a summary of PAF procurement plans is useful.

The 1988 Procurement Plan

Looking ahead twenty years, Pakistan decided on a force structure of:

- 111 F-16s
- 95 F-7Ps
- 100 Mirage III/Vs [2]

This total of about 300 fighters was thought adequate to defend against an Indian Air Force total of about 700 fighters around 2000. Why 300 aircraft? We can only speculate. The primary constraint on the PAF, in 1988 as always, was resources. The Army, of necessity, gets the bulk of Pakistan's resources. But to the extent that Pakistan could also have procured more F-7s, it probably felt that 300 was a reasonable minimum.

In 1965, Pakistan had 170 combat aircraft to India's 500, or a 1:3 ratio. In 1971 it had about the same ratio, 250 to 750. In 1965, Pakistan did not suffer from the discrepancy because India diverted 9 of its 23 combat squadrons to the China front, so the ratio was 1:2. Pakistan enjoyed other advantages which were mentioned in Part I of *Fizaya*: air-to-missiles, an efficient air defence radar system, and well-trained pilots (India was in the middle of its post-1962 expansion). In 1971, the IAF had about 500 combat aircraft in the West compared to Pakistan's perhaps 230, also a 1:2 ratio. In the East, however, Pakistan was outnumbered 10-1 in terms of squadrons. A plan to station an F-6 (MiG-19) squadron in the East never materialised. India would still have handily won the air war in the East; except its air losses would have been heavier. In 1971, the IAF completely outclassed the PAF in terms of equipment, and its pilots were now fully trained.

So, whereas a 1:2 ratio sufficed for a PAF success in 1965, it was inadequate in 1971. Currently, there has been yet another reversal. Assuming for simplicity that in a 2015 scenario India would keep five squadrons in the Northeast, the ratio again would be 1:2. But this time the quality of PAF aircraft would be much better equipped, with an air defence system well-tested by the Afghanistan War.

A recapitulation is necessary of why Pakistan feels comfortable with a 1:2 disadvantage. First, the PAF is primarily a defensive force, requiring fewer aircraft than the IAF, which places as much attention on ground attack as on-air defence. When resources are limited, the PAF's strategy is a sensible one. Second, correctly or otherwise, the PAF has always believed it has better pilots and the advantage of quality. Third, and this may be conceded, the PAF has traditionally been a more efficient organisation than the IAF, which despite its troubles is one of the biggest in the world and is sprawled across a land area five times larger than Pakistan. This requires many more fighters and SAMs than Pakistan. Because of India's northern commitments, the IAF also requires far more helicopters and transports. When one air force is built around 5-6 main bases, and another built around 25-30, perforce the larger air force's organisation will be more inefficient. It may also be added because the IAF has never faced the resource shortage experienced by the PAF from its birth, it's imperative to be as efficient as possible.

A last and subtle factor may be mentioned. This is the PAF's perception of itself vs the IAF, justified or not, is the moral/psychological factor, which cannot be quantified, but definitely exists. The PAF is publicly tight-lipped. The IAF, however, belongs to the 'let it all hang out' school. This is inevitably because India is a democracy with strong institutions while Pakistan has been a dictatorship as often as it has been a democracy. Even its democratic phases have been limited because the Army stands behind the politicians, looking over their shoulders to guide them at every stage. This creates a global impression that is favourable to the PAF as a tough, tight, scrappy air force, whereas the IAF is perceived as prone to accidents, bloated and inefficient. To what extent these images play into the PAF's self-image and influences its force structure is impossible to say, because these are subjective matters. But it seems likely they do play some part.

The Pressler Amendment devastates PAF planning

That the US Congress, press, and public knew about Pakistan's effort to develop N-weapons is no secret. As early as 1984, Senator Alan Cranston of California issued a highly-exaggerated report of Pakistan's capabilities, which had the country producing N-weapons on an 'assembly line' basis. This was amusing, as at the time and for years later Pakistan had no capability even for one weapon on its own. But the report played into the Indian Government narrative of Pakistan as a regional nuclear threat; and in any case it is not for the Indians to issue a countervailing report saying that a true Pakistan capability was probably 15-20 years in the future.[3]

Naturally, during the Afghanistan War, the US did not make an issue of Pakistan's N-program. But with the Soviet withdrawal completed, the US exhibited its usual disdain for vassal states by forbidding the delivery of any more F-16s. Pakistan had received 40, was due to receive 11 more for attrition replacements and to properly fill out its force, and ordered 60 more, paid for by its own funds, for a total of 111. Sometimes 113 F-16s are mentioned, likely a misprint.

The US, which is the first country to insist on the sanctity of contracts, not only broke its contract with Pakistan, but in an amazing act of fraudulence, refused to return Pakistan's money! As if this indefensible action was insufficient, the US started charging Pakistan money for aircraft constructed and put in storage! The US has never explained this astonishing behavior. Nor has this served as any warning to India, which, in the 21st Century, has been happily making multi-billion-dollar defence deals with the US. The Indians have been lulled by agreements with the US Government saying no restrictions will be placed on deliveries and necessary spares. But these agreements are not worth the paper they are written on, because the US Congress can at any time order the government to freeze or cancel deals.

Pakistan switches to more F-7s

To help make up for the non-availability of the F-16s, the PAF decided to buy 135 F-7s instead of Plan 1988's 95 aircraft. In 2000, yet another batch of aircraft was ordered, 57 F-7PG including seven trainers. This brought the total buy to around 190.

Table 2.1: PAF F-7 acquisitions

1988	20 plus four 2-seat trainers = 24 (No. 20 Squadron)
1988-89	60
1990-92	15 trainers
1993	40
2000	50 F-7PG, 7 trainers, No. 17 and 26 squadrons

The new aircraft equipped eight squadrons plus one squadron of the Combat Commanders School.

Eventually, 45 more aircraft were delivered through 2002, for a total of 235. Attrition, as we shall see from the PAF accident list, was low. The first 120 aircraft were P models for Pakistan while the last 60 were PG models, substantially superior to the P model.

The F-7s provenance comes from the Russian MiG-21. In 1961, the Soviets sold a complete production line to China. The F-7 has over 55 domestic and export variants, so keeping track of how the PAF aircraft are equipped is not easy. At any rate, in the 1980s, China embarked on a westernised version of the F-7, to appeal to air forces unused to Chinese equipment. This was the F-7M Airguard. The F-7 Skybolt is derived from the Airguard and is more advanced. Simultaneously, China began, with Pakistan, the Sabre II project, which, while the airframe and engine were of F-7 stock, was to be a Generation 4 fighter.

While the table below represents our best effort to sort out the different versions and different aircraft, readers should keep in mind that the distinction between the Super 7 and Sabre II is unclear.[4]

Table 2.2: Chinese F-7 versions actual and planned for PAF
F-7 versions for Pakistan

F-7	Basic Chinese MiG-21; WP-7 engine, 12,700-lb.s.t. on afterburner; 1 × 30mm with 60 rounds; 2 × AAM (short-range)
F-7M[5]	More powerful engine. Updated electronics (provided by UK's GEC): improved ranging radar, a head-up display weapon aiming computer (HUDWAC), an identification friend-or-foe (IFF) system, an air-data computer, a radar altimeter, and other improvements to the basic airframe. WP-7N engine; 13,450 lb.s.t. on afterburner.
F-7P	24 modifications for PAF, improved F-7M
F-7PG	Improved F-7P for PAF (G = gai, meaning improved); same as F-7MG; WP-13F engine, 14,650 lb.s.t. on afterburner; 2 x 30mm with 60 rounds each.

Sabre II	Radical update of F-7; terminated because of Tiananmen Square; Pakistan decided on cheaper F-7P, $4-million flyaway 1st batch; F-4-4 class engine, ~17,000 lb.s.t. on afterburner
Super 7	Redesigned nose to accommodate F-20 Tigershark avionics; GE 404 or PW 1120 engine, APG-66 radar. F-16 class. USD 10 million-unit cost. Grumman, China Aircraft Corporation, and PAF. Rejected by PAF in 1990; also, Tiananmen Square event forced Grumman to pull out of partnership with China. 1987-1990.

Pakistan inducted two versions of the F-7 in service: F-7P and F-7PG, about 120 and 60 aircraft respectively. There is mention in the literature of the F-7MP, which is clearly the -7M version for Pakistan.

F-7P

Addition of a Martin-Baker Mk. 10 ejection seat and the capacity to carry four AAMs, rather than only two for the F-7M. Total 24 modifications over F-7M, specific to PAF.

F-7PG

For orthographic and internal views to compare to F-7P, visit PAF Falcons.[6] The F-7PG has a double-delta wing with an aspect ratio of 2.4. As explained by the website PAF Falcons, the F-7MG airframe has essentially the same F-7P fuselage, inner wing portion, tail plane and fin. "The outer wing section incorporates the major change, with a reduced 42° sweep and automatic manoeuvring flaps. The F-7MG uses an improved and more powerful WP-13 engine, which is also operational on the F-7III (Chinese version of the MiG-21MF). Additionally, cockpit layout, avionics and several ancillary systems have been changed, in line with modern trends. The important systems that remain unchanged (compared to the F-7P) are the fuel system, weapons payload capacity and internal guns."[7]

A delta wing is good for high speeds, but a problem for keeping the nose up during low-speed manoeuvers. The regular wing is good for low-speed manoeuvers. So, the double delta is a compromise, and the PAF claims a greatly enhanced performance in the transonic regime, where much air combat takes place. It should be kept in mind that the MiG-21 was designed as a daylight high-performance, point-defence, single pass interceptor operating under ground control.[8] The clean endurance was around 30 minutes and fell below that if the afterburner was used. It was simple and cheap, in keeping with the Soviet weapons design philosophy of its time the 1950s.

That was both the time of bombers, with the US alone deploying something approaching 2000 B-47s and B-52s, and of lessons learned from Korea. As an air-superiority fighter, the F-7/MiG-21s armament of 60 x 30mm rounds and two short-range AAMs was perfectly adequate for its mission. It was task-specific, not a multi-purpose fighter, and again, in line with Soviet practice, was not over-designed as is the case with Western aircraft, particularly American. The MiG-21 was intended to make one pass, at most two, amounting to 5 minutes of combat, before shortage of fuel compelled it to break away and head home.

The aircraft can be compared to the US F-104, its contemporary, which started as the simplest possible lightweight air superiority fighter—the A version. It then became a ground-attack aircraft with its C version. And last, it morphed into a very sophisticated multipurpose fighter/ground-attack/nuclear weapons delivery platform, in its G version. Of course, the Americans being the Americans, could not resist the most advanced cannon possible, the M61 6-barrel Gatling gun with an enormous load of 725×20mm rounds!

But with the passage of time, as happened with the F-104, there were demands to turn the F-7 into an all-weather air superiority and ground attack fighter. In that sense, the F-7PG represents the final evolution of the MiG-21, and with Western avionics it may be rated as having a performance somewhere between an F-7 and an F-17.

Table 2.3: Comparison between F-7P and F-7PG[9]

Parameter	F-7P	F-7PG
Improvement in rate-of-turn		33 per cent to 66 per cent (5,000 & 15,000-feet) AMSL
Take off speed	310 kmph	280 kmph
Take-off length		35 per cent less than F-7P
Landing speed	290 kmph	270 kmph
Safe entry into loop	800 kmph at 5000 feet AMSL	600 kmph at 5000 feet AMSL
Radar	Grifo 7 (retrofitted)	Grifo 7
AAM	Sidewinder AIM-9L all-aspect	Sidewinder AIM-9L all aspect
Thrust-to-weight ratio	0.8	0.9

Mirage 3/5s

A fascinating aspect of the PAF's "chequered decade" was its push to build up its Mirage force as a way of overcoming its equipment deficiencies. This story is worth telling because it typifies the PAF determination to do the best possible with few financial resources.

As related in *Fizaya* Part I, the Mirage III entered service starting in 1968, when 24 D, E, and R versions were ordered. To counter the IAF buildup—by 1971 the IAF had 8 MiG-21 and 6 Su-7 squadrons—would have required at least 100 Mirages to offset. But for an air force used to paying nothing for its aircraft, the ~ USD 75 million required for 24 aircraft represented was a big financial stretch. Though in today's money that sum is only half-a-billion dollars, Pakistan's GDP that year was only USD 8 billion.[10] The deal as a percentage of the GDP was equal to USD 2 billion in today's GDP, a substantial amount. More than that, for 15 years the PAF aircraft/spares acquisition budget was near zero, as everything came under the US Military Assistance Program. The budgetary shock must have been substantial, even for this tiny number of aircraft.

Table 2.4: Mirage 3/5 purchases

Year	Aircraft
1967	18×3E, 3×3D, 3×3RP new (Indian Intelligence estimates 4 aircrafts from there are reports that 28 aircraft were bought.)
1973	28×5PA2 and 5PA3
1975	10×3RP new
1990	50×3O, 3D from Australia, 45 put into service
1996	34×5F, 6×3D from surplus French stocks, 20 put into service
2000	9×3EL, ex Lebanon, 600 to 1000 hours on airframes
2004	50×5DA ex Libya (3E with 5 engine), 150 engines (many sealed packages) mostly for spares
2004	33×5F ex France, at least 14 put into service

In all, the PAF purchased around 235 Mirages over a 27-year period.

The PAF, as usual, bargained hard. It obtained the Australian Mirages along with a large quantity of spares for just ~USD 23 million (Exchange rate USD 1 = AUD 1.28). And that too was a 7-year loan! Under Pakistan's peculiar budgetary process, half was paid from the PAF budget and half by the Government of Pakistan.

Another example of the unusual Pakistan defence budgetary process is the purchase of the Mistral SAM in 1991 which was affected by the PAF from its own budget, and later compensated by the Government of Pakistan. This raises a question. The Government of India would be most loathed to delegate comparable authority to the IAF. In 2012, after vocal criticism of the then MOD procurement policy, the limits on what services can purchase without higher clearance was lifted to about US$ 4 million per item. But this was for emergency purchases of spares. It is inconceivable that the IAF could, on its own, order two squadrons of Mistrals or equivalent.

Doubtless, the dual budget process leads to corruption. But as the Australian Mirage process shows, this also creates a sense of ownership, at least for the PAF. In the 1996 purchase of 40 Mirage 5s from the French Air Force, surplus stocks were priced at $150 million, including upgrades. The IAF would have simply put the figure before the government and stepped back. But the PAF bargained the French down to $125 million! When the French offered to sell 40 Mirage 2000s in the late 1990s for a negotiated price of $4 billion, the PAF insisted that the total include half a billion dollar update of the air defence system. The Pakistanis often derogatorily refer to the Indian '*bania* (trader) mentality,' but the only thing the Indians are good at is paying more than the contract agreement. The PAF would seem to outdo any Indian government *baniyas*.

The ROSE modernisation program (Retrofit of Strike Element)

This program was designed to bring second-hand Mirages up to reasonably modern standards by retrofitting electronic systems. The program substantially enhanced the PAF's ground-attack capability. Aircraft retrofitted were intended to serve for 10 years in the PAF, thus bridging the gap until the arrival of the F-17 Thunder. It seems that the retrofitted aircraft were issued to three existing and one newly formed squadron. The rest of the 180 aircraft purchased from Australia, France, and Lebanon were used to replace attrition and out-of-life aircraft or for spares.

Mirage IIIO ROSE I

Under this version, 33 ex-Australian Mirage 3s were upgraded. This process included at least two upgrades and included:

- Grifo M3 radar (Some problems surfaced later but the PAF said it resolved the issues)
- New HUD
- New HOTAS (Hands on Throttle and Stick), useful for High-G manoeuvering
- New Multi-function displays
- Inertial navigation system linked to GPS (SAGEM nav/attack)
- New Radar Warning Receiver
- New ECM suite
- New system for dispensing chaff and flares
- Air-to-air refuelling

The Grifo M3 provides Beyond Visual Range capability.

Mirage 5F ROSE II

This upgrade was applied to twenty aircraft from the batch of 40 purchased in 1995 and provided the PAF with a true night strike capability for the first time.

- Forward-Looking Infra-Red (FLIR) system by SAGEM
- Digital avionics by SAGEM
- GPS navigation
- Radar Warning Receiver/chaff and flare defence
- EW system
- HUD
- HOTAS
- Night Vision Goggles

Mirage 5F ROSE III

The third and last upgrade was applied to 14 of 33 ex-French Mirage 5Fs and issued to a new No. 27 Squadron ('Zarrar') for night strike. The main modification was the installation of a new SAGEM nav/attack avionics suite.

Search for new aircraft

The PAF appeared to have attained a brief relief from the US embargo thanks to the 1996 Brown Amendment. This allowed the delivery of withheld aircraft and spares, but without the vital F-16s. The amendment was helpful to the PAF; but in 1998, after Pakistan's nuclear tests, the Glenn amendment again terminated all deliveries. The unreliability of the US as a supplier was revealed when in 2002 discussions began on restarting deliveries. In a period of 12 years, the US changed its mind four times. We are left wondering at the enormous strain this must have imposed on the PAF's planners. Nevertheless, very quickly after the Pressler Amendment was enacted, the PAF began its search for alternatives.

MiG-29 and Su-27

Discussions on these two aircraft began in 1991 and ended finally in 1997 when Moscow announced it would not sell military equipment to Pakistan. The decision was in deference to India. Nonetheless, it is also clear that the PAF did not find the aircraft suitable, at least in the configuration offered.[11] Nor, apparently, were the Russians serious about selling the aircraft. They refused to provide documentation, would not make the aircraft available to Pakistan for testing, either in Pakistan or overseas, and generally dragged their feet. When they did agree to let Pakistan fly the two types, the PAF rejected them.

From this arises two questions. First, how is it that when Pakistan did not think enough of the MiG-29 and Su-27 to buy them, why did India so happily agree to their purchase? Was there some essential deficiency to the aircraft or were they simply unsuitable for Pakistan service? Second, a school of thought saying the Russians were merely playing the Indians using fake discussions with Pakistan. They knew from the start that India was by far the much larger market and had no intention of jeopardising their relationship with India, which extended far beyond just the Su-27/30. But they kept telling the Indians that they had Pakistan as a customer, and if India wanted exclusivity, it had better order fast and orders lots of aircraft. Perhaps it is not a coincidence that India signed a contract in 1996 and that shortly thereafter the Russians told Pakistan they had cancelled any potential sale for political reasons. If this is correct, did India lower its standards to accommodate the aircraft? At the very least it would have compromised India's will to negotiate a better deal.

J-39 and Mirage 2000

Some maintain the Swedish J-39 Gripen is the finest light fighter in the world. Certainly, Sweden offered the aircraft at an attractive price. But 20 per cent of its components were American, and the Pressler restrictions made a sale impossible.

The Mirage 2000 was probably the most thoroughly-tested aircraft the PAF has sought. Before it decided on the F-16, it had found the Mirage 2000 inferior for its purposes. In 1985 and 1987 the aircraft was tested again to see if the manufacturer had remedied the shortcomings. The PAF remained dissatisfied and decided to go ahead with an F-16 purchase using its own funds. After Pressler, in 1992, the PAF tested the -2000E, and found it was not up to specification. The price was also much too high. In 1995, Pakistan was ready to buy the -2000V version, but the Government of Pakistan said it lacked the necessary resources.

Aside from which Pakistan had made the decision to go in with China on the Super-7, from which evolved the FC-1/F-17 on which ultimately Pakistan settled. The F-17 story is detailed under the section 2000-2010.

Other Pressler-created difficulties

The PAF leased a number of T-37s that were the backbone of its training program. Development of a replacement trainer, the K-8, was begun in 1984, but the process was slow and only six aircraft were inducted by 1994, ten years later. Of course, the Indian aeronautical industry takes 20-30 years to bring anything into service. The point here is that when the T-37 lease expired, it could not be renewed and the aircraft had to be put into storage in Pakistan. This upset the training program. Eighteen T-33s were operated by the PAF for photo-recon and target towing. With spares cut off, the PAF could not afford to maintain the aircraft and they had to be phased out.

The PAF had 16 C-130s. Without the US spares, the fleet began to run down. The same thing happened to the TPS-43 air defence radars and automated air defence system.

Pakistan took immediate advantage of the minor relaxation of the US arms embargo permitted by the 1996 Brown Amendment. Though it could not obtain any of the mothballed F-16s, it accepted all the spares it had bought for the first batch of F-16s, and rejected spares purchased for the embargoed aircraft. Here, again, is an example of the PAF's negotiating toughness and its ability to move fast—Brown was implemented in February, and all deals had to complete by end-1996 to fall within the Brown window. Pakistan did not entirely get its way because it was forced to accept components with expired shelf lives.

Prior to this short respite, Pakistan had been buying F-16 spares from where it could get them and even embarked on an upgrade. The Pressler amendment did not prohibit Pakistan from buying spares on the commercial market. In some cases, prices were five time those of the government-to-government rate.

New purchases

Pakistan's purchases during this period included:

- 93 Mirage 3/5s, second hand, about 50 were upgraded
- 57 F-7PG new from China
- 55 F-7P new from China
- 2 squadrons of Mistral SAMs, possibly six flights each of five launch stations
- 1 Crotale 4000 squadron of 4 launchers
- 6 K-8 jet trainers
- Unknown number of domestically produced primary trainers (Mushak)
- 2 Y-12s from China, 11-seaters, for No. 41 Squadron
- Helicopters (unknown number)

Prima facie, adding 160+ fighters over 10-years is reasonable achievement for a small air force. The problem, of course, was that the PAF was inducting third-generation fighters, the Mirage 3/5s, and the equivalent of a modernised MiG-21 at a time the IAF:

- Had begun the process of modernising six MiG-21 squadrons (Project Bison, though because of delays the first squadron was not reequipped till the early 2000s);

- Started upgrading its Jaguars, particularly including a FLIR targeting pod, and preparing to order 37 more to keep the strike force to strength;
- Completed the induction of the MiG-29 plus the acquisition of attrition aircraft (Generation 4); and
- Started induction of the Su-30 (Generation 4).

No one familiar with the Indian Air Force will deny that it had its very own difficult decade between 1990 and 2000, largely due to massive incompetence at the Ministry of Defence level and the IAF's habit of casually acquiring new systems without extensive testing and refusal to compromise on standards (MiG-29), the opposite of the way the PAF functions.

Our intent is not to criticise the PAF. With Pressler wreaking havoc with its modernization plans, and its financial situation such that even just $100 million was a great deal of money, the PAF did a remarkable job of keeping itself in the air in the 1990s. The IAF's new aircraft budget for one year probably exceeded the PAF's entire 10-year budget!

Rather, our intent is to note that the PAF was having a most difficult time due to reasons beyond its control. The new acquisitions were thin gruel where trainers, transports, missiles, and helicopters were concerned. And the number of aircraft purchased was sufficient only to replace the Generation 2 MiG-19, whereas the need was to replace the Generation 3 Mirage 3/5 and to buy more Generation 4 aircraft like the F-16.

Notes

1. Pakistan Dawn Newspaper. 2019. *Scientist raises doubt about success of Indian N*-test. August 28, 2019. https://www.dawn.com/news/849091/newspaper/newspaper/column
2. This is an estimate. The actual figure is not available to us.
3. A report prepared by Ravi was not greeted by the Government of India with any interest, and his request for technical help and a grant to complete the story was ignored.
4. Global Security. 2011. *F-7P Sabre II Super 7*. November 4, 2011. http://www.globalsecurity.org/military/world/china/j-7p.htm#
5. Bitzinger, R. 1991. Chinese arms production and sales to the Th*ird World. Report produced for the RAND corporation* http://www.dtic.mil/dtic/tr/fulltext/u2/a256842.pdf
6. N.d. PAF Falcons *F-7MG/PG vital statistics*. http://www.paffalcons.com/gallery/f7/images/f7pg-17-large.jpg

7. Pakistan Defence. n.d. *F-7MG Trials with by Pakistan Air Force.* http://www.pakdef.info/pakmilitary/airforce/ac/f7pg.htm The URL has changed and is not traceable.
8. For an excellent brief history of the MiG-21 see Goebel, Greg. 2023. *MiG-21 Single Seat Variants.* October 1, 2023. http://www.airvectors.net/avmig21_1.html
9. Pakistan Défense *F-7MG Trials with by Pakistan Air Force*, op. cit.
10. Trading Economics. 2013. http://www.tradingeconomics.com/pakistan/gdp
11. 'The story of the Pakistan Air Force 1988-98', op.cit. pp. 93-96.

3
Kargil 1999

To understand the PAF's role, or rather the lack of it, during the war requires a diversion into the causes and aims on the war. This is particularly necessary as few authoritative details from the Pakistan side exist, with the exception of Kaiser Tufail's unbiased account.[1] As Director of Air Operations in Air HQ, he was at the scene.

The Kargil War was a strange affair. It came out of nowhere, lacked a geo-strategic rationale, suffered from a lack of tactical thought and was severely 'underfunded' in terms of the resources allocated. It was foredoomed to failure, as even a single hour of staff work at Pakistan GHQ could have predicted. To call the war an *ad hoc* affair is to insult the word *ad hoc*, because no thought whatsoever was devoted to starting the war or to conducting the war once it was underway.

Worse, it was dishonorably directed by a leadership that refused to claim responsibility for the soldiers who acquitted themselves bravely despite the perfidy of their generals. To term the North Light Infantry, elite mountain troops, as *mujahidin* volunteers spontaneously moved to gather in the remotest part of Kashmir to liberate occupied territory, and to insist the men fight out of uniform to preserve the *mujahidin* fiction, was an act of military baseness unprecedented in the annals of independent South Asian military history. Because so little is known about the war from Pakistan's side, and because readers from outside the subcontinent may have had little exposure to the story, a diversion is necessary to establish the background.

Pakistan has yet to publish an in-depth analysis of the war, and possibly never may because it was a disaster.

The Pakistani plan

Pakistan's plan was to infiltrate and seize the heights in the Dras-Kargil sector, thus gaining artillery control of the vital Sonamarg-Leh road, India's main logistics route from Kashmir to Ladakh. The infiltrators would take the heights without difficulty, as the Dras and Kargil sectors of North Kashmir, India vacated its posts during the winter. Dras has roughly 2 meters of precipitation in October-April, which could equate to 40 meters or more of snow depending on air moisture. In January, coldest month of the year, the mean minimum is -24°C, and it can dip to -40°C on certain days. No wonder India used to vacate its forward posts when the snow set in by November till the start of May. To add, this was a roadless area, served by animal tracks for use when the snow melted. The operation was to be completed by May, presenting the Indians with a *fait accompli* when they returned to occupy their posts.

Pakistan was hopeful that it could close and keep closed the road for the month of June. After that, the monsoon would shut down the road due to landslides, and also shut down Indian airfields in Ladakh, preventing reinforcement. "In October, the Pakistan Army would march up the Siachen ridges, encountering only the bodies of Indian soldiers dead from hunger and cold."[2]

The following is a precis of Tufail's article:

> The PAF was kept in ignorance of these plans until after the infiltration was complete. Only three Pakistan Army generals were fully informed: the COAS General Musharraf under whose aegis the operation was planned and conducted, the GOC X Corps, the corps commander for Kashmir, and the GOC Force Command Northern Areas, specifically responsible for the North Kashmir sectors. The trio believed that the Air Force was not required, and the PAF was kept in ignorance of the Army's plans.

The first time the PAF officially learned of the Army's action was two days after the Army began to occupy the heights in the Dras and Kargil sectors. It was passed off as nothing requiring the PAF, as the Army could hold off the Indian Air Force with its Stinger SAMs. When the PAF suggested that the Army might require its help neutralising Indian artillery, the Army confidently dismissed such a need, and said the Dras-Kargil arena was too narrow for India to deploy massed guns. Instead, India committed 300 guns, heavy mortars and rocket launchers gaining a devastating fire advantage.

Incidentally, why the Pakistan Army thought any Indians would die of cold and hunger is baffling because Siachen is kept well-stocked by helicopters year around. And knowing (in those days) that the Sonamarg-Leh road is closed by snow for seven months of the year, the Indian Army routinely stocks six months of supplies. Siachen is supplied through the Thoise air base, well out of Pakistani reach. Pakistani forward posts are about 1000-meters below Indian posts; the temperature is always below zero, and the oxygen level is 10 per cent of sea level. Surprise and/or a mass assault are all but impossible. The Pakistan Army's reckless bravery is well attested but an assault against Indian posts is not reckless bravery, but plain suicide.

IAF Deployment

According to the PAF, the IAF began positioning its fighter squadrons on 16 May, six days after Pakistan openly announced its infiltration. The IAF entered action on 26 May. This delay was not the IAF's responsibility: it has already been noted that massive confusion existed in Delhi as to what precisely was going on. The IAF is not maintained on a hair-trigger alert unlike the US air forces. Perhaps the IAF could have mobilised faster than six days after being warned, but this is quibbling. The delay after air mobilisation was political, as the government struggled to define its exact response.

Table 3.1: IAF deployment for Operation *Safed Sagar*[3]

Srinagar	34 MiG-21, MiG-23, MiG-27
Awantipur	28 MiG-21, MiG-29, Jaguar
Udhampur	12 MiG-21
Pathankot	30 MiG-21, MiG-23
Adampur	46 Mirage 2000, MiG-29, Jaguar

Srinagar and Awantipur are in the Kashmir Valley. Udhampur is near Jammu. Pathankot is at the junction of Punjab, J&K and Himachal Pradesh.

Adampur is in Punjab, near Jullundur. Of the approximately 150 aircraft, about half (the MiG-21s and MiG-29s) were deployed for air defence. The ground troops amounted to a reinforced division. As such the strike aircraft committed represented the largest number ever assigned to support an Indian Army division; larger, indeed, that committed even to a corps, which is what the Indian counter offensive finally built up to.

IAF Squadrons 'Safed Sagar' (Operation White Water)

- Mirage 2000: 1, 7
- Jaguar: 14, 27
- MiG-29: 28, 223
- MiG-27: 9
- MiG-23: 221
- MiG-21: 51, 108

A complete order of battle is available at *Bharat Rakshak.*[4] That source says that full squadrons were not deployed; usually detachment of 4-6 aircraft. The complete order of battle included aircraft from:

- 13 fighter squadrons
- 2 transport squadrons
- 4 helicopter units plus 1 flight
- 3 radar squadrons and 3 signals units
- 3 Mobile Observer Flights
- 3 SA-3 and 1 SA-8 squadrons, plus one flight SA-16

IAF Losses

The MiG-21 pilot left his formation when he saw the MiG-27 in trouble and tried to protect the bailed-out pilot. Consequent to a Stinger hit, he successfully bailed-out breaking a knee, but was subsequently shot and killed by Pakistani troops. This was discovered when his body was returned to India and caused great anger in the country. Unfortunately, since the first days of air warfare downed pilots have risked death at the hands of the enemy on the ground. The MiG-27 pilot was quickly captured by the Pakistan Army and severely beaten before the Pakistan Air Force took custody. Once with the PAF he was well-treated.

Table 3.2: IAF Losses Kargil 1999

Date	Aircraft	Squadron/HU	Cause
5/27	MiG-27	No. 9 Squadron	Gun gas ingestion while strafing caused engine flameout, Batalik
5/27	MiG-21	No. 17	Stinger hit while protecting MiG-27 pilot on ground, Batalik
5/28	Mil-17	No. 129 HU	3 Stinger hits operating against enemy, Tooling

In addition to the above losses, a PR Canberra of No. 106 Squadron suffered a Stinger hit while on a low-level reconnaissance mission, knocking out one engine. Had the aircraft been anything but a Canberra, it would surely have been lost. But the aircraft's two engines are mounted one under each wing, widely separated. So, the second engine was intact, and the pilot retained sufficient control to fly to Srinagar and land safely. Subsequently high- and fast-flying MiG-25R Foxbats of No. 102 Squadron had to take over the reconnaissance role.

Sorties

The PAF estimated that the IAF flew about 1200 sorties:

- Strike – 550
- Air defence – 500
- Reconnaissance and ELINT – 150

This figure was accurate but divided slightly differently.[5]

- Strike – 580
- Air defence – 460
- Reconnaissance and ELINT – 160

This is close enough not to matter. In addition, the IAF and Army Aviation flew 2500 helicopter sorties. Last, the IAF flew an unknown number of transport sorties. The combined total exceeded 4000.

Combat operations

In the initial stages, MiG-21s, -23s, and -27s were used for ground attack with rockets and cannon strafing. Jaguars covered by Mirage 2000 performed reconnaissance. The loss of a MiG-21, MiG-27, and armed Mil-17 helicopter in about 24 hours caused an abrupt cessation of offensive operations. Two days later, the IAF returned, this time at medium/high altitude, and using GPS as a workaround because the IAF lacked tools for the new air environment. The importance of this shift cannot be overemphasised. The IAF, like its former parent the Royal Air Force, had for fifty years worshipped at the altar of low-level strike. Attacking from medium- and high-altitudes, standard US Air Force doctrine, was considered heresy. The rapidity of the change reflects well on the IAF's flexibility.

The IAF had taken advantage of warming Indo-US relations in the 1990s to start acquiring Paveway kits for converting ordinary 'iron' or 'dumb' bombs to guided, or 'smart' bombs. But the US embargo on India subsequent to the 1998 nuclear tests reduced IAF capability in this field to zero. The Mirage 2000 had come equipped with the ATLIS targeting pod, but apparently the aircraft, foreseen for an air defence role by the IAF to counter the F-16, had no attack capability in the form of the hardware/software required to drop smart bombs. In a remarkable show of improvisation and flexibility, India quickly obtained the needed equipment and help from Israel, and the IAF had its smart bomb capability back by June 12.

A startling fact from the war is that despite the profusion of gun camera photos seemingly providing evidence of massive use of smart bombs, only eight were dropped by Mirage 2000s and one by a Jaguar! And even then, the smart bomb equipped aircraft were partnered with other carrying iron bombs. The smart bombs were to be used only if the iron bombs missed their target. It would appear the same images were repeatedly used by the media.

Nonetheless, those disturbed by this new IAF, suddenly a paragon of efficiency and flexibility, can comfort themselves with the same casual, disorganized IAF they have come to know and love. The IAF lacked the bombs needed for strike missions! Eventually, a stock of old Spanish 250 kg bombs bought for the Ajeet light fighter was found and converted to smart configuration!

The two Mirage 2000 squadrons, Nos. 1 and 7 flew over 40 per cent of the sorties during the war. This shows that while quantity in the air is important, quality is the main determinant. Among the Mirages' achievements were destroying the major Pakistan Army supply bases at Muntho Dhalo (Batalik), and Dras, and the smart bomb attack on the HQ of the Pakistan battalion defending Tiger Hill. Because resupplying the sector from Pakistan's side is difficult, the loss of the supply bases shortened the war. The Tiger Hill attack helped break the staunch defence of this vital feature. Being forced to fight up the mountain without cover, the Indian Army suffered heavy losses. The final assault on the ridge was a walkover for the Army.

The PAF in the Kargil War

Readers may be baffled by the short exposition of the PAF's role in the Kargil War; particularly because this book is about the PAF. The reason is that the PAF did very little in the war.

Figure 3.1: Pakistan Army Puma 330. Drawing © Tom Cooper

Foremost was the political decision not to employ the PAF to preserve the fiction of mujahedeen spontaneously organizing themselves to 'liberate' a part of Indian Kashmir. By political we do not mean a decision taken by the civil government, but by GHQ. The PAF chief sensibly refused to expand his operations without written orders, which the Pakistan Army was unable to produce. "*Mujahdin*" was an absurd fiction because the international community, to whom it was directed, did not buy it for a minute. Two points require discussion.

First, clearly Pakistan was worried about escalation if the PAF was used. This shows exceptionally poor planning. The attack plan was predicated on India being unable to escalate because of Pakistan's—at the time non-existent—nuclear deterrent. So, to decide India could not escalate, launch your attack, and then worry about India escalating is absurd.

Second, as Tufail makes abundantly clear, the PAF was in no shape to counter the IAF. This was because of the "chequered decade" of the US sanctions, which almost crippled the PAF. The Mirage 3/5 could not operate in the presence of MiG-29s and Mirage 2000s, both equipped with BVR missiles. The F-7 is a point defence fighter with short legs. A single flight of F-7s was sent to Skardu it could have provided some air cover. But the base is primarily for transports and Army Aviation and was considered too vulnerable to Indian attack. Moreover, there is the shocking information that this time the F-7, which was providing the backbone of the PAF, lacked intercept radar! The F-16 was available in limited numbers, and flown from Kamra Air Base, but spares were very short, and the PAF wanted to keep its F-16s in hand in case of escalation across the international border or in West Kashmir. No other aircraft had the range to provide air cover. After flying F-16 patrols for some days, the PAF told the Army it could not continue for lack of spares. Thereafter the sole PAF activity was providing air defence on a 5 minute alert.

The PAF could not attack across the border which would have risked escalation. Aside from this, it had no orders from the political leadership to attack. Ignorant of the PAF's limitations and its lack of orders, the PAF was unfairly condemned for inaction. Apart from this, the PAF asked how it was supposed to justify an air war against India to support *mujahadin*, since the Pakistan Army was denying it was in action.

In a good act of improvisation, the PAF managed to move a mobile radar to a point 12,000 feet altitude near Skardu. At least the PAF managed some radar coverage.

Both politically and operationally, the PAF was severely constrained in the Kargil War. Also, the casual arrogance by which the GHQ convinced itself that the PAF was not required at all surely was unhelpful.

But Tufail is objective enough to accept that, at least at the start, the Pakistan Army was correct in some assumptions. The 'Stinger on every hill' that would neutralise the IAF had worked. The army also told the PAF that the IAF bombing would not work because the targets were small, well hidden, and difficult to detect. This also proved correct. The Indians themselves have admitted it was difficult, especially as snow continued to fall on the heights. Particularly hard to detect were the camouflaged bunkers. What the GHQ did not foresee is how quickly the IAF would change tack. It is wrong to blame the GHQ for this omission, given the lackadaisical manner in which the IAF went about its affairs. Probably no one was more surprised than the IAF itself!

President Musharaff had his revenge on the PAF, a surprisingly malicious act seeing as he kept the matter a secret from the PAF and had no idea of the PAF's limitations of operating in the far north. When the existing Air Chief retired, Musharraf sidelined the five senior air marshals and appointed an officer who till a few weeks previous had been a two-star Air Vice Marshal. The speculation is that he acted deliberately, choosing a junior officer as PAF Chief who could not stand up to him. If this is true, he harmed the PAF.

Notes

1. Kaiser Tufail, PAF Group Captain (2009). Kargil Conflict and Pakistan Air Force. 2009, January 28. *Aeronaut.* https://kaiser-aeronaut.blogspot.com/2009/01/kargil-conflict-and-pakistan-air-force.html
2. Ibid. Please also see Sanjay Badri-Maharaj (2001) Operation Meghdoot: India's War in Siachen, 1984-2020. 2001. Helion Books: United Kingdom. Sanjay has a doctorate in war studies from Kings College, London and has written extensively on the Indian military.
3. Provided by Group Captain Kaiser Tufail, then Director Operations at PAF HQ, in http://pakteahouse.net/2009/02/12/paf-in-kargil-a-paf-warrior-speaks-out/
4. Bharat Rakshak (nd). "Order of Battle during the Kargil War: IAF OrBat and Honors." http://www.bharat-rakshak.com/IAF/History/Kargil/Orbat90.html
5. Sheneg, V. (October 16, 2009). Operation Safed Sagar. http://www.bharat-rakshak.com/IAF/History/Kargil/1055-VedShenag.html

4

2000-2010: The Opportunity Decade

Pakistan's relationship with the United States may well be the most dysfunctional between two so-called allies since the Second World War. The cause of the dysfunctionality is, oddly, India. What is odder is that India does not realise that it is at the core of US-Pakistan relations.

With the start of the Cold War, the US began to encircle the Soviet Union and China after 1950. The ring started in Western Europe and continued to Southern Europe (NATO). The Middle East and Iran were covered by the Central Treaty Organization. Eastward, the South East Asia Treaty Organisation took over. The right flank of the encirclement consisted of Japan and South Korea.

To fill the gap between Iran and SEATO, the US approached India. A newly decolonised India refused, wanting to have nothing to do with foreign alliances. Pakistan eagerly pushed itself as an alternative. The US knew that it was not much of an alternative—India was five times bigger, but because its war with the Soviets and Chinese was an existential one, Washington gingerly accepted Pakistan's offer, and Pakistan joined CENTO.

Nonetheless, the US always kept its eyes on India. The military assistance given to Pakistan was calibrated for two objectives: enough aid to stall a Soviet invasion through Afghanistan for the 7-10 days required for the arrival of US forces, but not enough aid to threaten India.

In 1962, India was forced to ask the US for assistance. With the prospect of winning India over, Washington promptly reduced aid to Pakistan. For example, a second F-104 squadron was not delivered. Nor was Pakistan's military equipment modernised. In the normal course of events, for example, Pakistan would have received M-60 tanks to replace its M-47/48s, and F-5s to replace its F-86s. The 1965 Indo-Pakistan War led to a total US aid cut-off. Pakistan wasted no time in allying with China, thus clearly showing its alliance with the US was based purely on expediency and not on any anti-communist ideology.

Between 1966 and 1979 the US made sporadic efforts to make up with Pakistan. Why? Because after the 1965 War, India voluntarily decided to hug the Red Bear, so Washington could not entirely write off Pakistan. The reasons for India's shift were many. First, the Soviets, from the 1950s, had patiently wooed India with economic investments. Second, India was angry with the US over military aid to Pakistan that culminated in the 1965 War. Also, India did not buy the US argument that Washington had turned to Pakistan only because of New Delhi's rejections. Until the 1980s, India was quite closed to the world. India had no conception of US Cold War imperatives or that the US was engaged in a war for survival with the Soviets. So, third, instead of seeing the US actions around the world as defensive, New Delhi saw them as attempts to impose a new white colonialism to replace the British Empire. The Indian elite, extending its visceral anti-colonial worldview to the US, was in a constant fervour against what it saw as US imperialism around the world, particularly in Indochina. Interestingly, while condemning America, a democratic India had no problem associating with the largest gathering of anti-democratic states ever assembled. This shows that India's anti-imperialism was born not of any ideology, but of anti-Americanism.

Last, the US refused to provide India with the arms requested after 1962. From the US' side the matter was simple: what was India prepared to give Washington in return? India's response was astonishment when the US asked for a *quid pro quo*. New Delhi truly believed Washington should hand over money and arms because Indians were, well, loveable and deserving. Thus, the tussle over India's request for 36 F-104s: the US hemmed, hawed and prevaricated. Meanwhile, the Soviets gleefully said: "You want 36 F-104s? Here, take 150 MiG-21s and we'll also build you a factory for domestic manufacture." In the wake of massive arms deliveries from the Soviet Union to India, the US felt it had no choice but to keep alive its Pakistan options.

Thus, happened the 1970 one-time exception arms deal for spares, some replacement aircraft, and M-113 APCs. The deal did not go through. In 1976, the US offered 110 A-7 attack aircraft if Pakistan would end its nuclear weapons program. Since Pakistan needed a minimum of $5 billion worth of arms aid (my back-of-napkin estimate) to counterbalance India conventionally, $500 million worth of A-7s did not suffice, and Pakistan sensibly refused. But here again we see India as being the US' main concern: to give Pakistan more would have threatened India's superiority over Pakistan, and effectively destroyed US relations with India. US military assistance from 1966-1982 equaled less than $70 million in 2009 dollars, effectively spelling the end of the military alliance between the two countries.

Table 4.1: Summary of US military aid to Pakistan 1955-2013[1]
(Military aid began in 1955)

Year	Economic Assistance, Total	Economic Assistance (through USAID)	Military Assistance, Total	Coalition Support Funds
1955	733.15	477.18	266	
1956	1065.67	700.89	1086.5	
1957	1079.65	619.9	437.59	
1958	968.22	589.59	533.13	
1959	1367.93	985.25	366.81	
1960	1689.84	1181.35	230.39	
1961	989.53	780.04	260.47	
1962	2334.65	1446.28	549.02	
1963	2066.77	1063.68	292.31	
1964	2222.66	1334.16	187.55	
1965	1928.9	1041.58	77.38	
1966	816.28	691.28	8.4	
1967	1213.36	719.38	26.33	
1968	1501.68	672.5	25.98	
1969	541.76	504.31	0.5	
1970	968.32	570.93	0.87	
1971	474.25	31.21	0.73	
1972	692.87	261.87	0.42	
1973	715.35	387.63	1.24	
1974	381.97	219.13	0.95	
1975	614.34	326.02	0.92	
1976	644.1	336.78	1.28	
1977	319.16	209.4	0.92	
1978	214.92	55.49	1.52	
1979	128.81	23.31	1.2	
1980	137.53	0	0	

1981	164.16	0	0	
1982	400.6	200.07	1.2	
1983	534.18	383.29	499.77	
1984	568.05	415.84	555.9	
1985	607.26	447.53	583.53	
1986	623.56	460.91	545.82	
1987	599.07	469.53	534.54	
1988	769.14	635	430.69	
1989	559.72	421.27	367.06	
1990	548.07	422.37	283.44	
1991	149.59	141.78	0	
1992	27.14	0.57	7.2	
1993	74.19	7.98	0	
1994	68.43	0	0	
1995	23.13	10.1	0	
1996	22.79	0	0	
1997	57.17	0	0	
1998	36.32	0	0	
1999	102.14	6.72	0.22	
2000	45.72	0	0	
2001	228.02	0.54	0	
2002	937.34	744.74	1739.7	1386.06
2003	377.93	284.81	1760.23	1450.98
2004	406.12	316.56	891.39	794.11
2005	490.42	374.04	1397.06	1050.15
2006	689.43	488.46	1246.1	916.13
2007	688.62	498.91	1079.72	755.74
2008	614.48	392.05	1378.32	1014.9
2009	1353.65	1076.25	1114.26	685
2010	1867.13	1529.53	2524.61	1220.5
2011[2]			1277	1118
2012			1273	1690
2013			1299	1750

Note: US$ (millions), in 2009 constant dollars.

In late 1979, the Soviet Union invaded Afghanistan. Ironically, this was precisely the threat that the first US alliance with Pakistan was supposed to counter. Between 1983 and 1990 the US provided $3.2 billion in military aid. But also, by now the US had managed to gain India's trust to the point relationships rapidly thawed. With the Soviets having withdrawn, the US wasted no time in shutting down aid to Pakistan for a second time. It can be agreed that Pakistan's attitude towards the US has been opportunistic. Yet, this no less opportunistic than the US' attitude toward Pakistan.

In 2001, the US invaded Afghanistan. Another irony: Afghanistan became the only country in the modern world to be twice invaded by a superpower—and by superpowers that were sworn enemies at that. In the following years, the US provided Pakistan with nearly $17 billion in military aid and Coalition Support Funds to defray Pakistan's alleged expenses in fighting the Taliban are extra. A considerable but unknown part of this has been diverted to the Pakistan military budget, though of late the US started checking receipts and denying some reimbursement.

Yet another irony: the US pays Pakistan to fight the Taliban, but the Taliban takes its orders, training, funding, and military leadership from Pakistan GHQ. So, in effect, the Americans are paying Pakistan to kill Americans in Afghanistan, aside from themselves spending nearly $100 billion/year in Afghanistan. Ever since the US shifted to an all-volunteer military, the American public has become increasingly detached from the US military. What takes the cake is the indifferent acceptance by the American public of this state of affairs. Who has ever heard of a state fighting an enemy, while giving money to the third party that hosts and controls the enemy? This shows the total breakdown of logic in the US Government. To make it yet worse, most American officials acknowledge the madness her/his government is engaged in, but the majority feel that the US cannot cut with Pakistan because now Pakistan at least gives *some* assistance in fighting the Taliban, or else it will give none. But the reason that the Taliban remain active and are spreading their control over Afghanistan is because of Pakistan. Effectively, the US is fighting itself!

Pakistan does launch anti-Taliban operations from time to time. But all are against Taliban factions that have gotten drunk on the notion of pan-Islamism and a revival of the Islamic Caliphate and consequently turned against the Pakistan state.

The F-16

Pakistan took delivery of 40 F-16A/Bs between 1983-87 (Peace Gate I and II, Block 15). In 1988, 11 more were ordered and manufactured as attrition replacements (Peace Gate III, Block 15 OCU, six A and five B). In 1989, an additional 60 were ordered (Peace Gate IV). Of these, 17 were manufactured by 1994 (eleven A and six B), making a total of 28 (seventeen A and 11 B).

Unfortunately for the Pakistan Air Force, all 71 aircraft under Peace Gate III and IV were embargoed because of US concerns about Pakistan's nuclear weapons program. With the Soviet withdrawal from Afghanistan starting in 1990, Pakistan lost any political leverage it might have previously enjoyed. The 28 already manufactured were stored in the US; the contract was 43 more aircraft was terminated (Block 15 OCU, 41 A and 2 B). The story of the 28 stored F-16s is long and tortuous. After failing to find other buyers, the US in 2002 assigned the aircraft to US Air Force and Navy aggressor training. The US, churlishly at first, refused even to return the money Pakistan had paid and charged Pakistan storage fees for the aircraft. Eventually, the money was returned.

After September 11, 2001, Pakistan's new and admittedly reluctant role as a key US ally in the war against Al Qaeda and the Taliban led to the reversal of the embargo, and in 2006 the US agreed to deliver 28 aircraft. On current information, at least 14 have been delivered, for which one serial is not identified.

Pakistan took the opportunity presented by the new alliance to formulate a requirement for 75 C and D Block 52s. The US refused to pay for these aircraft, given they were not needed in the war against terror or the Taliban. Washington's unwillingness to anger India also played a part in the decision. In the event, only 18 were actually ordered in 2006. An option for an additional 18 has not been exercised. The new program was codenamed 'Peace Drive.' Pakistan has said it did not take up the option because of the devastating 2005 Kashmir earthquake. Nonetheless, the relief costs were made up by international donations. It is not credible to believe that Pakistan cut its defence budget, depriving its air force of a critically-needed purchase, because of temporary financial constraints created by civilian relief. And in any case, seven years have gone by with no sign of additional F-16s. It is probably better to assume that the money, about $1.8 billion, was diverted to other Air Force programs and that the deficit in aircraft is to be made up by the JF-17 fighter.

The enormous escalation in modern weapons costs can be seen in the case of Pakistan's F-16s. For the 28 previously embargoed aircraft ordered in the late 1980s, Pakistan paid $35 million per aircraft. Less than twenty years later, it paid $85 million. The weapons package alone for the 18 F-16s is, at $650 million, more than the 28 aircraft, and is extra to the unit cost. It includes:[3]

- 500 AIM-120C5 Advanced Medium Range Air-to-Air Missiles (AMRAAM) plus 12 training missiles
- 200 AIM-9M-8/9 Sidewinder (one generation before the latest AIM-9X)
- 240 LAU-129/A Launchers for the SAMs
- 500 GBU-31/18 Joint Direct Attack Munition Guidance Kits
- 1,600 Enhanced Paveway GBU-12 (500 lbs.) and GBU-24s (2,000 lbs.) with dual laser/GPS guidance
- 800 MK-82 500-pound General Purpose (GP) and MK-84 2,000-pound GP bombs
- 700 BLU-109 2,000-pound bunker-buster bombs with the FMU-143 Fuse

Another way of considering weapons inflation is that in 1970, before the fateful 1971 war, Pakistan's defence budget was $3.9 billion in 2012 dollars.[4] The F-16 package including new aircraft, MLU, and other items is $3.6 billion. Yet another way of comparison is that Pakistan's 1970 GDP in 2012 dollars was about $72 billion, today it would be about $235 billion.[5] Its 1970 defence budget was about 5 per cent of the GDP; the F-16 package of just 18 new and 60 upgraded aircraft was 1.5 per cent of today's GDP. By contrast, India's purchase of 126 Rafale fighters could end up at $15 billion,[6] or 1 per cent of today's GDP (later $10 billion for 36 aircraft).

In microcosm, the above shows not just Pakistan's severe difficulties in trying to offset India, which has not just ten times the GDP, but a far higher percentage of GDP collected as tax.

According to one report, in 2012 the US Pentagon notified Congress of a proposal to sell 36 F-16C/D to Pakistan.[7] The last of the 2005 order of 18 F-16s Block 50/52 were delivered in February 2012,[8] so the inference has to be drawn that the 2012 deal is not for the 18 Block 50/52s optioned as part of the 2005 order, but for 36 additional aircraft. If this is so, Pakistan will attain its long-term goal of five F-16 squadrons. There is, however, no good identification if this is true.

What are the implications for Pakistan's long-envisioned goal of five F-16 squadrons? For a small air force, from a maintenance and training perspective, this is a reasonable number. Pakistan now has 78 F-16s. This could suffice for 4 squadrons (UE = 18 aircraft including two trainers), but Pakistan has only three squadrons.

The PAF appears split on the F-16 issue. One faction still wants an additional 30-35 aircraft. Another believes that the US is an untrustworthy supplier and nothing is gained by increasing dependence on Washington. Some in the first faction maintain that exchanging the US dominance for Chinese is hardly to Pakistan's advantage.

However, if the debate plays out, the F-16 may mark the last fighter purchase from the US, unless in the 2020s Washington clears the F-35 for Pakistan. Given the inevitable restrictions that will be imposed, not to mention the astronomical cost of the fighter (the unit price is low for a 5Gen aircraft, but the 30-years support cost is high) it is by no means certain that Pakistan would decide to buy F-35s. From many angles, a new generation Sino-Pakistan fighter may make more sense.

The PAF against the Taliban

Air Chief Marshal Rao Qamar Suleman, COAS of the PAF, gave some interesting statistics regarding the PAF's role in the war against the Taliban. He spoke on 12 November 2011, at the Dubai International Air Chiefs' Conference.[9] In one operation in August 2008, the PAF flew 650 strike sorties against 200 Taliban insurgents in the village of Loe Sam in Swat, North West Frontier Province; with 80 per cent of the ordnance dropped being smart bombs. He said that the Air Force had taken over the attack role from the Army aviation. In two years the PAF flew 5,500 strike sorties, dropping 10,600 bombs against 4600 targets. C-130s with FLIR were used for targeting to guide F-16s.

Unfortunately, unless it is assumed that the PAF is massively incompetent, something clearly not the case, these figures make no sense. Assume two bombs per sortie. Can it really be that the PAF flew 650 sorties against 200 insurgents, dropping 1300 bombs, 1100 of which were of the smart variety? Three sorties and almost six bombs, five of them guided, to kill one insurgent? We are assuming all 200 were killed. Far from reflecting well on the PAF's professionalism, if taken at face value, indicate an unprecedented misuse of airpower and astonishing ineffectiveness.

It is simpler to believe that (a) Pakistan has been getting rid of old bombs and using very few smart bombs; and (b) that Pakistan has been billing the US for sorties and ammunition expenditure that did not take place. While this is another story altogether, the US reimbursement to Pakistan for anti-Taliban operates has been characterised by shockingly loose controls. Though there is allegedly some tightening of procedures, the process has consisted of Pakistan presenting reams of invoices, and the US paying them after the most cursory of inspections.

The sums of money involved are hardly trivial. For Fiscal 2012 (1 October 2011, through 30 September 2012), the US allocated $1.69 billion for Pakistan via Coalition Support Funds. There is a separate counterinsurgency fund, independent of annual aid. The toughening of controls has meant that the US in 2011 was rejecting 40 per cent of bills presented for "military gear, food, water, troop housing and other expenses."[10] But only the most naïve will believe that Pakistan will fail to squeeze all money allocated out of the US, one way or the other. Pakistan has been amazingly sloppy in its invoicing. For example, it claimed money for the operation of US-supplied helicopters in anti-Taliban operations, whereas Pakistan actually sent them for UN peacekeeping in Darfur! It will simply be more careful now.

In an effort to keep US monies to Pakistan spent for the purpose allocated, and to appease India, the US has banned the US of any funds for purchase, modernisation or support of F-16s under the Kerry-Lugar Amendment. Money, of course, is fungible. So, if the US is aiding for weapons other than F-16s, this frees Pakistan's own funds for the fighter.

An issue ACM Suleman referred to was the initial problem(s) with UAV data links due to terrain masking. The PAF responded by flying its airborne relays higher. The PAF also outfitted a C-130 with the FLIR Systems Star Safire III EO/IR Sensor Ball to work with F-16s fitted with Goodrich DB-110 electro-optical reconnaissance pods. Five hundred sorties were flown by these F-16s and 650 by the C-130. The latter statistic does not look correct if there was just one C-130 with a Sensor Ball. The PAF apparently came in because Pakistan Army AH-1 Cobra attack helicopters had trouble operating at high altitudes—presumably, the heat did not help—and suffered from several losses.

Later I learned that Pakistan had four Sensor Ball FLIR aircraft. According to Scramble.nl,[11] these were C-130Bs construction numbers #3536 and #3689; C-130E No. 21 Squadron, Serial #119; and C-130E, Serial #180, written off on November 9, 2018 (ex-Australian A-97-190). For a short, generic description of Sensor Ball, see Teal Group.[12]

An Example of a PAF Orbat in the war against the Taliban

In October 2009 Pakistan launched Operation Raah-e-Nijjat. While it was billed as an anti-Taliban offensive, it was aimed only at the renegade Taliban that had taken over South Waziristan and were threatening other districts. Mandeep Singh Bajwa provided the following ORBAT:

Table 4.2: Air support to Op. Raah-e-Nijjat

Area of Op: South Waziristan Joint operation with the Pakistan Army PAF Commands: Central and Northern
38 Wing (PAF Musaf, Sargodha) • No. 9 Squadrons F-16 • No. 11 Squadron F-16 34 Wing (PAF Rafiqui, Shorkot Road) • No. 27 Squadron (Mirage 5E/F ROSE III) 36 Wing (PAF Peshawar) • No. 16 Squadron (A-5C Fantan) • No. 26 Squadron (A-5C Fantan) 33 Wing (PAF Minhas, Kamra) • No. 14 Squadron (F-7P) • No. 25 Squadron (Mirage 5E/F ROSE II) 35 Wing (PAF Nur Khan, Rawalpindi (Chaklala) • No. 6 Squadron (C-130) for paradrops Special Service Wing • No. 1 Special Operations Squadron • No. 2 Special Operations Squadron • No. 10 Squadron Special Reconnaissance Squadron

F-16 Serials

Summary of deliveries

- Peace Gate I/II: 40 aircraft, 28 A and 12 B
- Peace Gate III: 28 aircraft, 13 A and 15 B
- Peace Drive: 18 aircraft: 12 C and 6 D

Serials

The first 111 F-16s (delivered, embargoed and cancelled) had 6xx serials for the F-16Bs, and 7xx serials for the F-16A, in both cases preceded by the 2-digit construction year. Thus, the first F-16B for the PAF was 82601, and the first F-16A was 82701.

F-16s that were ordered but not constructed (cancelled) had PAF serials:

- F-16A Block 15 OCU: 742-782 (41 aircraft)
- F-16B Block 15 OCU: 628-629 (2 aircraft)

F-16s manufactured but embargoed had the serials (28 aircraft):

- F-16A Block 15 OCU: 729-741 (13 aircraft)
- F-16B Block 15 OCU: 613-627 (15 aircraft)

These aircraft were taken into service by the US given serials that are different. Also, each aircraft has a manufacturer's construction number. After the US invasion of Afghanistan, 14 were delivered to the PAF.

Below, a question mark after the date indicates uncertainty as to the delivery year.

Peace Gate I/II

Table 4.3: Peace Gate I/II

Serial	Model/Block	Delivery	Status
82601	B/15	1982	
82602	B/15	1982	
82603	B/20 MLU	1982	
82604	B/15E	1982	
82605	B/15M	1983	

84606	B/15M	1983	
84607	B/15N	1984	Written off
84608	B/15N	1984	
85609	B/15U	1985	Written off
85610	B/15V	1985	
85611	B/15V	1985	
85612	B/15V	1985	
82701	A/15E	1982	Written off 22 October 2004
82702	A/15E	1982	
83703	A/15M	1983	
84704	A/15 M	1983	
84705	A/15 N	1984	
84706	A/15 P	1984	
84707	A/15 P	1984	
84708	A/15 P	1984	
84709	A/15 Q	1984	
84710	A/15 Q	1984	
84711	A/15 Q	1984	
84712	A/15 Q	1984	Written off
84713	A/15Q, 20Q MLU	1984	
84714	A/15 R	1984	
84715	A/15 R	1984	
84716	A/15 R	1984	
84717	A/15 R	1984	
84718	A/15 S	1984	
84719	A/15 S	1984	
85720	A/15 S	1984	Written off
85721	A/15S	1985	Written off
85722	A/15S	1985	
85723	A/15 T	1985	Written off
85724	A/15 T	1985	
85725	A/15 U	1985	Written off
85726	A/15 U	1985	
85727	A/15U	1985	
85728	A/15U	1985	

Peace Gate III (All Peace Gate IV aircraft cancelled by US)
All Peace Gate III aircraft were constructed but placed under embargo. Fifteen went to the US Navy as aggressors. Later, all 28 aircraft were released to Pakistan.

Table 4.4: F-16 A/B

Serial	Model/Block	Delivery	Status
90613	B/15	2007	Embargoed
90614	B/15AM OCU	2008	Embargoed
90615	B/15AM OCU	?	Embargoed
90616	B/15AM OCU	2007	Embargoed
90617	B/15AM OCU; 20 MLU	2012	Embargoed
92618	B/15AQ OCU	2008	Embargoed
93619	B/15AR OCU	2008	Embargoed
92620	B/15AR OCU	2008	Embargoed; US Navy
92621	B/15AR OCU	2008	Embargoed
94622	B/15AS OCU	2003	Embargoed; US Navy
94623	B/15AS OCU	2008	Embargoed; US Navy
95625	B/15AU OCU	2002	Embargoed; US Navy
95626	B/15AU OCU	2002	Embargoed; US Navy
95627	B/15AU OCU	2002	Embargoed US Navy
91729	A/15AM OCU	?	Embargoed; Written off; US Navy
92730	A/15AM OCU	2002	Embargoed; US Navy
92731	A/15AM OCU	2002	Embargoed; US Navy
92732	A/15AM OCU	2002	Embargoed; US Navy
92733	A/15AM OCU	2002	Embargoed; US Navy
92734	A/15AQ OCU	2002	Embargoed; US Navy
92735	A/15AQ OCU	2004	
92736	A/15AQ OCU	2009	
92737	A/15 AQ OCU	2005	Embargoed
92738	A/15AQ OCU	2005	Embargoed; US Navy
93739	A/15AQ OCU	2002	Embargoed; US Navy
93740	A/15AR OCU	2002	Embargoed; US Navy
93741	A/15AR OCU	?	Embargoed; US Navy

Peace Gate

Serial	Model		
10801	D/52	2010?	
10802	D/52	2010?	
10803	D/52	2010?	
10804	D/52	2011	
10805	D/52	2011	
10806	D/52	2011?	
10901	C/52	2010?	
10902	C/52	2011	
10903	C/52	2010?	
10904	C/52	2010?	
10905	C/52	2010?	
10906	C/52	2011?	
10907	C/52	2011?	
10908	C/52	2011?	
10909	C/52	2011?	
10910	C/52	2011?	
10911	C/52	2012	
10912	C/52	2012	

F-16 Blocks as relevant to the PAF are provided in Table 4.5.

Table 4.5: PAF F-16 blocks

PAF F-16 Blocks	All to be given Mid Life Update (60 aircraft; 36 by TAI of Turkey)
Block 15 OCU	Operational Capability Upgrade; F100-PW-220 turbofan; AIM-120; 37,500 lbs. max.
Block 20 MLU	Mid Life Upgrade; bring aircraft to Block 50 specification
Block 50/52	F-100-PW-229; AIM-120, JDAM; long-range interdiction
Block 60	18 aircraft to or close to this standard said to negotiating in 2012

The two-letter codes after block numbers refer to sub-blocks; the implication is each sub-block is slightly different, no details are available. The MLU program will be complete by 2014.

Among the equipment Pakistan ordered are five reconnaissance pods for F-16s, the DB-100 for all-weather/day-night operations.

US Aggressor F-16s

The assumption concerning the 15 former US aggressor F-16s delivered to Pakistan is that the aircraft have been flown hard. Perhaps this is so. Be that as it may, Pakistan paid $151 million, or almost $11 million per aircraft, for three sets of upgrade work:

- Demodification, which means removal of US-specific equipment
- 14 structural upgrade kits
- 14 F100-PW-220E engines

F-16 engines

The Pratt & Whitney F100-PW-229 engine has a life of 4300 thermal cycles between depot inspections.[13] Engines from 2010 onward appear to have a 6000 cycles capability, good for 20 years between depot inspections. In the US Air Force, with its high flying rate, this is equivalent to seven years. The engine delivers a maximum of 29,160 lbs. static thrust. It features modular maintenance with real-time monitoring, permitting high availability.

The F100-PW-220E engine produces 23,770 pounds of thrust with the afterburner, and 14,590 pounds of thrust with the afterburner turned off. It has a 4000-cycle capability.

F-16 airframe life

The airframe is designed for a minimum of 8000 hours. Under the Mid Life Upgrade, the airframe should be good for another 5000 hours.

Mid Life Upgrade

All PAF F-16A/Bs will undergo the MLU. The use of the term 'Block 20 MLU' is slightly misleading, as in terms of electronic capability and weapons the MLU aircraft will equate to Block 50. The Block 40/50 have full night operational capability. The Belgian, Danish, Netherlands and Norwegian Air Forces coordinated their MLUs, with each aircraft requiring 2500-person-hours of work, or about 5 months. The key part of the upgrade is a new Modular Mission Computer, which replaces three previous computers. Of its 24 slots, ten are reserved for further growth.

Other improvements include:

- Upgrade of radar APG-68 version to latest version 9

- Advanced IFF
- Six new cockpit displays and indicators including side-slip stick and throttle

Improved electronics including
- Improved Data Modem
- New Electronic Warfare Management system
- Miniaturised GPS receiver
- Digital Terrain System

Additionally, cockpit layout is similar to Block 50, and Reece pod interface to be standard.

The new electronics are lighter, use less volume, and consume less power.

The Block 15s do not have digital flight controls, the Block 52s do. In the latter case, the aircraft can fly an automated terrain following path. In the former case, the pilot will follow the DTS's advice by manually flying on the Flight Path Marker in the HUD.

Block 50/52 aircraft

The weights for the new version are 18,238 pounds empty, 26,463 pounds normal loaded (air-to-air mission) and 42,300 pounds maximum takeoff. The aircraft has conformal fuel tanks giving it extended range; it is likely it can now cover a radius somewhat short of 700 km carrying a 3- to 4000-pound bomb load. It is the first F-16 version to integrate the Harpoon anti-ship missile. If used for maritime attack, though the number of aircraft is small, the plane will create a new complication for India because—especially with refuelling—the PAF can strike throughout the Arabian Sea. The old Exocet-armed Mirage 5s that were the standby for PAF's maritime strike are much less sophisticated. The APG-68v9 radar is far more advanced than the earlier versions of the APG-68 and performs both ground-targeting and air-to-air capabilities. It has significant growth potential.

When Pakistan obtained its first 40 F-16s in the 1980s, the Indian press was in an uproar about the threat these aircraft posed to India. As discussed in an earlier chapter, the aircraft's performance at low level was abysmal, understandable since it was designed as a fighter and since US attack doctrine calls for ingress into enemy airspace at 10- to 12,000 meters. There could be no comparison between the F-16 used offensively and the Jaguar, of which the IAF was then busy inducting three times as many. Ironically, with the new batch of 18 Pakistan has for the first time acquired a serious offensive capability. The aircraft, for example, has the electronic measures required to survive mid/high-level penetrations, and it certainly has the range to put all of India except the Northeast under the gun. Even the Northeast is in range assuming one aerial refuelling before departing Pakistan air space, and one over Tibet. Though there seems little point to flying all the way across India and then backing out, fighting IAF defences all the way. Now that the other 46 aircraft are being upgraded to becoming electronically on par with the Block 50/52, Pakistan has a meaningful offensive capability for the first time, at least to a distance out to 800 km from Pakistan.

Does it make sense for Pakistan to buy more F-16s?

Fighter aircraft prices are so opaque that only the broadest of generalization can be made when comparing two different types. So, it is with the JF-17 and the F-16. The F-16 Pakistan unit price of about $85 million is known. But how much does the JF-17 cost? Generally, $20 million for Block I, $25-million for Block II, and $35 million for Block III. One source has gone as low as $10 million, yet that hardly seems credible for a modern fighter, even if made by China and Pakistan and even if it includes only the airframe and engine with no electronics, spares, or support equipment. At the Dubai Airshow in 2011, the press spoke of Pakistan offering the aircraft at a cut price of $25 million to $35 million.[14] It is likely this is not a cut price, but the real one, particularly at the higher end. Thales had discussed a $1.2 billion contract for electronics and weapons for 50 JF-17s, suggesting these items alone cost about $25 million per aircraft.[15] This gives good reasoning for accepting a flyaway cost of $30 million as realistic.

With three JF-17s for the cost of an F-16, given Pakistan has limited resources and at least 10 squadrons of obsolete aircraft are in urgent need of replacement, the choice of the JF-17 appears straightforward. Yes, the F-16 is a better airplane, but perhaps one-and-a-half times better, certainly not three times better. And regardless, mass as well as quality is required in warfare.

The problem is that illustratively air forces spend 99 per cent of their time at peace, and only 1 per cent at war. So, life-cycle cost becomes important. While the life-cycle costs of the two aircraft are not publicly known, the F-16 will be far ahead in this regard. With upgrades, it lasts 40 years, its latest engine goes 10 years between depot maintenance and has low specific fuel consumption, and its electronics have high Mean Time Between Failure, plus are easy to upgrade. It is possible the F-16 has half the life-cycle cost of the JF-17.

The easy answer is that Pakistan needs both the F-16 and the JF-17. But along comes the J-10 (export version F-10 Vanguard), equivalent to the F-18.[16] If the J-10 is to be Pakistan's high part of the hi/lo mix, where does the F-16 fit in, particularly for a small air force with constrained resources? And this is without talking politics into account. So eventually perhaps there is no correct answer to the question: F-16 or JF-17?

An F-16 mystery

The PAF received 86 F-16s in all of which 8 have been written off. With 78 aircraft left, the PAF can equip four squadrons of 18 each, plus some for attrition. At least 12 aircraft will also be required for the Combat Commanders School. So why are there only three squadrons?

Figure 4.1: The picture is from Wikipedia; I was unable to obtain the original source. The PAF-16D is undergoing final testing in the US before delivery. (2009, September 30)

As NATO keeps continually reducing its military strength, F-16A/Bs will be available on the secondary market. For example, the Dutch and Belgians sold 20 surplus F-16s to Jordan.[17] Jordan had, in 2005, purchased 3 F-16Bs from the Netherlands. All US-origin equipment has to be cleared by Washington before being resold. Currently, Pakistan has good relations with the US and there should be little problem in gaining approval. It may be expected that, as usual, the PAF will drive hard bargains and likely miss some opportunities. As it did with the Mirage, it will likely buy all the airframes, engines, and spares it can obtain and then cannibalize or rebuild aircraft as much as possible.

Of particular interest is Israel's decision to put up its F-16A/B for sale.[18] These were Block 10 aircraft delivered in 1980-81 and have presumably seen hard use. Nonetheless, in the early 1990s all were rebuilt/upgraded to Block 30 standards (F-16C/D). About 70 A/Bs were new, originally destined for Iran and embargoed after the revolution. Another 50 were delivered used to Israel in the early 1990s.[19] Allegedly Israeli active-duty pilots fly 180 hours/year and reserve pilots 80. Including one airframe rebuild, the F-16 has a life of about 13,000 hours. So, the Is.AF aircraft should have a 50-year life. Including time spent in overhaul and rebuild, the 1980-81 batch should be good for use into the mid-2030s. Depending on how many hours the 1990s batch had before reaching Israel, these aircraft might be capable of serving into the late 2020s. Though the calculation is likely on the optimistic side, Pakistan should be able to get 12-20 years out of the Israeli aircraft, if purchased. This could help the PAF retire its F-7s and Mirages earlier than planned and provide added bulk to the PAF.

JF-17

The JF-17 has a long provenance. The Chengdu 7B, an advanced version of the Chengdu 7 (Chinese MiG-21) had made its appearance in 1984. Pakistan wished to acquire a more advanced version in the 7B to replace its large fleet of F-6 (Chinese MiG-19). In 1987, Grumman conducted studies, resulting in the Sabre II, also called the F-7S.

The F-7S is not to be confused with the Chinese Super 7, a separate project for China which ran almost in parallel and in which Pakistan was also interested. In the early 1980s the British helped China upgrade the F-7 into the F-7M. Subsequently, a further westernisation of the 7M was envisaged for export. This aircraft was named the Super 7, but the effort was abandoned because the aircraft was deemed too expensive. The Pakistan Air Force assisted with F-7M testing as the Chinese capability and experience with modern systems was limited.

For the Sabre II, Grumman redesigned the F-7M to include, among other advances, the radar from the US's F-20 Tigershark, which was the aircraft designated to replace the highly successful F-5 light fighter produced by Northrup for export to American allies. But subsequent to the Soviet withdrawal from Afghanistan in 1990, the US decided it no longer needed Pakistan, and imposed sanctions because of the Pakistan nuclear weapons program. This ended the Sabre II project. Meanwhile, further western involvement in China's Super 7 ended when sanctions were imposed on Beijing subsequent to the 1989 Tiananmen Square massacre. China announced it would continue the project on its own as the FC-1 Xiaolong (Fierce Dragon).

Figure 4.2: A No. 14 Squadron JF-17, now based Rafiqui Airbase. The squadron was the fifth to reequip with the JF-17 and previously flew first the Sabre, then the F-16, and then the F-7P. It scored a major victory in a 1965 raid on IAF Base Kalaikunda (F-86F) where it earned its slogan "Tail Choppers" and fought to the last, having to sabotage the last nine of 16 Sabre Mk. 6s on December 16, 1971, in Dacca 1971 (Canadair Sabre Mk 6 CL-13). Society of Aerospace Studies, New Delhi, on behalf of the estate of Pushpindar Singh Chopra

In 1995, Pakistan joined China in the FC-1's development. The first flight did not take place until 2003 when the first of five prototypes entered testing. Also, in 2003 Pakistan named its version of the FC-1 as the JF-17. The evolution of the JF-17 took almost twenty years. While several years were lost due first to Western sanctions and then to developmental difficulties, the lengthy period reflects the new reality of aircraft design. In the late 1940s, 1950s, and 1960s, twenty years could represent the complete life-cycle of fighter aircraft, from design to withdrawal from service, or at least to obsolescence. It is worth noting that work on the Indian Light Combat Aircraft began almost forty years ago.

Table 4.6: JF-17 Serials

JF-17 Serials	
07-101 (1st production aircraft)	12-213 (2-seater)
07-102	
07-103	
07-104 (26 Squadron)	
07-105	
08-106 (26 Squadron)	
08-107 (26 Squadron)	
08-108 (26 Squadron)	
09-109	
09-110	
09-111	
09-112 (26 Squadron)	
10-113 (26 Squadron)	
10-114 (26 Squadron)	
10-115 (26 Squadron)	
10-116 (26 Squadron)	
10-118	
10-119	
10-120 (26 Squadron)	
10-122 (26 Squadron)	
10-125 (16 Squadron)	
10-127 (written off)	

10-128 (16 Squadron)	
11-130 (16 Squadron)	
11-131	
11-132	
11-134 (16 Squadron)	
11-136 (16 Squadron)	

The table is compiled from data provided by *Scramble*[20] and miscellaneous photographs from the internet. It is likely the entire 1xx series is in sequence. The table is puzzling, because with the exception of one trainer no other aircraft from 2012 or 2013 have been identified.

Another puzzling matter is the two-seat JF-17B. This is said to be under development. But the single two-seater photographed in public carries the serial 12-213, indicating it is the thirteenth trainer. The PAF has said that the JF-17 is so easy to fly, only a few dual-seat versions are required. Could it be that 2012 production was dedicated mainly to this type?

Given that China is seldom forthcoming about its weapon developments, unsurprisingly many aspects of the JF-17's history are obscure. The aircraft was identified by Chengdu Aircraft Industrial Group in 1999 as the FC-1/Super-7.[21] This was at the time Pakistan and China signed their agreement for joint development. In a 2003 story by a Chinese online newspaper, Gao Zhicong is identified as the in-charge of the Super 7 project.[22] He says the aircraft will fly by year's end, and will replace the PLAAF's F-7s, and Q-5s. The news report says the plane is codenamed the Super-7/FC-1. While it can be accepted that the FC-1 is a development of the Super 7, to what extent does the design rely on the Russian Project 33?

This Russian project was misidentified as the MiG-33, which was a heavy fighter development of the MiG-29. The Project 33 was intended as an F-16 competitor for the low end of a hi-lo mix, but never materialised because the Soviets, and then the Russians, did not want the aircraft for their air force. It was cancelled in 1986. In 1998 China purchased all drawings and obtained Russian technical assistance in developing the plane. It is tempting to speculate that Project 33 designs were used to remedy problems that must have occurred when the US embargo terminated cooperation on the Super 7. Which leaves the question of why the FC-1 looks almost identical to Northrop's F-20 Tigershark.

The FC-1/FC-17 uses a single Russian RD-93 engine. This a development of the RD-33 for the MiG-29; Project 33 was to use the same engine. China purchased 100 RD-93s from Russia; the deal may have included an option for 400 more. At one point the Russians bowed to Indian protests and cancelled the sale, but later it was reinstated by Moscow. Further, JF-17s will use the Chinese version of the engine, called the WS-13. Some reports say the engine is a joint development between China and Pakistan. It has been under development since 2000 and was certified in 2007 with serial production from 2009. Pakistan may want the General Electric 404/414, but political and economic considerations make this an unlikely route.

A fascinating aspect of the FC-1 is that China has shown no interest in inducting the plane for its own use. Given the very large number of F-6/F-7 still in service, it would be thought the FC-1 is the ideal replacement. It seems that, however, China is content to continue working on the FC-1 in conjunction with Pakistan as an export fighter. Half the aircraft is manufactured in China. While Pakistan seems to have taken the lead on foreign sales, any exports benefit China equally. An unavoidable inference is that the PLAAF rejects the hi-lo concept and aims for the higher end with the FC-10 and stealth FC-20. If so, a drastic reduction in the size of the PLAAF may be expected. Insofar as China's main adversary is the US, and insofar as the US is itself moving away from the hi-lo mix, a focus on the high end is logical for China. The FC-1 is not survivable in a US F-35 environment; as such procurement would be a waste of resources.

At the same time, there is a baffling reference to a Chinese FC-1 squadron made by the defence minister, Chaudhry Ahmed Mukhtar, at the November 2011 Dubai air show.[23] He also mentioned Pakistan has three squadrons, though it was widely accepted the third squadron would be equipped in 2012. The third squadron has not been publicly identified as of mid-2013. Is it possible that the PAF has an JF-17 squadron in China? If so, what would be the point?

Adding to the confusion, in 2011 China was said to have gifted 50 JF-17 jets to Pakistan.[24,25] The Pakistan blogosphere says deliveries began in 2012.[26] But there is no sign of these aircraft. Might China have written-off its cost of the first 50 JF-17s and this is not a separate delivery? Some unverified reports even claim China has gifted a J-10 squadron.

Block I

Deliveries were to complete in mid-2012 if the delivery schedule is maintained but had not done so in mid-2013. This block includes the first 50 JF-17s. As of end-2011, PAF had logged 10,000 flight hours on the type.[27] With apparently no JF-17 delivered to the PAF in 2012 and at least for the first six months of 2013, two possibilities exist for the delay.

- A major production hitch has occurred
- Pakistan has decided to terminate Block 1 earlier in favour of Block 2

Block 2

This is supposed to encompass the next 50 aircraft. The enhancements will affect the data link and electronic warfare capabilities. An air-to-air refuelling capability will be added, as will new guided weapons. A two-seat variant is being developed, too. The current program schedule calls for the Pakistan-based factory to deliver the JF-17 Block-2 to the PAF from mid-2012 to 2015; as mentioned, however, there was no sign that Block I delivery had ended as of mid-2013.

Block 3

This batch of 50 is planned for delivery from 2016.

Squadron service

As of end 2011 the aircraft equipped Nos. 16 and 26 Squadrons, previously flying the A-5 Fantan, the Chinese ground-attack version of the F-6/MiG-19. In 2012 it was rumoured that No. 27 Squadron converted, but it appears the third squadron will be No. 17. The No. 27 Squadron has the latest rebuilt Mirage ROSE III night strike aircraft, and it would be surprising if the PAF had decided to reequip it. Rumour also mentions No. 15 Squadron at Masroor, which has been flying the Mirage 3, as the next candidate. Logic dictates the replacement of the Mirage 3 as the first priority because these aircraft were built in the late 1960s; the youngest would be over 40-years old, the oldest 45-years. The Mirage 5s should be next for replacement because they are between 35- and 40-years old. The oldest F-7s are 'only' 25 years old and can presumably wait for replacement.

The third squadron should have been delivered by early 2012. Instead, it will be delivered in 2013.

Prototypes

Six prototypes were built:[28]

- PT-01 First flight September 4, 2003, in Chengdu; first PAF test flights April 7, 2004.
- PT-02 Static load tests.
- PT-03 Chinese avionics; first flew April 9, 2004. Flight performance verification.
- PT-04 First flight April 28, 2006. Weapons integration and avionics testing.
- PT-05 Static ground testing for fatigue.
- PT-06 September 10, 2006; avionics testing.

Originally first PAF deliveries were scheduled for 2005. The flights with PT-01, however, revealed the need for major airframe design changes. This pushed deliveries to 2007. Development costs are given as $500 million and Block I unit costs as $15 million to $20 million. These figures should be treated with caution and are likely too low.

The first two production aircraft were delivered to the PAF on March 12, 2007, followed by six more in April 2008. Scramble.nl feels the prototypes/early production aircraft were turned into JF-17Bs.[29]

Armament

The JF-17 has seven hardpoints and a theoretical weapons load of 3.6 tons. In practice, the actual load will be considerably less because a fighter must carry external fuel-tanks for a useful range and two short-range AAMs for self-defence. Targeting and ECM pods further reduce the hardpoints available for weapons.

A typical air-to-air mission configuration consists of three stations for drop-tanks (total 3000 litres), two BVR and two short-range missiles.[30]

Typical attack configurations include three fuel tanks, two short-range AAM, and four Mk-82 500 lbs bombs (dual ejector racks); or two anti-radar missiles in place of the bombs; or one guided Mk-84 2000 lb bomb, two drop tanks, and two short-range AAMs.

Among the weapons being cleared for the JF-17 is the Chinese YJ-83 anti-ship missile. The C802 anti-ship missile (600 kg, 180 km maximum range) is also an option. Also cleared are the SD-10 4th generation BVR missile (200 kg, 70 km), the LT-2 1000-lb laser-guided bomb (10 km, total weight 564 kg), the WMD-7 laser-targeting pod (maximum 20 km range), and the LS-6 extended-range laser-guided bomb (454 kg, 80 km).

Engine

The RD-33 as first installed on the MiG-29 in the 1980s cannot be said to be a success.[31] 188 engines were procured for 70 aircraft. Seventy-four per cent of engines failed prematurely; one third of the 188 engines did not even reach 150 hours before failing. The first overhaul point was supposed to be 300-hours against the programmed 180 annual hours per fighter. Engine life was supposed to be 800-hours—itself nothing to celebrate by western standards, but actual life turned out to be less than 400 hours. Further, the engine produced significant smoke, a major problem particularly in the air-to-air combat mode. Moreover, at full thrust the engine used 238 kg fuel per minute—and double that for the MiG-29, which has two engines. Maximum thrust at sea level was even more expensive, reaching 1000 kg/minute fuel.

In defence of the Soviets/Russians, it needs reminding that they tended to design their weapons for wartime usage rates. Peacetime fighter hours were limited. Very high attrition wartime rates were expected, so engines with a life of 20 years or more made no sense. The Soviets preferred large numbers of any weapon system on the theory the high attrition environment likely in Central Europe meant numbers would decide the issue. Further, the Soviets had serious technician shortages at every level in every service, favouring the deployment of crude but simple weapons. And the MiG-29, like other Soviet fighter aircraft, was designed for primitive forward airfields with little maintenance support. Under these conditions it made more sense for the Soviets to produce a larger number of engines, simply swapping them out when they failed.

Production rate

There are two production lines for the FC-1/JF-17. One is at Chengdu producing 15 aircraft/year that will double to 30. The second is in Pakistan, producing two aircraft a month for a total of 24/year, though actual output has been lower. Some reports say the Pakistan line will increase to 36/year as of 2011; again, however, the indications are that production is substantially lower.

While China Aircraft Corporation and Pakistan Aeronautics Corporation own the venture 50-50, Pakistan makes 58 per cent of the parts. It is unclear if this is by value or by the number of parts. The engine and avionics are Chinese-supplied; at this point Pakistan is producing the airframe. It seems unlikely, either way, that Pakistan is producing half the aircraft.

The combined China-Pakistan production suffices to reequip two squadrons a year. By now there should have been signs of a fifth squadron but heading into Fall 2013 there still seem to be only two.

F-17 Block II

The Block II was supposed to enter service in mid-2012, but due to unspecified delays the date was shifted to 2013. Block II is supposed to feature air refuelling, cruise missiles, better data links with AEW aircraft, improved avionics, improved radar, and more advanced EW systems. Some of the 'improvements' may not really be so. For example, Block I already has air refuelling.

The issue of interest is the radar. Pakistan had planned to use the Grifo S7, but for unknown reasons this has not worked out so far. Block I aircraft use the Nanjing KLJ-7 radar. Another deal to equip the plane with French avionics and the Thales RC-400 radar does not seem to have materialised.

Aviation Week says that the Block II will feature a thrust-vectoring version of the WS-13 engine, a Chinese AESA radar, an improved infrared search and tracking module, new avionics, and the next generation version of China KG300G EW pod.[32] Further improvements include use of composites and radar-absorbing coating. Considering the Block II is supposed to be entering service, it seems unlikely that these developments represent Block II. Their inclusion in Block III, which will enter service in 2016, seems more reasonable.

This raises the separate question of what the Pakistanis mean when they maintain, as they did at the 2011 Dubai Air Show, that the FC-1 is a fundamentally different aircraft from the JF-17.[33] The sole clue is that the Pakistanis claimed that the FC-1 has all-Chinese avionics and will be delivered to the PLAAF. At the same time, there is no evidence yet that Pakistan has succeeded with a non-Chinese avionics suite, and certainly no serious efforts have been made for a different engine. It appears that Pakistan claims of a fundamentally different aircraft may, at this time, be hyperbole, as also Pakistan Aeronautics Corporation's claim that should export customers want a different engine, that can be arranged.

JF-17 vs Tejas

Table 4.7: JF-17 vs Tejas

JF-17	Tejas
Specifications Projected [1999] Actual [2004] LENGTH 13.95 meters 14.9679 m HEIGHT 5.02 meters 4.77485 m	**Specifications** Wing Span 8.20 m Length 13.20 m Height: 4.40 m (14 ft 9 in)
WING SPAN 9.5 meters 9.4646 m Wing area: 263 sqft MAX T-O WEIGHT 12,500 kg Empty weight 6,411 kg Normal take-off weight 9,072 kg Maximum landing weight 7,802 kg Fuel weight 2,268 kg Weapons load 3,629 kg Thrust/weight ratio >=0.9 MAX LEVEL SPEED 1031 knots Mach 1.6 MAX RANGE / Ferry range 864 nautical miles 2,037 km SERVICE CEILING 16,000 meters 15,240 m T-O RUN 500 meters 609 m LANDING RUN 700 meters 823 m	Wing area: 38.4 m^2 (413 ft^2) Empty weight: 6,560 kg (14,460 lb) Loaded weight: 9,500 kg (20,944 lb) Max. take-off weight: 13,300 kg (29,100 lb) Internal fuel capacity: 2,458 kg 3000 liters Maximum external fuel 4000 liters Maximum External Stores Load 4000kg (8818 lbs.) Maximum Speed Mach 1.7 Service Ceiling 50,000 feet. G Limits +9/-3.5

RD-93 Maximum thrust: 50.0 kN (11,230 lbf) Dry, 81.3 kN (18,285 lbf) Afterburning. Specific fuel consumption (SFC): 75 kg/(kN·h) (0.77 lb/(lbf·h)) dry, 188 kg/(kN·h) (1.85 lb/(lbf·h)) Life expectancy: 4,000 hours (actual Block I 3,000), first overhaul 1,200 hours The problem is that the SFC is higher than advertised; the overhaul and life hours exaggerated	F404-GE-IN20 turbofan (developed for India) Dry thrust: 48.9 kN (11,000 lbs.) Thrust with afterburner: 84 kN 19,000 lbs st Specific fuel consumption: *Military thrust*: 0.81 lb./(lbf·h) (82.6 kg/(kN·h)) *Full afterburner*: 1.74 lbs./(lbf·h) (177.5 kg/(kN·h)) FADEC, modular, special emphasis on stall free Full TBO: 6000 hours, but engines subject to extreme stress will be lower. Life of 8000 hours can be extended. Kaveri GTX-35VS turbofan rated at 20,200 lbs under development
Armament * 23 mm GSh-23-2 twin-barrel cannon Some combination of * 2 – PL-2 or AIM-9 AAM * 6 - PL-7 AAM * 6 - PL-10 AAM * ASMs, bombs	Armament *Internal GSh-23mm twin barrel gun with 220 rounds of ammunition Seven external hardpoints, can carry air-to-air missiles, air-to-surface missiles, anti-ship missiles, rocket launchers and ECM pods *Self Defence RWR system, jammer and chaff & flare dispensers.
	Kaveri Specific fuel consumption: *Military thrust (throttled)*: 0.78 lb/(lbf•h) (79.52 kg/(kN·h)) *Full afterburner*: 2.03 lb/(lbf•h) (207.00 kg/(kN·h)) Supercruise Tejas Mk. II ~2016 with GE 414, 22,000-lbst
Development cost: $500 million Prototypes: 6 Unit cost: Block I ~$20 million Block II ~$25 million Block III ~$30 million Up to 300 aircraft will be purchased Block I: 50 aircraft Block II: 150 aircraft Block III: 100 aircraft	$2.2 billion (take INR 45 = USD 1) Block I Prototypes: 20 $0.9 billion (take INR 45 = USD 1) Block II Unit cost: Block I $35 million As of 2012 180 aircraft are planned: Block I: 40 aircraft Block II: 100 aircraft (GE 414 engine, test flight 2015) Navy Tejas: 40 aircraft

Development

The extraordinarily long development period of India's Tejas light fighter has been unfavourably contrasted to that of the JF-17. It cannot be denied that India has the unique ability to drag out weapons development programs to the extent a single system becomes a multi-generational effort.

The requirement for what became the Tejas light fighter was formulated in 1969, at a time India already had the advantage of considerable experience with assembly, design, and production of combat aircraft starting with the Vampire in 1948, going on to the Gnat and the HF-24 Marut. The Marut, in developmental terms, can be compared to the JF-17 in that the airframe was designed in India, the engine was imported, and the avionics were also imported. In 1969, India was preparing to manufacture the MiG-21. India had an enormous lead over Pakistan in combat aircraft development and production, and then proceeded to waste the lead.

Twenty-five years passed before India seriously took up work on the Tejas in 1984. The first flight took place in 2001, seventeen years later, compared to eight years for the JF-17's flight after the 1995 Sino-Pakistan MOU. The Indian Air Force's No. 45 Squadron (Vampire, Gnat, MiG-21) will likely become operational in 2013, though it will include Limited Series Production test aircraft. Pakistan likes to say JF-17 development began in 1995, three Block I squadrons were in service by 2012, and by 2013 3-4 more squadrons will be in service, depending on the rate of delivery from Chengdu. Pakistan has completed production of Block I and is starting production of Block II. Tejas Block II will start production in 2016—by which time Pakistan will have started on Block III.

But is it fair to compare the development times for the two aircraft? First, the development for the JF-17 began ten years earlier than Pakistan says because the aircraft is based on the Chinese Super 7. Second, while Pakistani engineers participated in the design effort and the PAF made a valuable contribution to testing, this is a Chinese aircraft, not a Pakistani one. Third, that the plane went into production much faster than Tejas, the credit goes to China's formidable manufacturing base, not to Pakistan.

Tejas, in terms of its development, is quite different from the JF-17. To quote an American defence industry source, "Instead of buying finished and tested equipment from abroad, new designs had to be invented by government research agencies, then tested by themselves until they were ready, followed by integration testing with other elements. These choices were driven by India's desire for long-term self-sufficiency in many aircraft sub-systems, in order to reduce their dependence of foreign suppliers."[34] Further, Pakistan did not have to suffer engine-supplier embargoes: the Russians handed over as many RD-93s as China wanted, whereas supply of the GE 404 was blocked for years by the US.

None of this is to exonerate India and denigrate Pakistan. The latter has taken a huge step forward with the JF-17, considering how basic Pakistan's fighter development and production base was. In particular, there is no excuse for India's squandering of 25 years from the time it formulated plans for a 2nd generation fighter to the time it began work on the Tejas.

Comparing the two fighters

Ostensibly, the two aircraft appear so overtly similar in many characteristics that comparisons are inevitable. In reality, however, the two are quite different, if only because the JF-17 is a third-generation aircraft and the Tejas is a fourth-generation aircraft. For example, the Tejas airframe is formed from composites and JF-17 has an all-metal airframe. Tejas's flying control system is much more sophisticated. Despite claims by the Chinese and Pakistanis that the RD-93 has equivalent specific fuel consumption to the GE 404, this cannot possibly be the case. And the 404 most certainly has a much longer life. India disposes of ample financial resources to import the best technology from around the world; there are no political bars to it buying what it wants. China and Pakistan face considerable restrictions in acquiring top-of-the-line Western technology, even if cost is not a consideration. And because India does not need the Tejas to be a multi-purpose fighter, its plane can be optimised for the air combat mission whereas the JF-17 must be a jack-of-all-trades.

In a larger sense comparing the two aircraft is an unproductive exercise. For the IAF, Tejas is a low option intended to provide numbers. The IAF will be flying Rafales, Su-30s, and most importantly, the stealth FGA. For Pakistan, the JF-17 will equip all but two squadrons, which will take the FC-20. Indeed, there is no assurance Tejas will ever be procured in meaningful numbers. It is quite possible the Rafale buy will be doubled and the Tejas buy correspondingly reduced. If this happens, Tejas' function will have been to give India experience in the design, prototyping and production of a 4th generation fighter.

None of this is to denigrate the JF-17. Pakistan, before this aircraft, had no fighter design, prototyping, and production capacity. Undoubtedly most of the work has been done by China. But Pakistan has been present at every step. It has undoubtedly learned a great deal, and in one move has gone from repair/overhaul of 2nd generation aircraft like the F-7 and Mirage 3/5 to production of a 3rd generation aircraft. Considering how industrially backward Pakistan is, this is quite an achievement.

The use of composites in the LCA resulted in a 40 per cent reduction in the total number of parts compared to using a metallic frame. Furthermore, the number of fasteners has been reduced by half in the composite structure from the 10,000 that would have been required in a metallic frame design. The composite design also helped to avoid about 2000 holes being drilled into the airframe.

A further note on Tejas

Tejas employs C-FC materials for up to 45 per cent of its airframe by weight, including in the fuselage (doors and skins), wings (skin, spars, and ribs), elevons, tailfin, rudder, air brakes and landing gear doors. Composites are used to make an aircraft both lighter and stronger at the same time compared to an all-metal design.

The tailless delta is more manoeuvrable; Tejas in clean configuration has a lower wing loading of 51 lbs per square foot of wing area; JF-17 has 71. This gives Tejas a faster climb and instantaneous turn rate. Eurofighter, considered a highly agile aircraft has a wing loading of 64. It is said the JF-17 is likely superior in sustained turn.

Nonetheless, in the age of the BVR AAM, manoeuvrability may be less important than in the days of dogfights.

PAF's Surface-to-air missile defences

At the end of the 1980s, Pakistan's SAMs consisted of six Crotale 2000 squadrons, two Chinese SAM-2 squadrons, and Bofors RBS-70s with the Army. The Crotales were modernized to the 3000 version, and some squadrons were further modernized to the 4000 version. The PAF procured the Mistral for close-in defence.

Ten batteries of two sections, each of two launchers with six SPADA (Aspide) missiles are in service for air base defence. The first battery was procured in 2010, with the last likely by 2014. The original deal was for $650 million and included 750 missiles, and a maintenance/re-life complex in Karachi. The 2000 is an upgraded version of the original system. This gives a squadron of 24 ready missiles, compared to a Crotale squadron's 16 missiles. Each battery has a detection centre, hosted in a modularised shelter with air surveillance RAC-3D radar; a firing section has a tracking and illumination radar. Spada 2000 is able to detect targets up to 60 km and intercept them up to 25 km with the Aspide SAMs, a development of US Sparrow, which has a 25 km range.

Certainly, despite continuing Chinese upgrades the Red Flag is getting very long in the tooth, having originally entered service in the 1950s. Moreover, the missile is liquid-propelled—red nitrous oxide and kerosene, which means missiles have to be fuelled before launching, something unacceptable today because required reaction times are much shorter than in the 1950s. SAM-2 was designed as an anti-bomber missile. Soviet territory was vast, allowing ample warning of when bombers would be passing within range of a particular SAM-2 complex, so a long reaction time was acceptable. A squadron of six Red Flags requires 200 personnel, whereas a single SPADA launcher provides the same number of missiles.

The Crotale in France has seen constant modernisation with the 5000 and Nouvelle Generation following the 3000/4000 series. Pakistan began upgrading its Crotale 2000s in 2004, and the last missiles were upgraded as recently as 2007. This indicates Crotale should be good till 2017. Possibly further upgrades are planned.

At the same time, the older a system becomes the more expensive it is to maintain. The PAF is constrained for resources. Moreover, Pakistan is looking to buy 3 more SPADA batteries; the Navy wants four batteries for air defence of its naval bases. The Pakistan Army is also looking at 4-6 batteries. If these additional orders are placed, it might indicate that older missiles are slated to be phased out.

Chinese SAMs

Red Flag (renamed Black Arrow by the PAF) entered service in the 1970s. The Indian Air Force intelligence noted two squadrons into the 1980s. Though some sources have said that 12 batteries were purchased, this is more likely to refer to the number of launchers. Forty missiles were included—they are out of service.

The replacement is the HQ-9B, which the PAF says has a range of 125 km, and 25 km against low-level cruise missiles. It is a reverse engineered but much improved system, built with Israeli help. Four batteries are in service, six more are under delivery, A launcher has four missiles; reload missiles, 4 to a truck, are also in service. There have been rumours China to supply the HQ-9 in its export version, the FD-2000. 'FD' are the Chinese initials for the words 'defensive shield.' While the addition of HQ-9 will represent a powerful expansion of PAF's SAM capabilities, it must be kept in mind this missile is a reverse-engineered S-300. Each launcher carries 8 missiles, and in Chinese service, a battery is 8 launchers. This is a big, heavy, and complex system; the missile's maximum range is 125 km; it also has some capability against cruise and intermediate/medium-range ballistic missiles. While the need is urgent, it remains to be seen if the PAF can afford the HQ-9.

While the Pakistan Army is the main user of the Anza shoulder-fired SAM, it is likely the Air Force also uses it for close defence of its air bases. The Anza series produced in Pakistan are:

- Anza-1, based on China HN-5, itself based on SAM-7; about 1100 rounds; production ceased.
- Anza-2, based on China QW-1; about 1300 rounds; production ceased; allegedly a Stinger reverse-engineered by China.
- Anza-3, based on China QW-2; currently in production, equivalent to SAM-16 Igla I.

Anza Mk III / QW-2[35]

All aspect; fire-and-forget; infrared homer.

Table 4.8: Anza III/QW-2

System length: 1.590m
System weight: 18kg
Missile length: N/A
Missile diameter: 0.072m
Missile launch weight: 11.32kg
Propulsion: Single-stage solid rocket
Operating altitude: 0.01~3.5km
Operating range: 0.5~6km
Max speed: 600m/s
Guidance: Dual-band passive infrared homing seeker
Warhead: 1.42kg HE fragmentation
Weapon reaction time: <5 seconds

FN-6/16

SIPRI reports 1191 FN-6 and 806 FN-16 of these shoulder-fired SAMs sold to Pakistan.[36] The -16 is the upgraded version. Its details are:[37]

Figure 4.3: Chinese FN-6. Army Recognition (2018, December 19). FN-6 MANPADS Man Portable Air Defence Missile System, with IFF

Source: https://armyrecognition.com/china_chinese_army_missile_systems_vehicles/fn-6_man_portable_air_defense_missile_system_technical_data_sheet_specifications_pictures_video.html

- Seeker: multi-color infrared
- Range: 500 - 5500 m (FN-16 extended to 6000-meters)
- Altitude: 15 - 3800 m
- Speed: 600 m/s
- Length: 1495 mm
- Diameter: 71 mm
- Missile Weight: 10.77 kg
- Total Weight: 17 kg

Before analysts add HN-6/16 numbers to Pakistan's inventory total, a question must be resolved: are these missiles replacement for Mistral or are they net additions?

Current SAM units

Crotale

Five of six original squadrons remain as No. 451 was merged into No. 454. Squadrons are shifted around as dictated by operational requirements; the bases given here are not necessarily current.

- 451 Squadron Sargodha merged into 454 Squadron at Chaklala
- 452 Squadron
- 453 Squadron Masroor
- 454 Squadron Samungli (Training Squadron)
- 455 Squadron Crotale 4000 Chaklala
- 456 Squadron Kahuta

Mistral

- 242 Squadron Sargodha
- 249 Squadron (unknown base)
- A flight may have five firing posts; the number of flights in a squadron is not known but may be two flights each of 5 firing posts. One hundred rounds were purchased.
- Red Flag II
- (SAM-2 development)
- 471 Squadron Chaklala
- Unidentified squadron

In 2010, the PAF's chief apparently said at the Zhuhai Air Show that the air force was looking at several Chinese SAM systems, including the HQ-18.[38] This missile is a Chinese version of the Russian SAM S-300V (NATO SAM-12 Gladiator). This has a 75-km range and the tracked carrier has four missiles.[39]

It would seem something akin to the HQ-12/KS-1 SAM would be more economical than the HQ-18. The HQ-12 is solid fuel, with two missiles on a truck-based launcher. It will avail Pakistan little if it buys a battery of HQ-18 launchers when three HQ-12 batteries can be purchased for the same price.

TOE of a HQ-12/KS-1 SAM battery[40]

Since the PAF is to definitely purchase at least one Chinese SAM system, the TOE of the KS-1A battery is of interest because it is indicative of the way in which China does things. One regiment—presumably three batteries—was sold to Myanmar in late 2013. The missile also has ABM capability. The battery can simultaneously engage three targets, which seems on the low side.

- 6 × dual-launcher on 6 × 6-wheeled vehicle, 2 rounds each
- 6 × reload vehicles 6 × 6
- 3 × missile carrier vehicles, 8 rounds each
- 1 × SJ-231 ECC station
    * 1 × HT-233 radar (for 3-D target search, detection, acquisition, identification and engagement; clutter rejection and missile guidance)
    * 1 × Type 305A S-band 3-D mobile tactical air defence radar (with a 250 km range)
- Support vehicles
    * 1 × tractor
    * 1 × missile-test vehicles
    * 1 × electronics maintenance vehicles
    * 2 × tool vehicles
    * 1 × power supply vehicle

Radar Systems

The Pakistan Air Force's radar resources have increased manifold in the last two decades. The biggest addition has been AWACS/AEW aircraft, but there has been an expansion of other systems too.

Aerostats

Pakistan's six L-88 Aerostats are unique (a $155 million project total). The US uses ten of these blimp-borne radars for surveillance of its Caribbean and southern borders, and for protection for its Afghanistan bases. India has at least 5-6 Israeli radars primarily for defence against terrorist-flown aircraft. India is developing its own system. Radars are deployed in the Punjab, Rann of Kutch, Delhi, Agra, and possibly Jammu and Kashmir among other places.

The L-88 is a lightweight radar of 370 km range, and the aerostat can be hoisted to a maximum height of 4600 meters, providing excellent low-level coverage. These systems are not mobile, but of course are no more vulnerable than ground radar systems. Once raised on its tether, an aerostat will typically stay aloft for 30-days before being reeled-in for maintenance. Two radars are used: one for area surveillance, and one steerable that can focus on closer-in targets of interest.

VERA Passive Radar

Pakistan Air Force may have six, produced by a Czech firm now owned by Americans. This is an extremely complex matter and if you are interested in Pakistan radars, read *"The History of Downgraded Vera-E Radar Purchase by PAF"* which is based on Wikileaks cables.[41] The discussion is too dense for us enthusiasts. The radar, if in service comes in several versions and Pakistan may have for an early radar detection one.

The main point is that all of Pakistan's radars including Chinese are said to be degraded systems.

Radar Squadrons

400 (TPS-43; not confirmed)
403 (TPS-43) Lahore
408 (TPS-43) Malir
410 (TPS-43G) Sargodha
481 Control & Reporting Wing, PAF Lahore, 7 MPDR
482 Control & Reporting Wing, PAF Malir, MPDR
484 Control & Reporting Wing, PAF Chaklala, MPDR
486 Control & Reporting Wing, PAF Chaklala, MDPR (No. 904 Squadron MPDR-90 is part of this wing)

409 Wing, PAF Sargodha (There is a 4091 Squadron with MPDR-90 radar at Sargodha, likely a flight of No. 409 Squadron.)

Ground Combat Wings

Only one is identified, No. 314 Ground Combat Wing, Samungli (Quetta). The 'wing' may be a misprint for 'squadron,' assuming each wing such as No. 31 at Samungli has a ground protection squadron. Conversely, the wing designation makes sense if it contains several squadrons, each deployed to a PAF flying wing.

Radars

- The TPS-43 radars were modernised once the US aid resumed.
- 5 × China YLC-2 radar, 350-km, in 2003 and possibly 2 more in 2006.[42] Long Range Phased Array 3D. First at Sakesar replacing FPS-89/100. Presumably at Badin too.
- 6 × AN/TPS-77 radars; transportable, 2005 contract for $90 million. One at Masroor.
- Unknown number of FPS-117 replacing FPS-20.
- 6 × L-88 Aerosats.
- Thomson-CSF ATC radars have a dual role of Pakistan Air Traffic Control and early warning.

Low level radars

- *MPDR:* Major investment was made between 1979-80 in 45 Mobile Pulse Doppler Radars acquired from Siemens of Germany. These are called the SILLACS MPDR 45/E. SILLACS stand for Siemens Low Level Air Defence Control System. They are controlled from six Control and Reporting Centres, which are also mobile, and correspond presumably to the PAF's six MPDR wings. Each CRC can control up to 8 radars; the CRC is data-linked to the Sector Operations Centre. According to Janes Weapons System 1987-88 edition, there are two fully mobile versions one with 45 km range another with 60 km. There is a third version, transportable, with a 90 km range. The first two are single vehicle system with a radar mast extendable to 18 meters and a shelter for the operating crew. The CRC is in two units, a shelter with 4 workstations and two assistants positions and power generators on trailers. The MPDR project was the first phase of Project Crystal.

- TPS-70. One such buy for four low-level air defence radars was identified in a March 1990 list to the US Congress. The radar operating envelope is 3 meters to 30,000 meters, with a ~240-km range against a small low target. More may be in service.
- Up to 10 x YLC-6; detect range 150-km, mobile/dismountable, set up and dismantle time <10-minutes each, good low-altitude performance.[43]
- Air Traffic Control: 8 Thomson-CSF TRS-2215 and TRS-2230 type (mobile and fixed/relocatable systems).

Out of service

- FPS 89/100 10 units
- Condor
- Type 514
- FPS-20
- AR-1/6 Radar: In 1968-69 six AR-1 Plessey low level radars were installed, followed by 3 of the mobile versions, called AR-15. The range is about 150 km. Likely replaced by TPS-77.

Pakistan Air Defence Organisation

The Pakistan Army has the 3rd and 4th Air Defence Divisions which are integrated into the PAF's air defence network. Pakistan Army corps generally have an AD brigade each.

- Northern Sector PAF Chaklala, Rawalpindi (under Northern Air Command, Peshawar).
- Central Sector PAF Sargodha (under Central Air Command, Sargodha).
- Western Sector PAF Samungli (under Central Air Command, Sargodha).
- Southern Sector PAF Shere-e-Faisal (under Southern Air Command, Karachi).

Civil Air Traffic Control system

Today it is common practice to integrate civil ATC and military systems. A video explains how it is done in Italy and Germany.[44] The need to coordinate civil and military air traffic in peacetime is obvious; less clear is precisely what role the Pakistan civil ATC plays in wartime.

Pakistan ATC

Lahore Area Control Centre
Karachi Area Control Centre
Primary Surveillance Radars at
- Pasni
- Lak Pass (for Quetta)
- Rojhan (near Rahim Yar Khan)

Primary Surveillance Radars plus secondary Surveillance Radars at
- Islamabad
- Lahore
- Karachi

Aerostat/L-88 **As mentioned earlier, but to repeat:** Pakistan's six L-88 Aerostats were purchased under a $155 million project cost. The US uses ten of these blimp-borne radars for surveillance of its Caribbean and southern borders, and for protection for its Afghanistan bases. India has at least 5-6 Israeli radars primarily for defence against terrorist-flown aircraft. India is developing its own system. Radars are deployed in the Punjab, Rann of Kutch, Delhi, Agra, and possibly Jammu and Kashmir among other places.

The L-88 is a lightweight radar of 370 km range, and the aerostat can be hoisted to a maximum height of 4600 metres. It provides excellent low-level coverage. These systems are not mobile, but of course are no more vulnerable than ground radar systems. Once raised on its tether, an aerostat will typically stay aloft for 30 days before being reeled-in for maintenance. Two radars are used: one for area surveillance, and one steerable that can focus on closer-in targets of interest.

FPS-117

This is a low operating cost air surveillance radar with a range of 330 km (80 per cent probability against 1-meter-square radar cross section). No details of numbers or locations.

YLC-2

This is a modern Chinese long-ranged phased-array 3D radar. Five were delivered in 2003 and possibly two more in 2006.[45] The first was installed at Sakesar, replacing a US FPS-89/100. This implies that Badin, too, was upgraded. Also, in 2003, Karachi was upgraded to the YLC-2.

AN/TPS-77

This is a transportable version of the larger TPS-117. One C-130 or two medium trucks can move the entire system. It uses a crew of 6. Detection and tracking range is about 400 km. Six were procured in 2005 for $90 million. One is at Masroor.

Radar Squadrons

400 (TPS-43, unsure)
403 (TPS-43?) Lahore?
408 (TPS-43) Malir (both squadron and station are unsure)
410 (TPS-43G)

A 1990 notification to Congress spoke of four TPS-70 radars, which are designed as the successor to the TPS-43s. Retained TPS-43 radars were modernised once US aid resumed.

Low-Level Radar Systems

AR-1/6 Radar: In 1968-69 six AR-1 Plessey low-level radars were installed, followed by 3 of the mobile versions, called AR-15. The range is about 150 km. Likely replaced by TPS-77.

To repeat once again from previous pages:

MPDR: A very major investment was made between 1979-80 in 45 Mobile Pulse Doppler Radars acquired from Siemens of Germany. These are called the SILLACS MPDR 45/E. SILLACS stand for Siemens Low-Level Air Defence Control System. They are controlled by six Control and Reporting Centres which are also mobile and correspond, presumably, to the PAF's six MPDR wings.

Each CRC can control up to 8 radars; the CRC is data-linked to the Sector Operations Centre. According to Janes Weapons System 1987-88 edition, there are two fully mobile versions one with 45 km range another with 60 km. The there is a third version, transportable, with a 90 km range. The first two are single vehicle system with a radar mast extendable to 18 meters and a shelter for the operating crew. The CRC is in two units, a shelter with 4 workstations and two assistants positions and power generators on trailers.

The MPDR project was the first phase of Project Crystal.

TPS-70. One such buy for four low-level air defence radars was identified in a March 1990 list to the US Congress. The radar operating envelope is 3 meters to 30,000 meters, with a ~240 km range against a small low target. More may be in service.

YLC-6: Up to 10 x YLC-6; detect range 150 km, mobile/dismountable, set up and dismantle time <10 minutes each, good low-altitude performance.[46]

Cruise missile

- Haft 8 one carried on JF-17 centreline, 350-km range.

Stand Off

- AS-30L French laser-guided, 11 km maximum, 250 kg warhead. Obsolete.
- AGM-65 Maverick US 22 km maximum, 56 kg warhead, EO guidance.
- H-4 Pakistan design, 120 km range; possibly based on a Denel bomb; EO guidance.
- H-2 Pakistan design, 60 km range; possibly based on a Denel bomb.
- TAKBIR Series Satellite Aided Inertial Guided Bomb Family Pakistan design, likely uses US Paveway kit.
- GBU-12 US Paveway II; 500 lbs. Mk-82 bomb inventory may be 700.[47]
- GBU-10 US Paveway II; 2000 lbs. Mk-84 bomb; inventory may be 300.

Anti-Ship

- C-802 China, 165 kg warhead, 120 km range. Inertial guidance, then terminal phase by radar seeker.
- C-803 China, IR and Radar, 350 km, 165 kg warhead. Subsonic, terminal phase Mach 2.
- CM-400AKG Wrecker[48] China (export YJ-12), 2000-lb warhead, 1st guidance system Inertial/GPS 50-meters CEP, for terminal guidance

EO/IR for 5-meters CEP, 240-km maximum; two warhead types, 150-kg and 200-kg.

- Exocet AS 39; 50-70 km range depending on launch profile; 165-kg warhead.
- AGM-84 Harpoon 125+ km range, 210-kg warhead.

Anti-Radar

- AGM-88 HARM can be GPS guided depends on version, 100 km range.
- AGM-45 Shrike.
- MAR-1[49] (Brazil) × 100; 25 km, 200 lbs. warhead; GPS-guided.

(AGM-88 HARM and AGM Shrike turned out to be incorrect information. In any case, in our original draft we wrote about AGM-88 "If Pakistan had this type, it would not have had to buy the much more expensive Brazilian type.")

Notes

1. Provost, C. 2011. Sixty years of US aid to Pakistan. 2011, July 11. The UK Guardian. http://www.guardian.co.uk/global-development/poverty-matters/2011/jul/11/us-aid-to-pakistan Source: Wren Elhai, Center for Global Development, 2011.
2. Aid for Fiscal 2011, 2012, and 2013 from US Congressional Research Service (2013, April 11). Direct overt US aid appropriations for and military reimbursements to Pakistan, FY2002-FY2014. http://www.fas.org/sgp/crs/row/pakaid.pdf
3. Defense Industry Daily (2012, April 4). $5.1B Proposed in Sales, Upgrades, Weapons for Pakistan's F-16s. http://www.defenseindustrydaily.com/51b-proposed-in-sales-upgrades-weapons-for-pakistans-f16s-02396/
4. Pakistan Rupees 300-billion 1970-71, PNR 4.76 = USD 1, multiply by 6.12 for 2012 prices.
5. GDP calculated indirectly using UN Data http://data.un.org. 1970 per capita $205, population 59 million, say $12-billion 1970 prices and about $75-billion 2012 prices. GDP for 2012 estimated by International Monetary Fund; available at UN Data (2013). World statistics pocketbook. Downloaded May 13, 2013. http://data.un.org/CountryProfile.aspx?crName=Pakistan#Summary
6. Indian Rupees 75,000 crores, or approximately $1 billion. The program was originally costed at $10.8 billion or Rs 42,000 crores, but because of inflation and rupee depreciation, the cost will likely near double in rupees and increase 50 per cent in dollars. Figures from Ajai Shukla (Broadsword Blog, February 12, 2012) http://ajaishukla.blogspot.com/2012/02/indian-air-force-may-get-126-

rafale.html Shukla is a former military officer and correspondent for the Indian economic daily, the *Business Standard.*

7. US Defense Industry Daily, April 4, 2012; op. cit., 35.
8. Syed, B. (2012, February 7). Pakistan receives F-16 planes from US. *Dawn.* Downloaded August 9, 2013. http://beta.dawn.com/news/693664/pakistan-receives-f-16-planes-from-us
9. No author identified (November 15, 2011). "Air force dropped 10,600 bombs in two years: Qamar". Reprinted from *The News* by Pakistan Defense Forum. http://www.defence.pk/forums/military-photos-multimedia/140404-dubai-airshow-2011-a-37.html#ixzz2Zbl9bsV4
10. Entnous, A. 2011. "U.S. Balks at Pakistani Bills" 2011 May 16) *Wall Street Journal.* http://online.wsj.com/article/SB10001424052748703730804576321570902617838.html
11. Scramble.nl Pakistan Military Database https://www.scramble.nl/database/military/pk#results
12. David L. Rockwell (2019, November 25). "Raytheon's Airborne FLIR Sensor Ball Systems Drawn From: Military Electronics Briefing" 2019 Teal Group. https://tealgroup.com/index.php/teal-group-media-news-briefs-2/teal-group-news-media/item/raytheon-s-airborne-flir-sensor-ball-systems
13. Pratt & Whitney (n. d.) Pratt & Whitney's F100-PW-229. http://www.pw.utc.com/media_center/assets/f100_pw_229_white_paper.pdf
14. No author (2011, November 13). Pakistan offers cut-price JF-17 fighter jet at Dubai Air Show. *Reuters.* http://tribune.com.pk/story/291210/pakistan-offers-cut-price-jf17-fighter-jet-at-dubai-air-show/
15. Defense Industry Daily Staff (2011, November 14). Pakistan & China's JF-17 Fighter Program. http://www.defenseindustrydaily.com/stuck-in-sichuan-pakistani-jf17-program-grounded-02984/

16 As usual with Chinese fighters, there is much confusion on designations. The export version of Chinese FC-20 is also referred to as the J-10B, of which Pakistan is said to have purchased 36. But the FC-20 is a stealth F-18/Su-27 class aircraft.

17. Defense Industry Daily (2008, September 10). Jordan Buys 20 F-16 MLU from Holland, Belgium. http://www.defenseindustrydaily.com/jordan-buys-20-f16-mlu-from-holland-belgium-updated-02176/
18. Zitun, Y. (July 12, 2013). "IDF to offer tanks, planes, missile boats for sale". *Ynetnews.com* Downloaded July 20, 2013 from http://www.ynetnews.com/articles/0,7340,L-4404232,00.html See UPI's story July 15, 2013 for more details: "If you're looking for a cut-rate F-16 or Merkava tank". http://www.spacedaily.com/reports/If_youre_looking_for_a_cut-rate_F-16_or_a_Merkava_tank_999.html Though it is not specified these particular aircraft are the F-16s for sale, disposals have to be of the A/B versions.

19. F-16.net (2013). Cheil Ha'avir: Israel Defense Force/Air Force - IDF/AF. Downloaded July 24, 2013. http://www.f-16.net/f-16_users_article7.html
20. Scramble is a society of aviation enthusiasts and aircraft spotters. http://www.scramblemagazine.nl/index.php?option=com_mildb&view=search
21. Flight Magazine (1999, July 14). China and Pakistan agree on Super-7 fighter development work. http://www.flightglobal.com/news/articles/china-and-pakistan-agree-on-super-7-fighter-development-53912/
22. China.org.cn (2003, June 13). Super-7 fighter jet to make test flight. http://www.china.org.cn/archive/2003-06/13/content_1066954.htm
23. Ibid.
24. Lubin, G. (2011, May 20). Pakistan's "Best Friend" China Agrees To Provide 50 New Fighter Jets". *Business Insider.* Downloaded December 1, 2012. http://www.businessinsider.com/china-pakistan-jets-2011-5#ixzz2awQzVgoDhttp://www.businessinsider.com/china-pakistan-jets-2011-5
25. Waldron, G. (2011, May 20). China to expedite 50 JF-17 delivery to Pakistan. *Flight Global.* Downloaded December 1, 2012. http://www.flightglobal.com/news/articles/china-to-expedite-50-jf-17-kits-for-pakistan-357062/
26. Farhan_9909 (2012, August 21). 50 JF-17 from China delivery started. *Pakistan Defense* http://www.defence.pk/forums/jf-17-thunder/203150-50-jf-17-china-delivery-started-9.html
27. http://chinesemil.blogspot.com/2011/11/china-pakistan-jf-17-fighter-ready-for.html
28. (na) (nd) JF-17 Thunder (FC-1/ Super-7). http://www.pakakhbar.com/military/airforce/super7.html
29. Scramble. Pakistan Military Database. https://www.scramble.nl/database/military/pk
30. Pakistan Aeronautics Complex (2013). JF-17 Aircraft, Downloaded December 6, 2012. http://www.pac.org.pk/jf17.html . [If the site does not come up, go to pac.org.pk; click on "Products" and then on JF-17]
31. Details taken from Indian Comptroller and Auditor General report as cited in http://forum.keypublishing.co.uk/showthread.php?t=50771
32. Johnson, R. (2011, November 13). JF-17: the world's next best-selling light fighter?" *Aviation Week.* As reproduced in http://www.zinio.com/reader.jsp?issue=416198869&o=ext
33. Ibid.
34. Defense Industry Daily Staff (2013, April 23). LCA Tejas: An Indian fighter – with foreign help. *Defense Industry Daily.* http://www.defenseindustrydaily.com/india-lca-tejas-by-2010-but-foreign-help-sought-with-engine-01901/#tejas-program-india-exports
35. Sinodefence.com (2007). QW-2 Man-Portable Surface-to-Air Missile. http://www.sinodefence.com/army/surfacetoairmissile/qw2.asp

36. SIPRI (2023) Arms Transfer Database. https://armstransfers.sipri.org/ArmsTransfer/CSVResult
37. Defense Updates (2012, December 11). Chinese FN-6 / FN-16 MANPADS.http://defenseupdates.blogspot.com/2012/12/chinese-fn-6-fn-16-manpads.html
38. Haider (2011, January 22). Pakistan evaluating HQ-18. *Pakistan Defence Forum* Air Force to Downloaded August 4, 2013. http://www.defence.pk/forums/pakistan-air-force/89926-pakistan-evaluating-hq18.html
39. Federation of American Scientists (2000, June 30) S-300V. http://www.defence.pk/forums/pakistan-air-force/89926-pakistan-evaluating-hq18.html
40. Sengupta, P. (2014, January 14). KS-1A MR-SAM Scores First Export Success. Trident-Trishul Blogspot. http://trishul-trident.blogspot.com/
41. Pakistan Defence & Military Forums (November 24, 2017). The History of Downgraded Vera-E Radar Purchase by PAF. https://pdf.defence.pk/threads/the-history-of-downgraded-vera-e-radar-purchase-by-paf.530145/
42. Wise, J. (2009, January). PLA Air Defense Radars. *Air Power Australia* Technical Report APA-TR-2009-0103. Downloaded August 9, 2012. http://www.ausairpower.net/APA-PLA-IADS-Radars.html#mozTocId769296
43. Ibid.
44. Euro News (nd). Fly Series 1 – civil-military cooperation in European skies. Downloaded August 8, 2012. http://youtube.googleapis.com/v/dqQmLRZjnHk
45. John C. Wise (2009, last updated 2024. January 27). NRIET/CEIEC/CETC YLC-2/YLC-2A/YLC-2V High Guard 3D Long Range Surveillance Radar. PLA Air Defense Radars. *Air Power Australia.* http://www.ausairpower.net/APA-PLA-IADS-Radars.html
46. John C. Wise (2009, last updated 2024. January 27). PLA Air Defense Radars. Air Power Australia. http://www.ausairpower.net/APA-PLA-IADS-Radars.html
47. 1000 kits were delivered in 2010 for use against insurgents. We assume Pakistan will want to maintain this level of inventory. http://www.reuters.com/article/2010/03/02/usa-pakistan-weapons-idUSN0217277420100302
48. http://missilethreat.com/dubai-china-details-performance-of-carrier-killer-missile-for-jf-17/ DUBAI: China details performance of 'carrier killer' missile for JF-17
49. Price paid $1.1-million including support (n.a.) (2008, December 7.) Air Weapons: Brazilian HARM For Pakistan *Strategy Page* http://www.strategypage.com/htmw/htairw/20081207.aspx

5

2010-2020: The Best Decade

Pakistan plans a force level of 20 fighter squadrons, a number that realistically gives it a strong defence against the IAF, and enough of a strike capability to tie up a large number of IAF air defence squadrons. This may be the first time since its inception that the PAF will have this capability, and it will help make 2010-2020 into the PAF's best decade. The 2015 and 2020 squadrons are estimates that assume funds are available for additional JF-17s and F-20s.

Table 5.1: Estimated PAF squadrons 2010-2020

	Squadrons			
Type	2010	2013	2015	2020
J-10	0	0	2	6
F-16	2	3	3	4
JF-17	2	3	7	10
J-7	7	6	5	0
Mirage 3/5	6	5	0	0
K-8	0	1	1	1
Transport	3	3	3	3
ELINT	1	1	1	1
Tanker	0	1	1	1
AWACS/AEW	0	2	2	2

Note added in 2024: you can see Pushpindar and I overestimated the rate at which new aircraft were acquired by the PAF; as of end 2023 seven F-7/Mirage squadrons were still in service.

Note

- It is assumed that Pakistan will obtain a fourth F-16 squadron. If it continues to be resource short, this may consist of used, rebuilt F-16A/B. The PAF is believed to have had an option for a second batch of F-16C/D, which was cancelled or put on hold because of resource shortages. Non-official sources say the PAF has asked for delivery of the second batch.

- The Chinese weapon systems each have several designations, particularly in the case of export versions. The F-20 is not the alleged 5th Generation Chinese Stealth Fighter. That is the J-20. A new purported stealth fighter is the J-31, currently undergoing tests. The FC-20 is the export version of the PLAAF's J-10. Two squadrons were signed for in 2006 for 2014-15 delivery. The lengthy gap between the contract and delivery is not explained, except that Pakistan says that it has co-developed the FC-20. If so, the delay might have arisen because of the need to "Pakistanise" the aircraft. The table below is from Andres Parsch,[1] and is a good summary of the Chinese fighter numerical designations. Please consult this source for designation of other aircraft such as trainers, bombers, transports, and helicopters.

Table 5.2: Chinese Fighters

Designation	Manufacturer	Model; Remarks
J-2	Mikoyan	MiG-15; versions include **J-2** and **JJ-2** (MiG-15UTI); J-2/JJ-2 designations questionable!
J-4	Mikoyan	MiG-17F; versions include **J-4** and **JJ-4** (MiG-17U); J-4/JJ-4 designations questionable!
J-5	Shenyang/ Chengdu	MiG-17PF built in China; versions include **J-5**, **J-5A**, **J-5R**, **JJ-5** and **JZ-5**
J-6	Shenyang	MiG-19 built in China; versions include **J-6** (Mig-19S/SF), **J-6A** (Mig-19PF), **J-6B** (Mig-19PM), **J-6C** (Mig-19SF), **J-6bis** (improved J-6), **J6Xin** (improved J-6A), **J-6I**, **J-6II**, **J-6III**, **J-6IV** (cancelled), **JJ-6** ('MiG-19UTI') and **JZ-6** (MiG-19R)
J-7	Chengdu	MiG-21F built in China; numerous versions, most important are – based on MiG-21F-13: **J-7**, **J-7I**, **J-7II** (export: **F-7B**), **J-7IIA**, **J-7H** (**J-7IIH**), **F-7M** *Airguard* (export), **F-7P/MP** *Airbolt* (export) – based on MiG-21MF: **J-7C** (**J-7III**), **J-7D** (**J-7IIIA**) – 3rd generation J-7: **J-7E** (**J-7IV**), **J-7EB**, **J-7EH**, **J-7G**, **F-7MG/PG** (export) – trainer: **JJ-7** ('MiG-21U'), **JJ-7A**, **FT-7P/PG** (export)

J-8	Shenyang	Developed from MiG-21 (NATO 'Finback'); versions include **J-8, J-8A** (J-8I; 'Finback A'), **J-8B** (J-8II; 'Finback B'), **J-8C** (J-8III), **J-8D** (J-8IIA; J-8II with AAR), **J-8E** (J-8A with new radar & avionics), **J-8F** (J-8IIF), **J-8M** (J-8IIM; improved J-8II; 'Finback C') and **JZ-8**
J-9	Chengdu	Single-engine Mach 2.4 fighter project (1970s; canard layout); not built (reports referring to J-9 as a CATIC fighter project based on MiG-23 are probably in error).
J-10	-	Swing-wing all-weather fighter project (late 1960s); not built, number later re-used.
J-10	Chengdu	Multi-role fighter; versions include **J-10A** (single-seater) and **J-10B** (two-seater).
J-11	Shenyang	Single-engine lightweight fighter design (late 1960s); not built, number later re-used.
J-11	Shenyang	Sukhoi Su-27SK (also two-seaters Su-27UBK and Su-30MKK) built in China; versions include **J-11, J-11A** and **J-11B.**
J-12	Nanchang	Single-engine ultra-lightweight STOL fighter project (1970s); prototypes only; number might be re-used.
J-12	-	Possibly reserved for XXJ project; designation unconfirmed!
J-13	Shenyang	Advanced single-engine fighter project (1980s); not built; number will most likely be re-used.
J-15	Shenyang	Chinese multirole naval aircraft
J-16	Shenyang	Chinese strike aircraft
FJ-17	Chengdu	China-Pakistan collaboration 'Thunder'
J-20	Chengdu	5th generation stealth fighter in development
J-31	Shenyang	5th generation stealth fighter in development

J-10/FC-20[2]

(Please note the nomenclature FC-20 is no longer used; otherwise, the FC-20 was allegedly the export version of the J-10. The J-10 has been exported to the PAF as the J-10CE. The number 20 is used for the J-20 stealth fighter.)

This is the first Chinese fighter designed from the outset for ground attack.

Powerplant: 1 X Russian Salyut AL-31FN turbofan

Thrust (dry): 76.2kN (7,770kg, 17,130 lbs.)

Thrust (afterburning): 122.55 kN (12,500 kg, 27,557 lb)

In-flight refuelling: Yes

Weapon: 23mm single-barrel cannon

External Hardpoints: 11 (five under the fuselage centreline; six under the wings)

Design: tailless canard delta wing; inherently unstable; controlled by Fly By Wire, giving it high manoeuvrability, especially at supersonic speeds.

Load for long endurance air-to-air mission:

- 2 × PL-11/PL-12 MRAAM
- 2 × PL-8 SRAAM
- 2 × 1,600 litre drop tanks
- 1 × 800 litre drop tank

Load for ground attack mission:

- 2 × PL-8 SRAAM
- 6 × 250 kg LDGP bomb
- 2 × 1,600 litre drop tanks
- 1 × 800 litre drop tank

Nonetheless, from cryptic statements made by senior PAF officers from time to time, there are indications that the J-10/FC-20 deal is by no means done. The problem appears to be on China's side. There are two possibilities:

- China is not proceeding in timely fashion on customising the aircraft for the PAF, which is a condition of purchase;
- China is asking for more money than previously agreed.

Future Procurement

J-20

The Chinese stealth fighter tail number 2002 undertook its fifteenth test flight on 14 August 2012.[3] The tail number indicates it is the second aircraft in the series. This is a rapid development considering that flight tests with tail number 2001 started only in January 2011 and that there are three prototypes (tail number 2003 has not yet been identified in flight). Thus, the total number of flights likely exceeds 20.

Considering that India is developing 200 FGFA stealth fighters with the Russians, Pakistan likely has looked at the J-20. It would have almost certainly concluded that the aircraft is unsuited for Pakistan. Even the PLAAF is unlikely to buy it. An aviation analyst has described the plane as 'cobbled together' with some stealth elements, but far from being a stealth fighter.[4] For example, the engine nozzles are not stealthy, and the canards compromise stealth. Of course, much could change with future prototypes because the aircraft may simply be a technology demonstrator. The Chinese may have been under pressure to prematurely reveal and fly the J-20 to show the US that the latter's naval and air forces out to the Second Island Chain (1500 nautical miles) are vulnerable.

It will likely be years before China has a true stealth fighter. Even then, will China be willing to export it? Could Pakistan afford it, assuming the plane can be customised to Pakistan's requirements? Most importantly, is this big, heavy, long-range air defence fighter even appropriate for the PAF, given that from the Indian border to Peshawar is merely 500 km? The J-20 is perhaps equivalent to the MiG-25 Foxbat, in that it is optimised for range and speed. The MiG-25, of which the IAF operated one squadron, was a fighter designed to intercept the US' proposed B-70 high-altitude, high-speed bomber which was cancelled.

Pakistan could consider something like the Eurofighter Typhoon as a counter-Indian stealth platform. The Typhoon is ten to 100 times less stealthy than the US standard[5] ('golf-ball' or 'insect-sized'). But it is an excellent visual-range fighter that has, in exercises, held its own against the F-22 Raptor.[6] Is it not the idea of a stealth fighter to stay outside the adversary's detection range and use Beyond Visual Range missiles? At least the US Air Force's think tank, RAND, says BVR has been oversold:

> "In a 2008 study … the Air Force-funded think tank RAND warned against assuming long-range missiles will work. RAND looked at 588 air-to-air shoot-downs since the 1950s and counted just 24 that occurred with the attacker firing from beyond visual range. Historically, American

long-range air-to-air missiles have been 90-percent less effective than predicted, RAND asserted."[7]

The close-in versus BVR debate, however, is contingent entirely on the performance of BVR. This may not be adequate at this time. But will it be true ten years from now?

Nonetheless, what is clear is that Pakistan cannot afford to get a western stealth fighter. Currently the only one available is the F-35, at a unit cost of $176 million (Fiscal 2013 buy).[8] That suggests a lifecycle cost of perhaps $300 million over 20 years, or $12 billion for 40 aircraft. That is hardly feasible for Pakistan.

Table 5.3: J-20 vs HAL FGFA

Chengdu J-20[9] Black Eagle	Sukhoi/HAL FGFA[10]
• Crew: 1 • Length: 64-feet • Wingspan: 41-feet • Height: 4.45 m (14 ft 7 in) • Wing area: 630-ft² • Empty weight: <17,000 kg • Max takeoff weight: ~35,000 kg • Powerplant: 2 engines, combined 60,000 lbs after burning • Maximum speed: Mach 1.8 • Combat radius: 2,000 km	• Crew: 1 • Length 22.6 m • Height 5.9 m • MTOW 34,000 kg • Range 3880 km • Speed Mach 2 • Max Weapon Load 2.25 Ton (Int.) & 5.75 Ton (Ext.) • Thrust Vectoring w/ Nozzle (±15°) • Engine Thrust 2×14000 kgs

See http://warfare.ru/?lang=&linkid=2280&catid=255 for a much more detailed exposition[11]

F-20

Unlike the JF-17 program, which was freely discussed by the PAF for many years, almost nothing definitive is known about the PAF and the Chengdu F-20. In PLAAF service, it is called the J-10. Some reckon it is equivalent to the F-18E Super Hornet. Such judgments should be made cautiously, however, because more and more, fighter aircraft are becoming platforms for electronics, computers, and weapons, and their performance characteristics are becoming less important. Unless it can be shown that the Chinese have equalled the US in these areas, claiming that the J-10 equals the F-18E becomes meaningless. Characteristics such as speed, rate of turn, manoeuvrability in the transonic range and so on have fairly much been the same for thirty years. Short of shifting to UAVs, there is little prospect for improvement here.

Flight International's 'World Air Forces 2011/2012' credited China with 200 J-10s. This is in contrast to the JF-17, which China developed and produced, but did not introduce into its own service. Pakistani sources claim the J-10 was co-developed with Pakistan; more likely the PAF has been helping Chengdu customise the aircraft for Pakistan service. The figure commonly used is that 40 aircraft are contracted[12] for 2015 delivery, and that 150 are required. While the contract was signed in 2009, has the Pakistan Government cleared funding? The unit cost is in the range of $30 million, twice that of the JF-17.

Periodically there are reports that the PAF is unhappy with the FC-20 and may not buy it. Are these reports motivated by Pakistan's wish to gain leverage vis-à-vis the Chinese? Or are they genuine expressions of concern about the aircraft?

Table 5.4: J-10C vs Su-30MKI

J-10CE	**Sukhoi Su-30MKI**[13]
• **Crew**: One **Powerplant:** 1× WS-10B • **Thrust:** claimed 31,000 lbs. max; may as yet be only 27,000 lbs. • **Dimensions:** 16.9 m × 9.8 m × 5.7 m • **Take-off:** 14,000 kg/19,227 kg **Weapon:** 23mm single-barrel cannon; external 5,000 kg fuel/pods/weapons Air-to-air 4 AAM, 4000 litres external fuel • **Attack** 2 AAM, 2 × 500 kg, 4000 litres external fuel	• **Crew**: Two • **Powerplant:** 2 × Salyut AL-31FP • **Afterburner:** 2 × 27,500 lbs. • **Dimensions:** 21.9 m × 14. 7 m × 6.4 m • **Take-off** 24900 kg; max 38800 kg • **Fuel Normal:** 5270 kg Max 9640 kg • **Take-off** run 550 m landing 750 m Max • 30mm Gsh-30 with 150 rounds

Notes

- WS-10B might not be 31,000 lbs yet as claimed by China
- J-10C is the latest version, 'E' export
- J-10 was initially designed around AL-31N engine
- It is primarily air defence, whereas Su-30MKI is multirole but with excellent air-to-air manoeuvring.

K-8P

Jointly developed with China, the aircraft is produced at the Pakistan Aeronautical Complex. China and Pakistan have sold 600 aircraft since they entered service in 1994, two thirds for the PLAAF. The PAF version has a modern glass cockpit and electronics as specified by it.

The aircraft is not normally armed but can be equipped with a 23mm gun pod (centreline); two fuel tanks, and two AAMs. Its maximum speed of 0.75 limits its role to a point-defence fighter backing up regular air defence squadrons. It is not known if the PAF plans to use its K-8s for this role. It can also be used for light ground-attack.

With the completion of recent orders, the PAF will have around 90 of these trainers.

Crew: 2 (in tandem)

- Empty weight: 2,687 kg (5,924 lbs.)
- Max. take-off weight: 4,330 kg (9,546 lbs.)
- Powerplant: 1 × Garrett TFE731 (3,600 lbs.)

Armament

Table 5.5: K-8P Armament

Air-to-Air	Air-to-Ground	Air-to-Ground	Air-to-Ground
23mm cannon	23mm cannon	23mm cannon	23mm cannon
2 × 360 litre tanks	2 × 360 litre tanks	2 × 360 litre tanks	4 × 250 kg bombs
2 × PL-5 AAMs	2 × 57 mm pods	2 × 250 kg bombs	

Saab 2000 AEW & C[14]

Pakistan was originally to buy 7 of these aircraft from Sweden. This would have permitted two on station at all times to cover 1200 km of the front, for short periods. This is hardly ideal. For example, one aircraft in the north and one in the south leaves the central front (Multan and Bhawalpur) and western front (Balochistan) unprotected. True, the AEW aircraft do not circle one spot when airborne. They fly racetracks that can be 100-300-km long. So, within a 30 minute period most of the front is covered at least once. For maritime surveillance this is adequate. Over land, it does mean coverage compromises have to be made. But of course, this would have been a big jump compared to no high-altitude coverage before.

Figure 5.1: Saab 2000 AEW of No. 3 Squadron 'Angels' Serial #11-045. Drawing © Tom Cooper

The order was cut to four, and the reason could be that Pakistan was getting a better deal by buying four Chinese AWACS. The matter is discussed in greater deal under the ZDK-03 entry as the Chinese would take PKR payment versus hard currency to Sweden.

The Saab 2000 has a maximum operating ceiling of 9000 meters. Its patrol speed is 160 knots. At that height the radar can detect fighters or warships at about 300 km, and cruise missiles at about 150 km.

The system has two operating restrictions. First, there are only five operator console systems. Second, in practice the radar is likely limited to 120 degree sectors on either side of the aircraft. This is not, of course, what the manufacturer says: a greater coverage is claimed.

Against that, the system has two advantages.

- The operating costs are much lower than those of a mid-size AEW such as one based on a Boeing 737 airframe.
- The radar can simultaneously cover different sectors, possibly 60 degrees each, in air-to-air and air-to-ground. Depending on the resolution of the air-to-ground mode, Pakistan will have the capability of detecting Indian armoured formations, a major tactical advantage.

An open question is if five operator stations are too few in the South Asian context. In the context of the US E-3, the Inner German Border was about 750-km long and the first day of war might have seen 3000 or more aircraft in the sky. And given the US is a global power, with no consideration for operating costs, something with long-range becomes a priority—a big, heavy aircraft like the Boeing 707 fits the bill. The Japanese use the 767 because of their long-range maritime needs. South Korea and Turkey use the smaller 737.

Other details

- The aircraft has a significant self-defence and ESM capability
- 2 flying crew
- 5 operator stations, with four jump seats behind for additional watch officers
- Rest area for six, bunks for four
- One lavatory, a galley, and baggage storage space
- Secure communications
- Theoretical maximum endurance 9.5-hours, theoretical maximum range 3000-km
- Take off 1400-meters, radar comes on three minutes after take-off; time to 25,000-feet = 15-minutes
- Laser and missile warning systems, chaff

The situation regarding these AEWs in PAF service is difficult to assess because apparently two were completely destroyed in a terrorist attack on the base. One was damaged and is being repaired by Saab. There are suggestions that a new aircraft has been ordered.

ZDK-03

This aircraft is referred to as the 'Karakoram Eagle' in the Pakistan media. The aircraft's flyaway cost appears to be in the $70 million range, which by today's standards is quite inexpensive for a full-scale AWACS. There is speculation the radar may not be as advanced as that on PLAAF AWACS, though how that compared to western AWACS is unknown. The airframes are new.

Specifications for Y-8F-600 aircraft

This is the platform for the radar; it is an updated design produced in conjunction with Ukraine. Some sources say the Y-8F-600 is the same as the Shanxii Y-9 transport.

Table 5.6: Y-8F-600

Range	4500 km
Cruise speed	550 km/hr
Max altitude	30,000-feet
Climb	600 feet/min
Engines	4 × P&W PB150B turboprop engines; quieter, better fuel economy, improved hot & high
Electronics	Modern western systems

The big question is why did the PAF buy this aircraft? Not only will its maintenance/flying costs be substantially more than the Saab 2000, the PAF is complicating its maintenance by having two completely different early warning aircraft. Given how careful the PAF is about spending money, this is surprising.

The reason could not have been radar performance. 300 km radius is standard for AWACS/AEW type aircraft. For example, the Australian 'Top Hat' radar has a range of 'more than' 200 nautical miles, equal to 340 km.[15] Under real-world operating conditions, about 300 km is likely to be practical range. Moreover, the Chinese radar cannot be as advanced as the Swedish.

At least one senior PAF officer, an Air Chief Marshal commanding the force, has said he was told by then President Musharraf to cut the Saab order to 4 aircraft and buy 2 ZDK-03 in the place of the additional Saabs that had been contracted for. He indicates that the PAF was opposed to this.

A short review of Chinese AWACS

China originally intended to mount an Israeli radar system on an Il-76 airframe, the same as the IAF has done. The project was cancelled in 2000 because of US pressure on Israel. China then developed the KJ-2000, mounting its own radar on the Il-76. At least four aircraft are in service and many more are to come.

As a hedge against failure, China developed the KJ-200, which features an Erieye type radar mounted on a Y-8. The aircraft has Pratt & Whitney Canada

PW150B turboprops, reducing noise and fuel consumption, and Honeywell avionics. As a hedge against failure of the radar development, China developed a Y-8 with a rotodome—which is what the ZDK-03 is.

It is probably reasonable to assume the ZDK-03 has the same engines as the KJ-200, and almost certainly it has Pakistan-specified avionics. It is supposed to have an Airborne Steerable Electronic Array (ASEA) type radar like the KJ-200.[16] But if so, why the rotodome? An advantage of the ASEA radar over a rotodome is that it is lighter, and maintenance is easier. Designers do not go back to rotodomes if the flat panel arrays are available. For example, both the Boeing 737 and 767 AWACS use flat panel arrays. So does the rotodome mean (a) China does not want to share its AESA radar with Pakistan; or (b) the radar has not worked out in development and Pakistan did not want it? In either case, why did Pakistan not buy more Ericsson radars from Sweden and use the Y-8 as a platform?

Part of the answer has to lie in cost. Had it purchased five Saab 2000s, Pakistan would have paid $170 million per aircraft.[17] The ZDK-03s are about $70 million each. That might be a flyaway cost, unlike the Saab 2000s, which likely includes several years of spares. Nonetheless, it is possible that the life-cycle cost is less than the Saab 2000. The PAF, being careful with its money, probably has computed on a life-cycle basis. It might also be the Chinese accepted Pakistan Rupees or accepted offsets, say in the production of K-8s and the JF-17 when the latter succeeds in obtaining export orders. If this line of reasoning is correct, the ZDK-03 may make more sense than the additional Saab 2000s.

Pakistan UAVs

Burraq UACV

(Named after the Prophet's winged steed that brought Him from heaven.)

Might enter service in 2013, said to be domestically designed. At best, it uses a variety of Chinese components. Payload is 200 kg. The Chinese have developed a laser-guided missile of about 40 kg weight and this might be a weapon for the Burraq.

Figure 5.2: Picture of what appears to be 12 Burraq UCAV. © Pakistan Interservices Public Relations

Source: https://thediplomat.com/2015/09/pakistan-uses-indigenous-drone-to-strike-terrorists/

Falcon (Selex Galileo)

The Falco has a night/all-weather capability over land and over water, with 8-14 hours of endurance. Maximum weight is 420 kgs, wing span 22 feet, and a top speed of 120 mph.[18] Four UAVs are controlled from three vehicles: Ground Control Station (GCS), Ground Data Terminal (GDT), and Ground Support Equipment (GSE). Payload is 50+ kg, and ceiling is about 15,000 feet.

Payloads include EO/IR, Laser designator, SAR, Maritime surveillance radar, ESM, Chaff/Flares dispenser, NBC sensors, and Hyperspectral sensor.

The PAF obtained 25 Falcos (5 systems x 4 UAVs, plus one spare) and likely has them in 2 UAV squadrons.

Flamingo

Though this UAV is probably an Australian civil design and is available in Pakistan (domestic manufacture) it is unclear if it is only on offer or has been inducted by the PAF. The payload bay permits swapping in and out of any payload within the weight limit.

A medium-range UAV with a 6-8-hour endurance, it has a 200-km range with a 30-kg payload. It is controlled from the ground, with two operators working from a truck module. It can fly a pre-programmed path that can be altered immediately via manual interruption. The weight is 240 kg, a maximum altitude 12,000 feet, and a wing span of 22 feet.

Jasoos II Bravo+

(The name means investigator, spy, detective.)

This 5-hour endurance drone is a Pakistan-built version of the Bravo that entered service in 2004. Its payload is 20 kg (electro-optical sensor package, live video) and maximum range is 100 km. The engine provides 38 horsepower. Maximum take-off weight is 140 kg, wingspan is 15 feet, and a maximum altitude of 10,000 feet is attainable. The drone has proved reliable in PAF service.[19] Though nothing remarkable, a major advantage is that it is inexpensive.

Mukhbar

It is a scaled down Jasoos for Pakistan Army use, with a 40 km range and a 10 feet wingspan. Its take-off weight is 40 kg, and payload 5 kg. 45 aircraft were ordered. More orders remain a possibility.

PAF Wings

All wings have a Station commander's Flight on the MFI-17. The 8x squadrons are actually SAR flights.

Table 5.7: PAF Wings

Wing	Station	Squadrons
31 Fighter	Samungli (Quetta)	17, 23, 85
32 Fighter Ground Attack	Masroor (Karachi)	2, 7, 8, 22, 84
33 Fighter Multi-Role	Minhas (Kamra)	14, 25, 87
34 Fighter	Rafiqui (Shorkot Road)	5, 15, 20, 27, 83
35 Composite Air Transport	Chaklala	6, 12, 21, 41, TCS
36 Tactical Attack	Peshawar	16, 26, 81
37 Combat Training	Mianwali	1, 18, 19, 86
38 Multi-role	Sargodha	9, 11, 24, 82, CCS
Flying Training College	Risalpur	1 & 2 PFT; 1 & 2 BFT

PAF Squadrons

Table 5.8: Summary of PAF Squadrons

Squadron	Nickname	Year Raised	Aircraft
1	Rahbars	1978	K-8
2	Minhas	1956	F-7P
4	Karakoram Eagles	1959/2008	AWACS
5	Falcons	1947	F-16C/D
6	Antelopes	1946	C-130
7	Bandits	1960	Mirage 3 ROSE 1
8	Haiders	1960/1982	Mirage 5
9	Griffens	1943	F-16A/B
10	Bulls	2009	Il-78
11	Arrows	1949	F-16A/B
12	Globe Trotters	1953 (1950)	VIP
13	Unknown	2009	Saab AEW
14	Tailchoppers	1948	F-7P
15	Cobras	1956	Mirage 3
16	Panthers	1956	JF-17
17	Tigers	1957	JF-17? (Was F-7P)
18	War Hawks	1958	F-7P
19	Sherdils	1958	FT-7
20	Eagles	1956	F-7PG
21	Burraqs	2006	C-130
22	Ghazis	1984	Mirage 3
23	Talons	1961	F-7PG
24	Blinders	1962/1988	Falcon DA-20
25	Night Strike Eagles	1966	Mirage 3 ROSE I/II
26	Black Spiders	1967	J-17
27	Zarrars	2007	Mirage 3 ROSE III

Note: Squadrons with two raising dates means they were deactivated and raised again. For No. 12, I have two raising dates. For No. 13, Kaiser Tufail informed there has never been such a squadron. Wikipedia mistakenly attributed the squadron to Alan Warnes, whereas when I got his book courtesy of Society for Aerospace Studies, it was clear that he said no such thing. The correct reference was No. 3 Squadron.

Notes on PAF Squadrons[20]

Sherdils (Serials from scramble.nl)

The team flies nine aircraft, but there are additional aircraft assigned.

Table 5.9: Sherdil serials

06-09-807	06-09-808	06-09-809	06-09-810	06-09-811
06-09-812	06-09-813	06-09-814	06-09-817	06-09-818
08-09-821	08-09-822		831	835

No. 1 Squadron

It is the PAF's fighter conversion squadron is based at Mianwali. It is at last rid of obsolete aircraft and now is equipped with the K-8P Karakoram. With the completion of recent orders, the PAF will have around 55+ of these trainers, and the PAF Academy's Advanced Flying Squadron also with K-8s is at Risalpur.

No. 2 Squadron

It flies F-7Ps from Masroor AB for the air defence of southern Pakistan. Because of the time spent over the sea and coast, its aircraft have corrosion-resistant engines. It also serves as a training squadron.

No. 3 Squadron

This is the old Transport Conversion School (TCS) squadron. The TCS exists, but the number was plated in 1982. Reraised on Saab AEW.

No. 4 Squadron

This was the old SAR unit and number plated since 1969; in 2008 reraised with ZDK-03 AWACS. The platform is the Chinese Y-8, similar to the An-12.

Table 5.10: ZDK-03 serials

11-001
12-002
13-003
14-004

Figure 5.3: ZDK-03 of No. 4 Squadron Serial # 12-003, probably over Arabian Sea. From US Public Broadcasting System

Source: https://pbs.twimg.com/media/FxMf_9eaAAEk8tb?format=jpg&name=medium

In the late 1980s, at the height of the Soviet-Afghanistan War, Pakistan asked for the US E-3. Unsurprisingly, this was refused and the E-2 offered. Pakistan refused this because of the poor performance over the mountains. Pakistan had to do without an AEW until 20 years later when the Saab 2000 entered service.

No. 5 Squadron

After flying Mirage 3s for 43 years, in 2010 the squadron began transitioning to the F-16C/D. Raised August 15, 1947, this is one of the PAF's oldest squadrons, with a 65-year history. It was the first Mirage unit, reequipping in 1968.

No. 6 Squadron

It is one of two C-130 squadrons and the PAF's main air transport squadron, equipped with the Lockheed Hercules. In 40+ years the squadron has lost 9 C-130s, including one that was sabotaged, President General Zia being killed. The squadron has been a major beneficiary of the US assistance after the US invasion of Afghanistan in 2001. Based at Chaklala, along with the two other PAF transport squadrons, Nos. 12 and 41, currently it has:

- 11 C-130E (six delivered in the 2000s, 5 US Military Assistance Program 1960s
- 5 C-130B (US Military Assistance Program aircraft)
- 1 L-100 civilian model

Aircraft in service have upgraded engines, modernised cockpits, and extended fatigue lives.

The US provided 9 B models, 4 more came from Iran for a total of thirteen.

Six of the E models are ex-Royal Australian Air Force aircraft originally built in 1965 or 1966 and refurbished for delivery to the PAF at a cost of $76 million. They were originally returned to Lockheed in 2000. Five E models, not listed below, came from Iran- the circumstances being unclear.

Table 5.11: C-130 Serials[21]

PAF Serial	Model	Comments
58-0739	B	MAP
61-2646	B	MAP
61-2648	B	MAP
62-4141	B	MAP
62-4142	B	MAP
64145	L-100	
65-12896	E	Ex-RAAF
65-12900	E	Ex-RAAF
65-12902	E	Ex-RAAF
65-12903	E	Ex-RAAF
65-12904	E	Ex-RAAF
65-12906	E	Ex-RAAF

Of the aircraft written off, seven were B models, one an E, and one was an L-100.

No. 7 Squadron

It flies Mirages for the attack mission with its home base at Masroor.

No. 8 Squadron

It is the dedicated maritime attack squadron, also at Masroor. Its Mirage 5s will be replaced by JF-17s carrying Chinese C-802/803 air-to-ship missiles. It is unclear if the aircraft has been tested with these missiles yet. Pakistan says the Chinese C-400AKG Mach 4 anti-ship missile has been integrated with the JF-17. The missile weighs 400 kg and has a range of 180+ kilometres.

No. 9 Squadron

An F-16 squadron. The purchase of one trainer for every single-seater raises a question we had asked in the first part of the book, and to which there is still no answer: why does Pakistan buy so many F-16 trainers? Forty percent of its inventory consists of trainers. Yes, they are fully combat-capable. But the second seat takes away valuable space that could be better utilised. Normally, for three squadrons, the PAF should require two trainers on establishment per squadron, and perhaps 4-6 for operational conversion.

Part of the answer may lie in that most of the aircraft manufactured but stored under embargo and then released (Peace Drive III) were B models. The Peace Gate IV aircraft, almost all A models, were never manufactured. This would mean the PAF ended up with more trainers than it needed for its reduced force. The original plan was for 111 aircraft, and while 24 trainers may seem a lot, it is probably not particularly disproportionate. Twenty-five trainers for 39 single-seater forces are definitely disproportionate, but Pakistan was in a limited position to bargain when the US resumed arms supplies. The PAF was down to 33 A/Bs. Getting 14 A/Bs from storage or withdrawn from US Navy aggressor training and refurbished, all at no cost to Pakistan was a quick, practical solution to the problem.

No. 10 Squadron

This was the B-57 training unit until number plated in 1960; reactivated in 2009 on Il-78 with 4 Midas Il-78MP air tankers with 3-point refuelling capability. One of the aircraft is a converted Il-76. The planes were constructed in 1987-88 and were in storage in the Ukraine. The payload is unclear but is probably around 40,000 kg. The aircraft can be quickly reconfigured for cargo, permitting something around 25 tons delivery to Skardu.

The tankers provide Pakistan with important new capabilities including:

- Extending F-16 CAP time to 5-hours; JF-17 time to about 4 hours
- Doubling Mirage 5/naval attack range and Arabian Sea surveillance range
- Permitting F-16Cs/F-20s to attack as far east as Calcutta and as far south at Cochin. The first would require refuelling over Tibet.

Table 5.12: Il-78 serials

R09-001
R10-002
R11-003
R12-004

No. 11 Squadron

On F-16: both an operational squadron and an OCU for the type.

Figure 5.4: F-16A-15OCU-CF No. 11 Squadron 'Arrows.' Serial #92731 Drawing © Tom Cooper. One of the aircraft Pakistan paid for but was embargoed and served with US Navy Aggressors before being refurbished and returned to Pakistan

No. 12 VIP Squadron

Table 5.13: Squadron Aircraft

Aircraft	Serial
Citation 560 Excel	J-754
Gulfstream IV-SP	J-755
Gulfstream IV-XG450	J-756
Airbus 310	J-757 (Given to PIA, the civil airline)
Citation 560V	0233
Boeing 707-351B	68-19635
Boeing 707-340C	68-19866
Citation 500 Bravo	1003

No. 13 Squadron

Raised 2009 on Saab AEW. (*This was actually No. 3 Squadron, misreported as No. 13)*

No. 14 Squadron

It is a rare case of stepping-down in terms of air capability. It was converted in 1993 from an F-16 unit to an F-7 squadron because of the shortage of aircraft following the US embargo. Its base is Minhas AB (Kamra). Its mission is the air defence of northern Pakistan. It routinely sends detachments to Skardu. It also flies reconnaissance with Mirages transferred from No. 5 Squadron when that unit converted to the F-16C/D.

No. 15 Squadron

Flies Mirages from Rafiqui and is qualified on stand-off weapons like the Chinese air-to-ground H-2/4.

Figure 5.5: Mirage 5DA (twin seater) of No. 15 Squadron Serial 90-601 ex Australian A3-101. Drawing © Tom Cooper

No. 16 Squadron

It was the first JF-17 Squadron, converting from the A-5C.[22] It flies in the air defence role, but also serves as a Test & Evaluation unit. All new production JF-17s are tested by this squadron and, on clearance, are declared operational. About 90 A-5Cs were delivered to the PAF. It is believed Pakistan may have obtained its A-5s for a million dollars each. If so, this would have proved a boon at a time Pakistan was very short of money. Even though the aircraft had a very low engine time-between-overhaul and airframe life, it was simple and robust. How simple? Two 23mm cannon with a hundred rounds each, a practical payload of 2 × 500 kgs with a centreline tank and Western avionics.

Yet oddly the PLAAF had much faith in this aircraft and kept asking the manufacturer to produce new versions. It cannot be determined what systems the PAF may have used, but by the 1990s this plane was being offered with western systems, for example, the avionics from the Italian light strike AMX fighter. New versions could even drop laser-guided bombs! The A-5 was the PAF's equivalent of the Indian Ambassador car: simple to the point of being crude, but capable of running no matter how matter how abused.

Nonetheless, the PAF must have been relieved when the JF-17 arrived and the A-5 could be honourably retired. Perhaps one day the PAF will write a history of their A-5s, and it is bound to be fascinating.

No. 17 Squadron
Flies from Samungli on the F-7PG.

Figure 5.6: F-7PG of No. 17 Squadron Serial # 01-816. Drawing © Tom Cooper

No. 18 Squadron
Dual role, operational squadron and OCU.

No. 19 Squadron
A dual operational squadron and an OCU.

No. 20 Squadron
An F-7 squadron.

No. 21 Squadron
It flies C-130s from Shere-i-Fasial. This identification is given by *Scramble*, a very large worldwide group of enthusiast air spotters.[23] It is also given by PAF Falcons.[24] In the age of the Internet, there is much cross quoting, so these cannot be taken as two independent sources. *Scramble* generally will not list a unit unless it is confirmed by its enthusiast observers. No other confirmation.

No. 22 Squadron

Flies Mirages from Masroor; its role is unclear. It is also an OCU.

No. 23 Squadron

An F-7 squadron flying from Samungli (Quetta).

No. 24 Squadron

This squadron used to fly the RB-57F 'Droopy', two of which were loaned by the US to the PAF for nuclear air sampling and ELINT missions against China and the Soviet Union. A most fascinating story that emerged in a Pakistan think tank journal only in 2010 details how the then Foreign Minister Z. A. Bhutto tried to persuade PAF COAS Air Marshal Asghar Khan to misuse the aircraft for missions over India. The Air Marshal refused as this would violate the terms of the US loan. Eventually, when the Air Chief Marshal resigned, Bhutto got his way.[25] It is remarkable what a high standard of honour the Air Chief Marshal exhibited and it speaks well of the old PAF.

One aircraft was lost to Pakistan army flak over Rahiwali in 1965 when the squadron leader, unhappy at the PAF's inability to destroy Amritsar (India) radar, decided to refine his pathfinder tactics against a Pakistan radar. The second aircraft was hit by a SAM-2 (or multiple near SAM-2 explosions) on its way back from Agra, where it had gone after the 1965 War for reconnaissance. Why is not known? The aircraft made it back to Peshawar and was taken away by the US. The story mentioned above contains speculation that the aircraft, which could fly up to 80,000 and should have been out of SAM-2 range was flying much lower. This was because PAF aircrew did not like the cumbersome high-altitude suits and had no patience with the procedure to wear them and in any case preferred low-level missions.

When the squadron was reraised in 1988, it was equipped with two Dassault Falcon 20F for ELINT and EW. It was joined later by J-753, a Falcon 20E converted from the VIP role ex-No. 12 Squadron.

J-753 'Mir'[26]
J-468 'Lodhi'[27]
J-469 'Iqbal'[28]

Figure 5.7: No. 24 Squadron 'Lodhi' Falcon 20F Serial J-468. Photo by Panagloffs A. Pletris, taken at Athens. Greece. The plane was headed west, destination not declared

Source: https://www.airpics.net/photo/J-468-Dassault-Falcon-20F-Pakistan-Air-Force/17470/L

A fourth ELINT/EW aircraft in Pakistan is PKN-101 (Navy) Raytheon Hawker 850XP. The aircraft is also used as a corporate jet for the Pakistan Navy chief.

No. 25 Squadron

Flies night-attack Mirage ROSE from Shabaz AB (Jacobabad).

No. 26 Squadron

Was the second JF-17 squadron, replacing A-5C. It flies in the air defence role and may also serve as a Test & Evaluation unit.

No. 27 Squadron

Raised 2007. It flies night attack Mirage ROSE IIIE/F from Rafiqi AB (Shorkot Road).

Then the youngest PAF fighter squadron. It has participated in the North West Frontier air campaigns. In 2012 the squadron was reported as converted to the JF-17, but this does not appear to be correct.

No. 41 Light Communication Squadron (Chaklala)

It is unclear if the squadron's single PA-34 is still in service.

Table 5.14: Squadron aircraft

Aircraft	Serial
Embraer 500/Phenom 100	V-4101
Embraer 500/Phenom 100	V-4102
Embraer 500/Phenom 100	V-4103
Embraer 500/Phenom 100	V-4104
Harbin Y-12 II	96-035
Harbin Y-12 II	96-091
Cessna 172	91-661
Cessna 172	

The aircraft's name is Phenom 100, but was certified as the Embraer 500, thus accounting for the double name. It is a very light executive jet.

2 crew + 4	passengers
2 × 1695	lb. static thrust Pratt & Whitney (Canada) engines
449	mph maximum speed
41,000	feet ceiling
2000	km range (4 occupants)

Harbin Y-12II

Distinguished chiefly by more powerful Pratt & Whitney (Canada) PT6A-27 engines, 680 shp:

- 2 crew + 16 passengers (maximum)
- Empty 6,600 lb.
- Maximum 11,700 lbs. (likely slightly higher)

Special Services Wing

Lacking verified information on the PAF's SSW organisation, we have relied on Wikipedia.[29] Readers are warned that none of this information is authenticated, and no sources are provided in the Wikipedia article. Several sources mention the wing and its history, proof that it exists. For example,

PAF Falcons has a video on YouTube stating that the Wing got its own anti-terrorist training centre in 2010.[30]

Supposedly, Air Commodore Dogar, PAF, a veteran of the Chindit operations in Burma pursued the idea of setting up a special operation unit. He is said to have done this in 1966; the wing was disbanded in the 1970s, then revived in 2001.

312th Special Service Wing

- No. 1 Special Operations Squadron
- No. 2 Special Operations Squadron (clandestine missions)
- No. 3 Special Operations Squadron (Anti-Terrorist and Hostage Rescue)
- No. 4 Special Operations Squadron (VIP protection)
- No. 5 Paratrooper Training Squadron (5th PTS)
- No. 10 Special Reconnaissance Flight (Clandestine flights)

Figure 5.8: Fast Roping from Pakistan Navy SH-3s, Karachi. Provided by Pakistan Air Attache, New Delhi, but taken from Airliners.net, Syed Zohair Zaidi. From the Estate of Pushpindar Singh Chopra, Society of Aerospace Studies, New Delhi

Combat Commanders School

The CCS is composed of the PAF's best pilots and has two squadrons of 12 aircraft each, one on Mirages ('Dashings') and one of F-7s ('Skybolts'). The CCS may now also be flying JF-17s, which might account for some of the aircraft produced in 2012 that have not shown up elsewhere.

Table 5.15: PAF Squadrons by type aircraft

F-7P/PG	Mirage III	Mirage V	F-16	JF-17	Transport	Other
2	7	8	5	16	6	4
14	15	25	9	26	12	10
17		27	11	17?	21	13
18					41	24
19						
20						
23						

PAF Inventory July 1, 2013

This is an estimate based on several sources. We believe that the number of Mirage 3/5s is overstated by many sources.

Table 5.16: PAF Aircraft Inventory

Aircraft	Number
J-17	100
F-16	61 (26 A, 19B, 12 C, 6 D)
F-7P	70
F-7PG	60
Mirage 3/5	120
K-8	55 (there may be more)
Saab 2000 AEW	4
ZDK-03 AWACS	4
Il-78 tanker	4
C-130B/E/L-100	17
C-235	4 (including 1 VIP)
ELINT/EW	3 including 2 Falcon DA-20
Helicopters	Total unknown: Mi-171, Alouette 3

Figure 5.9: Starboard underwing armament for airbase attack. From left to right: PL-5E-II AAM, 500-lb low-drag bomb, middle rear MAR-1 anti-radiation missile, middle front Durandal airfield attack bomb, 500-lb high drag bomb, 1000-lb low-drag bomb. Society of Aerospace Studies, New Delhi, estate of Pushpindar Singh

Low-drag bomb is for higher altitude bombing. High-drag has a parachute to slow down bomb and is used for low altitude bombing so that aircraft can be out of blast range. Otherwise, you could blow yourself up.

The Brazilian MAR-1[31] is used for SEAD (Suppression of Enemy Air Defence) and equips both the JF-17 and Mirage III ROSE/Mirage 5 ROSE. It has a 60-100 km range, with six modes, one of which is selected by the pilot. Pakistan purchased 100 missiles in 2008, and it was integrated with the JF-17 in 2011.[32] It has a passive seeker, 60-100 km range and comes in two versions.

Pakistan Navy Aviation

A brief mention of Pakistan Navy aviation is helpful because it provides a picture of Pakistan's sea frontier. Given that Pakistan has only 800 km of coast as the crow flies, its Navy aviation resources are considerable. Interestingly, the Navy's P-3 Orions are used over the North West Frontier Province for reconnaissance, ELINT, and bombing.[33]

Table 5.17: Pakistan Navy Air Squadrons

Squadron	Aircraft	Number	Serials
27	Fokker 27 MR ATR-72-500	3 2	
28	P-3C	9-11	See Table 33
29	Atlantic Hawker 850XP	1 1	 101

Before the arrival of the two ATR-72s to replace Fokker F-27s, five of the latter were in service. These three were used for MR, and two for moving personnel and freight. It is presumed the ATR-72s for No. 27 Squadron, purchased slightly used from civil sources, will replace F-27s in this role.

P-3B/C

Three P-3C-II3/4 were purchased with Pakistan's own funds, and then embargoed in 1991 before delivery, even though Pakistan had paid for them and had taken ownership. The aircraft were cleared for delivery in 1996. One (serial #27) was lost in a crash in 1999. In 2004 the US agreed to sell Pakistan 8 Orion P-3C-Is in an almost $1 billion deal. Of these, two were lost in a terrorist attack on PNS Mehran and one was written off in a ground collision. US agreed to deliver two replacement aircraft. All aircraft from the batch of 8 were delivered by 2012. The aircraft have under gone considerable upgradation and modernisation under the Pakistan Upgrade Program. The aircraft are equipped with Harpoon Extended Range Standoff Land Attack Missiles said to have a 240 kilometre range, in addition to depth charges and torpedoes for anti-submarine warfare. This version of the Harpoon (AGM-84H) can also be used against surface warships. Pakistan purchased one P-3 for spares but is refurbishing the aircraft for service.

A Pakistan blog says that the serial numbers have been changed.[34]

Table 5.18: P-3 Serials

#81 (earlier #25)	In service
#82 (earlier #26)	In service
#83 (earlier #27)	Lost 1999 off Pasni
#84	Destroyed by terrorists on ground 2011
#85	In service
#86	In service, arrived 2010
#87 (presumably earlier #31)	Destroyed by terrorists on ground 2011, arrived 2010
#88	In service, arrived July 2012
#89	In service, arrived July 2012
#90 (presumed)	In service
#91 (Presumed)	In service unless delayed, was due 2012

Note:

Naturally one speculates what happens to No. 29 Squadron. With just one Atlantic and one Hawker 850 aircraft, is it worth Pakistan's time operating the Atlantic and will the squadron reequip with P-3s?

At any rate, 15-16 MR aircraft for just 800-km coastline represents a formidable patrol capability.

Mirage 5 MR Strike rumour

Some sources say that the PAF's No. 8 Mirage 5 maritime strike squadron has been given to the Pakistan Navy. This is incorrect: the squadron continues with the PAF.

Helicopter squadrons

Table 5.19: Pakistan Navy helicopter squadrons

Squadron	Aircraft	Number	
111	Sea King	20	A number are being delivered from Qatar
222	Z-9EC	4-6	Shipboard; serials #21, 22, 25, 41
333	Alouette	2	Training; serials 34, 36 (-316 model)

The Lynx helicopters of No. 222 Squadron are in storage. Serials #21, 22, and 23.

Figure 5.10: Pakistan Navy Z-9 #25

Source: https://www.reddit.com/r/Helicopters/comments/1aes8y0/pakistan_navys_harbin_z9b_1170x1171/#lightbox

***Sea King Serials* (first ten only + ex-Qatar)**

10	Written off – 4 September 2023
11	
12	
13	Written off – February 1986
14	
15	
16	
17	
18	Written off – 31 August 2018
19	
50	Ex-Qatar
54	Ex-Qatar
55	Ex-Qatar
56	Ex-Qatar
57	Ex-Qatar

First 10 from Scramble.nl; next five from M. Umar Aziz.

Seven acquired from UK for spares. Ten acquired from Qatar in 2021 including #50, #54, #55, #56 #57 M Umar Aziz photos. The rest of #5x series are not identified; but likely to be 51, 52, 53, 58, and 59.

Other squadrons

No. 93 Squadron is operated by the Pakistan Maritime Security Agency. It has 1 F-27 modified for ASW and 3 Defender BN-2T surveillance aircraft. Serials #08, 42, and 46.

No. 659 UAV Squadron is equipped with the Mukhbar (scaled down Jasoos II) UAV. Probably intended for coastal surveillance east of Karachi. Can also be used for shipboard use.

Pakistan Army Aviation

This is a large force, in flux because of re-equipment. Very approximately, its inventory consists of:

Table 5.20: Pakistan Army Helicopters

Type	Number of aircraft
AH-1F/S attack	30
Eurocopter A 550 light attack	20 including under delivery
Bell 412	60 including 40 under delivery
Mi-8/17	90
SA 330 medium transport	30
SA 319	15
Bell 206	8

Pakistan Maritime Surveillance Agency

The Agency has one squadron, No. 93, with 1 F-27 Friendship and 3 BN-2 Defender.

Pakistan Strategic Forces Command

No information is available on the PAF's contribution to this joint services command. Two or three fighter squadrons are assigned to the command. Missiles appear to be controlled by the Army.

Figure 5.11: Pakistan Maritime Security Agency BN-2 Defender from https://pmsa.gov.pk/pmsa-bases. Serial #46. Other two aircraft are #08 and #42. Pakistan MSA does not list the single F-27

Source: Which Scramble has as scrapped with no date and https://www.airliners.net/photo/Pakistan-Navy/Fokker-F-27-200MAR-Maritime/649091/L has as "Closed."

Terrorism

The Pakistan military has been subject to terrorism. Generally, official figures are that three non-operational aircraft were destroyed. Other sources give a total of 14, including F-7 (non-operational) and K-8, and 14 personnel killed.[35]

Figure 5.12: The third PAF Il-78 air tanker of No.10 Squadron. Provided by Pakistan Air Attache, New Delhi, but taken from Airliners.net, Syed Zohair Zaidi. From Estate of Pushpindar Singh Chopra, Society of Aerospace Studies, New Delhi

Note on Balakot 2019

This incident is not discussed here because it is highly controversial, unnecessarily so in my opinion. The main reason is that I did not get a chance to discuss this with Pushpindar and it is unfair to include the event in a book where he is my co-author.

Balakot is a storm-in-a-teacup because statistically we have a sample size of n=1. That has no significance. True, that is not *always* true. If, for example, if your hypothesis is there are no aliens, then meeting just one shows your hypothesis is wrong. N=1 is adequate. But one limited encounter between the IAF and PAF tells us nothing about them that can be a guide. All we know is that the PAF took the encounter seriously enough that it has systematically remedied the gaps it saw. As for the IAF, I at least don't know what gaps the encounter exposed or what lessons, if any, the IAF learned.

You can read Pakistan's version at Alan Warnes.[36] I have not included India's version because this is a book only about Pakistan.

Notes

1. Parsch, A. (2012) Chinese military aircraft designations. http://www.designation-systems.net/non-us/china.html
2. Sinodefence.com (2009, March 2011) Jian-10 Multirole Fighter Aircraft. Downloaded August 8, 2013. http://www.sinodefence.com/airforce/fighter/j10.asp
3. China Defense Mashup (2012). Fifteenth flight of No. 2002 J-20 on August 14th. http://www.china-defense-mashup.com/the-15th-flight-of-no-2002-j-20-fighter-on-august-14.html This URL is no longer available.
4. Hodge, N. (2011, January 11). China's J-20 fighter: stealthy or just stealthy-looking?" *Washington Wire* http://blogs.wsj.com/washwire/2011/01/19/chinas-j-20-fighter-stealthy-or-just-stealthy-looking/
5. Kopp, C. (2000). "Eurofighter Typhoon: Demon or Lemon?" Downloaded July 4, 2013. http://www.ausairpower.net/Analysis-Typhoon.html
6. Axe, D. (2012, July 30). "How to defeat the Air Force's most powerful fighter". *Wired* . Downloaded July 8, 2012. http://www.wired.com/dangerroom/2012/07/f-22-germans/
7. Axe, D. (2012, July 30), op. cit.
8. Department of the Air Force (2012) FY 2013 President's Budget: Table P1 Page 28. http://www.saffm.hq.af.mil/shared/media/document/AFD-120210-115.pdf
9. Figures are taken from several sources including Thompson, L. (2011, March 2) "New Details On China's J-20 Fighter Provide More Nuanced View Of Threat".

Lexington Institute http://www.lexingtoninstitute.org/new-details-on-chinas-j-20-fighter-provide-more-nuanced-view-of-threat?a=1&c=1171

10. Hindustan Aeronautics Ltd. (2012) "Our Products". Downloaded February 17, 2013. http://www.hal-india.com/futureproducts/products.asp
11. See http://warfare.ru/?lang=&linkid=2280&catid=255 for a much more detailed exposition
12. "Pakistan buying Chinese J-10 Fighters" *Defense Industry Daily* (US). Downloaded February 11, 2013. http://www.defenseindustrydaily.com/Pakistan-Buying-Chinese-J-10-Fighters-05937/
13. VayuSena (2009, February 28). "Irkut/HAL Su-30MKI Air Dominance Fighter" Downloaded July 8, 2013. http://vayu-sena.tripod.com/info-su30mki.html
14. Saab Technologies (2012) "Saab Erieye 2000 AEW & C". Downloaded December 16, 2012. http://www.saabgroup.com/Global/Documents%20and%20Images/Air/Airborne%20Solutions/AEW_C/SSS08_0061_Datasheet_Saab_2000_ERIEYE_AEW_C.pdf
15. Air Force Technology (2012). Boeing 737 AEW&C Wedgetail Early Warning Aircraft, Australia. Downloaded February 19, 2013. http://www.airforce-technology.com/projects/737aewc/
16. Waldron, G. (2010, November 24). "Pakistan to receive first ZDK-03 AEWC aircraft". Downloaded January 25, 2013. http://www.flightglobal.com/news/articles/pakistan-to-receive-first-zdk-03-aewc-aircraft-350025/
17. The contract for five was for Swedish Kroner 6.9 billion (2006), approximately US$ 1 billion. See Asian Defense "Pakistan has now an eye in the sky (Saab-2000 ERIEYE AWE&C". http://theasiandefence.blogspot.com/2009/12/pakistan-has-now-eye-in-sky.html
18. SELEX Galileo (2010) "Falco UAV System". http://www.selexgalileo.com/EN/Common/files/SELEX_Galileo/Products/FALCO.pdf
19. Satuma Pakistan (2013). "Tactical Range UAV - Jasoos II (Bravo+)". http://www.satuma.com.pk/Detail.aspx?ProdID=2
20. Sources used include Khan, N. (2011, November 13) "Thunder's next squadron!". Downloaded July 28, 2013. http://pafwallpapers.com/blog/2011/11/thunder%E2%80%99s-next-squadron/
21. Many serial numbers are from RZJets. http://rzjets.net/aircraft/? parentid=6739&typeid=134&frstatus=1
22. Pakistan A-5C descended from the PLAAF Q-5, itself descended from The MiG-19/F-6 with Italian avionics and equipped with 2 × 23mm cannon, AIM-9 and Matra missiles plus 4 × 500 lbs bombs. With centre line fuel tank, 2 × 500-lb bombs. It was lightly armoured against ground small-arms fire. 90 were delivered between 1983-1994 and was agile in the air-to-air role. https://wiki.warthunder.com/A-5C.

23. Scramble "Pakistan Air Force Order of Battle" http://www.scramble.nl/mil/3/pakaf/orbat.htm
24. PAF Falcons "Battle lines of the PAF" http://www.paffalcons.com/bases/index.php
25. The letter was written by USAF Lieutenant George Singleton, posted to Pakistan at that time. It is available at http://www.defence.pk/forums/military-history-strategy/60610-1965-war-role-rb-57f.html
26. Presumably named after ACM Mushaf Ali Mir (1947–2003), killed in a Fokker 27 accident
27. Presumably named after Flight Lieutenant Saifullah Khan Lodhi of No. 24 Squadron killed in action on a reconnaissance sortie over Amritsar in the 1965 War.
28. Presumably named after Sqn Ldr Muhammad Iqbal, killed in the 1965 War.
29. Wikipedia (2012) Special Service Wing, Downloaded November 23, 2012. http://en.wikipedia.org/wiki/Special_Service_Wing
30. FAF Falcons (2010) "PAF sets up Commandos of SSG training center for Anti-Terrorism operations - May 14, 2010" http://www.youtube.com/watch?v=eQLcqvL2rrg&feature=player_embedded
31. See Alexandre Beraldi (2007, April 27). MAR-1. Latin American Aero and Defense. Defesa Net. http://www.defesanet.com.br/laad07/3_cta_mectron.htm
32. Alexandre Galante (2011, June 6). MAR-1 is integrated with Pakistan JF-17. http://www.aereo.jor.br/2011/06/06/mar-1-esta-integrado-ao-jf-17-do-paquistao/.
33. Macey, R. (2011, May 23). Before attack, Pakistan Navy boasted of role in fight against Taliban. http://thelede.blogs.nytimes.com/2011/05/23/before-attack-pakistans-navy-boasted-of-role-in-fight-against-taliban/
34. Khalid, O. (2011, May 27). "Target: Orions". http://www.pakwheels.com/blog/2011/05/27/target-orions/
35. Republic World (n.d.). 14 Aircraft Destroyed In Terror Attack On Pakistan Mianwali Airbase. https://www.youtube.com/watch?v=igtfOyfFp5Q
36. Alan Warnes. "Operation Swift Retort: One Year On." Air Forces Monthly. April 2020, p. 35. URL: https://airforcesmonthly.keypublishing.com/the-magazine/view-issue/?issueID=8176

6

2020-2024

To remind: This chapter was written four years after the final draft of PAF 1990-2020 was finalised. The final draft for 1990-2020 has been left as is, with the information available at the time. Only some egregious errors in the 2010-20 chapter were corrected.

The chapter on 2020–2024 is new. Luckily, just before submitting this book to the publisher, on 29 March 2024, Bilal Khan[1] of the Pakistan defence magazine Quwa.org (Quwa = force) wrote a comprehensive article on the PAF's new initiatives. Though this meant a delay in publication, his article enables us to double-check some of our information (including articles by Bilal) and to obtain a wider perspective on its plans.

To understand the background of what is happening in 2020-2024, please consider that Pakistan thought just because it had nuclear weapons, it could approach its modernising and conventional forces with casual insouciance. Interestingly, the Pakistan Army made no such assumption, and even before India's Cold Start era, it began assiduously to counter Cold Start, which was rendered obsolete before India had fully formulated it. As I explained at great length elsewhere,[2] Cold Start was a faulty doctrine, and so was Pakistan's belief it could deter India with tactical nuclear weapons.

The Balakot 2019 incident however made the Pakistan military understand that tactical N-weapons were no panacea. Discussion of the subject has no relevance here. This chapter is concerned simply with how the PAF reacted to Balakot has led to a wholesale reorganization of the PAF. The PAF has focused on increasing its combat capability by adding force multipliers; and of course, on getting new aircraft to replace its large numbers of obsolete combat aircraft, namely the F-7 and Mirage. The force multipliers are not cheap but increase combat capability at a fraction of the cost of new aircraft.

Bilal's assessment of the PAF 2020-2030 plan is

- Replacing Legacy Platforms
- Taking a Holistic Approach to Area Denial
- Enhancing Tactical and Strategic Situational Awareness
- Incorporating Drones into the Air Attack Element
- Expanding Air Lift and Logistics Capabilities
- Revising the Advanced Air Training Regimen
- Building Dedicated Offensive Wings

The main areas of our focus are tactical rather than Bilal's strategic:

- Replacing legacy fighters
- A gap-free radar ground network
- Completing its airborne electronic surveillance and control
- Multiplying the number of UAVs and UCAV
- Introducing large number of guided weapons
- Networking is air assets
- Proliferating UAV/CUAV

This translates into:

- Continuing production of the JF-17, possibly planning a Block IV version now called the JF-17PFX and preparing to bring Block I and II to Block III standard. It will rebuild JF-17s when necessary and to the extent possible.
- Acquiring J-10CE Firebirds from China. (No word on the J-10S 2-seater).
- Partnering with Turkey for development of the 'KAAN' 5-Gen stealth fighter (2028 introduction into squadron service in Turkey, if Pakistan continues with the program and if affordable, likely some in PAF by 2030).
- Acquiring the dual-seat L-15B trainer/light fighter.
- Increasing the numbers of C-130s (second hand).

- Adding to the number of helicopters and shifting from SAR to CSAR.
- Continuing modernization of its F-16s.
- More AEW.
- Installing its own SAM network
- Indigenous AAM including BVR; developing indigenous mobile SAM (no word on if PAF plans to buy these); deploying cruise missiles (<300 km and 550 km); possibly inducting an indigenous anti-ship cruise missile.
- Proliferating more UAV and UCAV across the board.

Figure 6.1: A handsome and trim Turkish Aviation Industries test pilot. Note, he wears a Türkiye patch, not a PAF patch. The PAF patch of the star within the crescent moon is astronomically impossible. This photo is taken by the late Pushpindar Singh Chopra, probably at a Paris Air Show. Society of Aerospace Studies, New Delhi

Outline of HQ Organization

Table 6.1: PAF HQ

Chief of Air Staff	
Principal Staff Officers	
Vice Chief of The Air Staff	VCAS
Deputy Chief of The Air Staff (Operations)	DCAS(O)
Deputy Chief of The Air Staff (Engineering)	DCAS(E)
Deputy Chief of The Air Staff (Administration)	DCAS(A)
Deputy Chief of The Air Staff (Training)	DCAS(T)

https://www.brecorder.com/news/40281711

Figure 6.2: Air Chief Marshal Mujahid Anwar Khan, 15th PAF Air Chief. From Society of Aerospace Studies, New Delhi on behalf of the estate of Pushpindar Singh Chopra

Air Force Strategic Command Islamabad
Northern Air Command Peshawar
Central Air Command Sargodha
Southern Air Command Masroor
Western Air Command Quetta

Air Defence Command, Chaklala (Rawalpindi)
Cyber Command, Islamabad
Space Command, Islamabad

Main Schools

Pakistan Air Force Academy, Risalpur
Combat Commanders' School (CCS), Sargodha
PAF Airpower Centre of Excellence (PAF ACE), Sargodha
PAF Air War College, Karachi
Air University, Islamabad

Weapons Production Establishments

Pakistan Aeronautical Complex (PAC), Kamra
Air Weapons Complex (AWC), Kamra

Table 6.2: Ranks

Marshal of the Air Force O-11	Chief Technician	OR-9
Air Chief Marshal O-10	Senior Technician	OR-8
Air Marshal O-9	Corporal Technician	OR-8
Air Vice Marshal O-8	Junior Technician	OR-7
Air Commodore O-7	Senior Aircraftman	OR-5, OR-6
Group Captain O-6	Junior Aircraftman	OR-4
Wing Commander O-5	Leading Aircraftman	OR-3
Squadron Leader O-4	Aircraftman	OR-1, OR-2
Flight Lieutenant O-3		
Flying Officer O-2		
Pilot Officer O-1		

Pakistan also uses Warrant Officer (JCO) ranks of Chief Warrant Officer, Warrant Officer and Assistant Warrant Officer.

Table 6.3: PAF Squadrons by type aircraft March 2024

F-7	J-10	Mirage	F-16	JF-17	Tpt	AEWC	Others	UAV	SAR
17	15	7 (III)	29 CCS	2	6	3	10 Refuel	60	85
20		22 OCU		8 (Blk 3)	12	4 (note)	24 ECM	61	89
23 CCS		25 (V)	19	14	41	53	1 FCU	62	86
		CCS See Note		18 LIFT	52			63	88
		50	5	16 (Blk 3)				64	81
			9	26				65	82
			11	27				66	84
				28 CCS					87
3	*1*	*4*	*5*	*8*	*4*	*3*	*3*	*7*	*8*

- CCS Mirage "Sky Bolts" was number plated in January 2024 as PAF continues to retire its Mirages; presumably, the aircraft in good condition will go to No. 50 Squadron; rumoured J-10CE will replace in CCS.
- No. 4 AEWC disbanding as of January 2024, presumed replacement Saab AEW Mk. 2.[3]
- No. 8 Squadron at the time of writing (April 3, 2024) was the latest squadron to reequip, with JF-17 Block 3.
- Prasun Sengupta says No. 7 and No. 22 Squadrons are awaiting J-10C
  Saab 2000 AEW and AEWC Serials from *Scramble.*

Table 6.4: Saab AEW Serials

10-025[4]
10-040
11-045
18-060
18-081
20-057
23-058 (new version)
J-038
J-068
10-045 written off
10-049 written off

In 2024-2030, you may expect the following, approximately:

- 1 less F-16 squadron (unless Pakistan manages one more rebuilt squadron; currently that Ukraine is mopping up available second-hand aircraft, these aircraft will be in short supply. Pakistan could also decide to standardise F-16 squadrons to 12 or 14 aircraft.
- All seven F-7 and Mirage squadrons out.
- First two JF-17 squadrons were rebuilt and upgraded.
- More JF-17 squadrons.
- 3 more J-10C squadrons (See entry on J-10—there may be more and no further new JF-17 squadrons).
- Add 2 L-15B light fighter squadrons. When this arrives No. 18 LIFT squadron may transfer its JF-17s to another squadron.
- The JF-17 squadrons are to get two JF-17B two-seat combat-capable trainers. Some likely have them already, as Pakistan has 26 B versions.
- For a total of 21-22 combat squadrons. Remember, CCS squadrons have the best pilots and are fully combat squadrons!

You will notice the PAF has 22 combat squadrons, not the 20 I assert would be more than sufficient to check India. Why it has gone to 22 by keeping obsolete F-7 and Mirage in service at a horrifying cost in pilots is beyond my comprehension. The explanation may lie in the PAF aims for a 1:1.35 parity with the IAF, i.e., 400 vs 540 fighter aircraft which is historically very high.

I also don't know why Pakistan has veered into the 50 series of squadrons. Before that, the PAF had a sensible sequential numbering, which stopped at No. 29 Squadron.

The CCS squadron used not to have squadron numbers even though they were, in effect, combat units with the best pilots. Now they have No. 28 (JF-17) and No. 29 (F-16). No. 23 CCS is an F-7 unit, and often referred to simply by its squadron number.

Bilal Khan, the energetic and loquacious editor of the *Quwa* defence magazine says that Pakistan can be expected to induct at least ninety fighter aircraft of a basic design. That plan for the F-16 went awry because of political and financial reasons and the PAF had to stop well less than the 111 it had ordered; the US delivered only 58 and Pakistan had to buy about 35 second-hand. The JF-17 has already exceeded that minimum of 90; perhaps there will be more than the 162 ordered or in service. The rumour is Pakistan is to buy only 30 Block III aircraft versus the 50 planned. 50 Is, 62 IIs including 26 B versions, and 50 IIIs followed by an emphasis on the J-10CE. But this is speculation, plus as of the end of 2024, it is irrelevant, though as of the date of writing (15 March 2024), there are no signs of a 2024-built aircraft.

Major Air Exercises

This is not a complete list of PAF training exercises. The PAF exercises vigorously, both at home and abroad. The US estimates that 90 per cent of pilots downed in combat have ten or fewer sorties; the concept of these exercises is to provide pilots with a Realistic Combat Manoeuvring experience against adversary aircraft. The US Red Flag (Nellis AFB, Nevada) from 1975 is the inspiration for such exercises and takes place three-to-six times a year throughout the year; and features different scenarios like 6 vs 6 and 6 vs 8.

Indus Shield 2023[5] staged in December at an unidentified air base in Pakistan appears to be a new exercise. Participating were Pakistan, Turkiye, Saudi Arabia, Qatar, UAE, Egypt, Oman, Bahrain, Azerbaijan, Indonesia, Morocco, Uzbekistan, China and Hungary.

Shaheen PAF-PLAAF air exercises

Table 6.5: Shaheen Sino-Pakistan air exercises

Exercise	Year	Duration	Location	Note
I	2011		PAK	
II	2013		PRC	1st ever foreign air exercise in China
III	2014	21 days	PAK	
IV	2015		PRC	
V	2016		PAK	
VI	2017	21 days	PRC	Xinjiang
VII	2018		PAK	
VIII	2019	15 days	Hotan, PRC	Biggest ever; PAF = 6 each Mirage 5. F-7PG, JF-17; PRC= J-10B, J-11A, Su-30, Y-8EW, Y-8GX4 ELINT (both 1st time)
IX	2022	23 days	Bolari	
X	2023	33 days	PRC	

Shaheen: Enhancing Joint Warfighting

To give readers an idea about the Shaheen exercises, read the following from Prasun Sengupta of Trishul-Trident Blog:

Ex Shaheen-VIII, PLAAF-PAF's joint exercise, was conducted in mid-August 2020.

"Although the air forces of China and Pakistan have been conducting bilateral air exercises since early 2011, it was only over the last two years that such exercises have acquired criticality, with the People's Liberation Army Air Force (PLAAF) increasing its reliance on the Pakistan Air Force (PAF) for accessing critical operational inputs on the warfighting capabilities of the Indian Air Force (IAF). Hence, it came as no surprise that within five months of the IAF-PAF clash over Jammu on February 27 (when the PAF launched OP Swift Retort), the eighth in the series of PLAAF-PAF air exercises—codenamed EX Shaheen-VIII—was conducted at Hotan air base in China's Xinjiang Uygur Autonomous Region over a 15-day period in mid-August that year.

"This was the largest of the bilateral air exercises ever to be conducted over a 15-day period, beginning on 23 August 2019 and concluding on September 10. More than 50 combat and combat-support aircraft took part, with the PAF pitching in with six each of its Mirage-VPs, F-7PGs and JF-17s, while the PLAAF, in addition to its J-10B, J-11A and Su-30MKK combat aircraft and KJ-200 airborne early warning & control (AEW & CS) platform, also brought in for the very first time its dedicated airborne electronic warfare platforms, the Y-8EW for electronic jamming and the Y-8GX4 for conducting ELINT missions. Together, such platforms for the very first time were exercised for missions ranging from air superiority, suppression of hostile air defences, deep and tactical interdiction, to joint air defence.

"Following this, the two air forces began the process of creating a networked airspace surveillance grid covering both Pakistan-occupied Kashmir (POK) and southern Xinjiang, and this involved the dispatch by Beijing of a JY-27A Skywatch-5 VHF radar to the PAF's Mianwali air base (for training purposes), which will ultimately be permanently located at Skardu airport in Baltistan and will be able to conduct bistatic operations with a similar JY-27A located since late 2019 in Kargilik in southern Xinjiang. Since then, several sorties by the PAF's IL-78MKP multi-role tanker transport aircraft carrying PAF electronic warfare specialists were flown to the PLAAF's Dingxin Test & Training Base in China's Gansu province last October for helping the PLAAF optimise the performance (when operating against the IAF) of its latest airborne electronic warfare platform, the Y-9G.

"Later, on December 7, a PLAAF combat aircraft contingent comprising four J-10Cs, two J-11As and two Su-30MKKs, and accompanied by two Y-20 airlifters, a KJ-500 AEW & CS platform and a Y-9G, arrived at the PAF's air base in Bholari."

"More than 50 combat and combat-support aircraft took part, with the PAF pitching in with six each of its Mirage-VPs, F-7PGs and JF-17s, while the PLAAF, in addition to its J-10B, J-11A and Su-30MKK combat aircraft and KJ-200 airborne early warning & control (AEW & CS) platform, also brought in for the very first time its dedicated airborne electronic warfare platforms, the Y-8EW for electronic jamming and the Y-8GX4 for conducting ELINT missions. Together, such platforms for the very first time exercised for missions ranging from air superiority, suppression of hostile air defences, deep and tactical interdiction, to joint air defence."

Also see:

> Shaheen X: August 28 to September 30, 2023. Jiuquan in Gansu Province and Yinchuan in the Ningxia Hui Autonomous Region. "The exercises focus on actual combat operations against a common near-peer adversary using interoperable integrated forces, and train for OCA, DCA, SEAD, DEAD, AD, CAP, OECM, EW, AEWACS and CAS missions."[6]

Anatolian Eagle

A Turkish air exercise of about ten days in which Pakistan takes part, along with other countries. The following years are when Pakistan participated.

Table 6.6: Anatolian Eagle Exercises

Exercise	Year	PAF aircraft
AE-4 III	2004	
AE-5 II	2005	F-16 Block 52; No. 5 Squadron
AE-6 II	2006	
AE- 7 II	2007	
AE-8 IV	2008	
AE-9 IV	2009	
AE-11 II	2011	
AE-12 II	2012	
AE-15 I	2015	6 x F-16; No. 9 Squadron
AE-16	2016	6 x F-16
AE-19	2019	5 x JF-17; No. 28 Squadron
AE-21	2021	JF-17; No. 2 Squadron; maybe F-16; Pakistan Navy
AE-22	2022	6 x F-16; No. 11 Squadron
AE-23 II	2023	5 x F-16 Block 52 No. 5 Squadron

Sometimes there is more than one exercise in the year. The venue is No. 3 Jet Base at Konya, which is configured for exercises. A typical exercise involves (from www.Sramble.nl):

Combat Air Patrol (CAP), Fighter sweep and Fighter escort.
Air-to-ground
Suppression/destruction of Enemy Air Defences (SEAD)
High-value asset protection
Reconnaissance
Close Air Support (CAS)
Slow mover protection
Combat Search and Rescue (CSAR)

Other exercises the PAF has or participates in
(incomplete list, illustrative)

Red Flag (US)

The 2023 article says first time participation, but this is not correct.[7]

2016 Six F-16 C/D from No. 5 Squadron.[8] USAF aerial tankers supported as the F-16 cannot refuel from the Il-78.

2010 (First time) 6 x F-16 No. 9 Squadron; USAF 77th Fighter Squadron.

2009 (Invited and apparently did not attend).[9]

2006 No. 9 Squadron exercised with USAF 9th Air Force in Southwest Asia.

Bright Star **(US-led, Egypt) (very occasionally)**

High Mark

"Exercise High Mark is the PAF's largest and most comprehensive exercise and is held about every five years. In 2010, it lasted for forty days and covered air defences across the entire country. Recently it has included army and naval units."[10]

2005

2010

Zilzal I 2000 With Qatar

Zilzal II 2004 With Qatar

Wide Awake

Wide Awake (15 hours' notice; all operational squadrons participate, every six months)

Flat Out (every six months, tests surge capability)

Spears of Victory 2023 (Saudi equivalent of Red Flag)

Tornado IDS from 7 Squadron at Dhahran/King Abdulaziz Air Base

F-15C/D Eagle from 13 Squadron at Dhahran/King Abdulaziz Air Base

F-15S/SA Strike Eagle from 6 Squadron at Khamis Mushayt/King Khalid Air Base

Typhoon F2/T3 from 10 Squadron at Taif/King Fahd Air Base

F-16C/D Fighting Falcon from PAF 5(MR) Squadron Falcons at Jacobabad/Shahbaz AB and JF-17 Thunder from 14(AS) Squadron Tail Choppers at Rafiqui

US Air Force: F16C/D Fighting Falcons from 120 Fighter Squadron / CO ANG Cougars at Aurora/Buckley AFB

Bahrain, Jordan, UAW

Spears of Victory 2022 (first exercise)

PAF contribution: No. 5 Squadron F-16

Qatar 6 Typhoon
Saudi Tornado, Typhoon, F-15
RAF
USAF F-16C No. 120 Squadron, Colorado Air National Guard

Desert Flag VIII 2023 (Previously Called Iron Falcon)

Desert Flag is hosted by the UAE. In this year, UAE, France, Kuwait, Australia, the UK, Bahrain, Morocco, Spain, the Republic of Korea, and the USA participated, according to the official release. India was present with five Tejas and two C-17.

Desert Flag VI 2021

UAE, France, Kuwait, Australia, UK, Bahrain, Morocco, Spain, ROK, India (6 X Sukhoi 30 MKI from No. 30 Squadron)

Not held in 2019 and 2020 due to Covid epidemic

2009

2004

Saffron Bandit (Preparedness against India, full-out exercise, every 2-5 years)

1992

1994

1997

1999

2009

2012

2017

These are the years for which we have dates, there may be others. The exercises take place over months, two squadrons up at a time.

Sea Spark is a Pakistan Navy tri-service exercise.

ACES Meet

"... is an international air exercise hosted and organised by the Pakistan Air Force, which aims to improve the combat preparedness of air forces by providing them with realistic training in air combat and counterterrorism operations. Participants in the exercise include contingents from several air forces throughout the world, including combat pilots and ground support troops with their fighter aircraft."[11]

PAF Inventory January 2024

This is an estimate based on several sources. We believe that the number of Mirage 3/5s is overstated by many sources because a large number have been procured for spare parts. In any case, the aircraft are being phased out rapidly. Nonetheless, keep in mind the PAF squeezes every last ounce out of its assets. For example, thanks to updates, the PAF still has a use for its F-7PGs. These are likely to remain till the L-15B trainer/LCA arrive.

Table 6.7: PAF aircraft inventory

Aircraft	Number
J-10	20 delivered as of end-2023; 16 on order; 72 by 2026[12]
J-17	130+, and 20+ to be delivered
F-16	74 A/B/C/D
F-7P/PG	70 and 60; likely less
Mirage 3/5	60 estimated
K-8	35+; additional 13 with Sherdils aerobatic team
Saab 2000 AEW	9
ZDK-03 AWACS	3 was 4, phasing out
Il-78 tanker	4
C-130B/E/H	13 + 7 H arriving ex-Belgium
C-235	4 (including 1 VIP)
ELINT/EW	3 Falcon DA-20
Helicopters	6 Mi-171, 12 AW139, 4-5 Bell 205 type, 10? SA-3160, some 316 (training)

New aircraft

F-10C

J-10CE serials (*Scramble. Nl.*) (E = Export). PAF name Firebird. PAF seems to have seen enough of the PLAAF "Dragons"!

Figure 6.3: J-10C No. 22-206 of No. 15 Squadron

Source: https://www.reddit.com/r/WarplanePorn/comments/tgr6yc/pakistan_took_one_of_the_highest_quality_j10c/

Table 6.8: J-10 serials

22-101	22-102	22-103	22-104	22-105
22-106	22-107	22-108	22-109	22-110
22-111	22-112	22-113	22-114	22-115
22-116	22-117	22-118	22-119	22-120
23-121	23-122	23-123	23-124	23-125

[Last five assumed] 22-107 may have been renumbered as 23-107.

The first batch of six was delivered in March 2022, a year after the order was finalised. This is an extraordinarily rapid induction and suggests that China diverted the aircraft from its own requirement. By the end 2022, another 14 were delivered, and 16 more are under delivery. No. 15 Squadron was the first, to replace Mirages, and No. 8 Squadron is the new squadron, also to replace Mirages. These were for maritime strike. Accordingly, it is being speculated that so are the latter, but there is no hard information on that. In early January 2004, it was reported the PAF had accepted another batch.[13] Is this the remaining 14 for the order for 36? An article suggests Pakistan plans to get another 100 in addition to the first arrival of 22.[14]

Important: Andreas Rupprecht, the expert of Chinese military aviation, says so far there is no sign the PAF's J-10C has thrust vectoring. Whereas it has been seen on some Chinese J-10Cs, for example the Zhuhai air shown in 2018.[15]

Pakistan is to be commended for its speed, especially compared to India. Nonetheless, after Balakot, Pakistan had no choice. Its need for a new fighter was urgent, and since the US was consistently refusing to supply new F-16s, Pakistan had to turn to its ally China. It is fair to compare the F-16 and J-10CE fighter since they have a similar weight and fuel load. The J-10CE has an ASEA radar and 145-km range PL-15 BVRAAM.

That said, however, the F-16 is Class A compared to China's F-10, which would be Class B. The US spends a whopping $145 billion on defence RDTE (FY 2024) and calls on global talent—including Chinese! The Chinese steal the US RDTE, but the US steals Chinese RDTE right back, something the US forgets to mention in its pious condemnation of Chinese theft. And of course, it has genuine Chinese talent from those students who decide not to return.

Fighter prices are notoriously difficult to compare. One example is Bahrain's recent order for F-16 Block 70s at $69 million each (presumably flyaway). China offered the J-10 for $40 million at the 2019 Bahrain air show. These prices mean nothing because no one with the money is going the Chinese fighter in preference to the American and say, 'the performance is equal.' First, the performance is not equal. And second, the life cycle cost is seldom in favour of the Chinese aircraft.

Stratcom Bureau avers that Pakistan paid $60 million per J-10C.[16] This grainy picture below from Stratcom Bureau shows a J-10C fully loaded for an air-to-air mission, with 2 x PL-10 and 4 x PL-15 AAMs and three drop fuel tanks. Approximate performance figures are given in Figure 20.

J-10 is descended from the cancelled Israeli Lavi, but the Chinese insist its progenitor was the very ambitious J-9, intended as the successor to the J-7. This is partially true but is known Lavi was a factor in the J-10 design.[17] The J-9 was cancelled in 1980, a year before its first flight, after fourteen years of development as it did not meet requirements.[18] The Lavi has a fascinating history but beyond the scope of this book. China has approximately 600 J-10s.

Please note *Militaryfactory.com* calls the Pakistani J-10 "Vanguard," which may be the case ten years ago when Pakistan seriously began looking at the J-10. There were even reports it had been ordered.

J-10 is intended to be in the F-16 class, indeed Israel replaced the cancelled Lavi program with the F-16.

Figure 6.4: J-10 on a full load interception mission. Source unknown; any infringement of copyright is inadvertent

Figure 6.5: J-9. This was first proposed as early as 1964, an ambitious effort considering China was very much a 3rd world country, and cancelled because it failed to meet targets. China J-10 is developed from the J-9 and not from the Israeli Lavi as was commonly believed

Source: From Wikipedia https://en.wikipedia.org/wiki/Chengdu_J-9.

L-15B Lead in Fighter Trainer/Light Combat Aircraft

This purchase was confirmed in late 2023 by China expert Prasun Sengupta of India. The number of aircraft is not yet known. Bilal Khan estimates 12 to 16 in the first batch, and then 20 to 24 in a second.

Now, why would Pakistan purchase a second LIFT, right after it designated the JF-17B (No. 18 Squadron) for the mission? Bilal Khan explains that the PAF's original plan was to graduate K-8 pilots straight to the JF-17B. Pakistan figured out that a LIFT costs as much as an operational aircraft, so why waste money? But the plan did not work out, and in a near-instantaneous change of plan, the PAF bought the L-15B, which it has been looking at since 2015. After all, the L-15B was a perfectly adequate light fighter, so by its purchase, it would not be losing fighters.

The Mach 1.4 speed is suited for dog-fighting, which takes place mainly at subsonic speed, with the higher thrust reserved for breaking away or getting a superior position against the opponent. The L-15B can carry a weapon load of 3500 kg across nine hard points. Each wing holds three hard points, while each wing tip accommodates a single hard point. The under-fuselage of the aircraft also holds a hard point for weapons carriage. So, it can also be used as a light-strike fighter.

Hongdu L-15B design and features (*courtesy of PAF Falcons*[19] *and Quwa magazine*)[20]

The L-15B combat trainer features a blended wing-body configuration and medium-aspect ratio wings with extended leading edges for enhanced aerodynamic performance. The empennage includes a single vertical tail and a full-motion horizontal tail.

The aircraft is fitted with a retractable tricycle landing gear, including a single nose wheel unit and two main wheel units. The L-15B trainer is 12.4m long and 4.7m-high and has a wingspan of 9.4m and a maximum take-off weight of 11.6t.

With a design service life of 10,000 hours, the trainer aircraft offers superior flight performance and safety, a broad operation envelope and a high cost-efficiency ratio.

Figure 6.6: Two views of the L-15B Light Combat Trainer

Source: https://thaimilitaryandasianregion.wordpress.com/wp-content/uploads/2015/10/kam46.jpg?w=624

Cockpit and avionics

The advanced glass cockpit of the aircraft features a head-up display for the front cockpit, multi-colour head-down displays for the front and rear pilot stations, and hands-on-throttle-and-stick (HOTAS) flight controls. It accommodates two crew members, including a student pilot in the front seat and an instructor at the rear in a tandem layout.

The modern cockpit is covered by a large glass canopy and offers space, comfort and superior all-round field of vision for the pilots. The aircraft is also equipped with a three-axis digital fly-by wire system, which allows the pilots to simulate the flight characteristics of some of the most modern fighter jets.

The extended nose section of L-15B differentiates it from the L-15 trainer. The nose section houses a passive electronically scanned array (PESA) radar. The X-band PESA radar can guide air-to-air and air-to-ground missiles to a maximum range of 111 km.

The trainer integrates a radar warning receiver (RWR) on the vertical stabilizer. The nose also features fin antennae for an identification friend or foe (IFF) system. The L-15B can also be equipped with dedicated electronic warfare jamming pods.

The advanced avionics aboard the JL-15B ensure the student pilots to handle the complex digital cockpits on modern Chinese fighters.

Armament

The L-15B can carry PL-10 infrared-homing, short-range, air-to-air missiles, PL-12 active, radar-guided, beyond-visual-range, air-to-air missiles, and PL-8 infrared-guided, short-range, air-to-air missiles, as well as LT-2 laser and LS-6 precision-guided bombs.

Engines and performance

The L-15B combat trainer is powered by two Ivchenko Progress AI-222-25F turbofan engines with an afterburner. The engines are equipped with a full-authority digital engine control (FADEC) system.

The power plant provides a maximum speed of Mach 1.4 and an operational range of 2600 km, which can be further extended with the integration of fuel drop tanks.

The L-15 aircraft also features an additional head-up display for the front cockpit, and hands-on-throttle-and-stick (HOTAS) flight control.

The Incorrect Report of Qatari Sale of Mirage 2000

In 2023, stories appeared about a Qatar sale of Mirage 2000 to Pakistan. This is incorrect.

- First, years ago the PAF rejected the purchase of new Mirage 2000s because India was acquiring them. Personally, I don't see the logic of that decision, but then India did the same when F-16V was offered by the US, even given that while the V version used the same airframe that outwardly was a F-16, it is actually a very advanced new aircraft for all practical purposes.
- Second, when the PAF already had the J-10 entering service, there is no need to acquire a new type.
- Third, what would the PAF do with just 12 aircraft?
- Last, and most compelling, is that the Qatari aircraft are very much in service.

For the analyst, the lesson is that, however severally something appears on the web, it does not mean that the sources are independent. Churchill allegedly once said that a lie is already half way around the world before the truth gets its pants on. In the internet age, a lie crosses the world 10 times over before truth has even had its morning beverage before s/he sits down with the computer. An analyst must consider the whole picture from a variety of angles, and waste considerable research time before s/he has the story right.

For example, no one even knows who said it first, but Churchill was not the origin![21] In the US, the quote is often attributed to Mark Twain. 'Professor Buzzkill' traces the quote to Jonathan Swift 1710! And I should indubitably look at least one other scholarly source, shouldn't I?! ('Professor Buzzkill' is in reality Joseph Coohill, a doctorate from Oxford with several history publications.)

The Mirage 3/5 Rebuild Story[22]

One of the most remarkable PAF achievements is rebuilding its Mirage III/Vs, often three times over. Though in later years this has cost the PAF in accidents, it has enabled PAF to keep up its numerical strength during a period when it has faced mass obsolescence.

Alan Warnes has enjoyed unprecedented access to the PAF by telling its story from its side. Unfortunately, many of his PAF articles are paywalled, and I am already past my small budget for research materials. Neither Alan nor the formidable—and scrupulously fair—Kaiser Tufail (much admired by Pushpindar) responded to my questions for certain details for this volume.

The keys to the Mirage rebuilding, in my opinion, is that the airframe is good for a remarkable 8000 hours, widespread availability of used aircraft worldwide and ingenuity of Pakistan aeronautical engineers.

According to the Pakistan Defence Forum, the following are the purchases:

Table 6.9: PAF Mirage Acquisitions

Blue Flash I	1967/1968: 24	18 x IIIEP, 3 x IIIRP, 3 x IIIDP[23]
Blue Flash II	1970: 30	28 x VP, 2 x 5DP
Blue Flash III	1977: 10	10 x IIIRP
Blue Flash IV	1978: 32	30 x VPA2/3, 2 x VDPA/3
Blue Flash V[24]	1990: 50	42 x IIIEA, 8 X IIIDA
Blue Flash VI	1996: 39	33 x VEF, 6 x IIIDF

Notes:

(a) Please don't utilise complete letter designations for professional use as they might be wrong in some cases.

(b) Flight Global[25] says 40 aircraft; refurbished in France.

(c) Project ROSE is summarized by Wikipedia.[26]

(d) Though many sources say Egypt agreed to supply 36 Mirage 5s to the PAF in 2019, I don't think the deal was finalized.[27]

(e) Please note Mirage 5P was for Peru. Pakistan Mirage 5s were -5PA x 18-5DPA2 x 2, -5PA2 x 18 Agave radar, and -5PA3 12 x for maritime strike.

(f) Pakistan Mirage IIIs were named IIIDEP (5 x trainers), IIIRP (13 x photo recon), IIIEP (18 x strike).

In 2001/02, the PAF acquired 10 Mirage-IIIs (9 Mirage-IIIEE and 1 Mirage-IIIDL) from Lebanon, which were stored since 1980s. All these aircraft had flown 300-600 hours and were a good choice for the PAF.

In 2003, the PAF purchased 12 Mirage-IIIEE and 1 Mirage-IIIDE from Spain. All of them were bought as spares; none was made operational.

In 2004, the PAF purchased 76 Mirages in two batches from Libya, which were stored for past 15 years. The first batch of 47 was 4 Mirage-VDR, 6 Mirage-VDD, 12 Mirage-VD and 25 Mirage-VDE. In 2007, 29 more were acquired. Oddly, though the aircraft had only 3-400 hours only 14 of the 76 were put into service, and the rest used for spares. Pakistan also acquired a large package of spares, including 150 Atar engines still in their original sealed packages.[28] While Pakistan Defence Forum does not explain why only 14 aircraft were used, presumably they were improperly stored, despite being in the desert, normally ideal conditions for preservation.

Mirage Serial numbers

The PAF uses the year of induction as the first two digits, followed by the three-digit aircraft number. Thus, the first Mirage (nicknamed 'The Old Baba') was 67-101.

Table 6.10: Mirage serials

100 series Mirage IIIEP (18 aircraft ordered 1967/1968)
200 series Mirage IIIRP (Ordered in 2 batches, 3 in 1968 and 10 in 1977)
300 series Mirage IIID and Mirage VD (3 ordered in 1968, 3 in 1970, 2 in 1979)
400 series Mirage V (28 Mirage VPA in 1970, 30 Mirage VPA2/3 in 1979)
500 series Ex-RAAF Mirage IIIO designated as Mirage-IIIEA (1990)
600 series Ex-French AF Mirage-IIIDA (1968)
700 series Ex-French AF Mirage VEF (ordered in 1996)
800 series Ex-RAAF Mirage IIIDF
900 series Ex-Lebanese 9 Mirage-IIIEL, 1 Mirage-IIIDL (2001/02)
000 series Ex-Libyan 14 Mirage-VDD

Not counted above are:

39 Mirage 5 ex Belgium 1996

13 Mirage 3s from Spain 2003

36 Mirage Vs from Egypt 2019

F-16

Table 6.11: F-16 Losses

Date	Serial #	Comment
18 Dec 1986	81-1502	Boar hit during take-off; both pilots saved
29 April 1987	81-0918	Blue-on-blue kill; pilot ejected, saved
04 Sept 1989	81-0910	Pilot disoriented during night sortie; killed
16 Jun 1991	81-0921	Night training crash due engine failure
27 Oct 1991	81-0923	Crash due unauthorized engine part; pilot saved
10 Nov 1993	81-0936	Bird hit crash; both pilots saved
17 Mar 1994	81-0919	Crashed/killed on daylight flight disorientation
22 Oct 1994	81-0899	Bird hit, pilot safe
17 Jul 2009	92- 0405	Pilot killed on routine night flight
11 Mar 2020	92- 0406	Pakistan Day parade; pilot killed
22 March 2022		Both pilots killed in routine sortie

(11 total)

Figure 6.7: Airliners.net. PAF F-16A

Source: https://www.airliners.net/photo/Pakistan-Air-Force/General-Dynamics-F-16A-Fighting-Falcon-401/6366393

In 2022 a $450 million sustainment package from the US was agreed on. It includes:[29]

- Participation in F-16 Aircraft Structural Integrity Program

- Electronic Combat International Security Assistance Program
- International Engine Management Program
- Engine Component Improvement Program, and other technical coordination groups
- Aircraft and engine hardware and software modifications and support
- Aircraft and engine spare repair/return parts
- Accessories and support equipment
- Classified and unclassified software and software support
- Publications, manuals, and technical documentation
- Precision measurement, calibration, lab equipment, and technical support services
- Studies and surveys
- Other related elements of aircraft maintenance and program support.

$450 million seems like a lot of money but of course, we don't know how much is for spares and for aircraft/engine hardware/software modifications/ support. Conversely, just one program for India calls for $4 billion cost for 31 Predator MQ-9B, or $130 million per unit.[30] Military hardware/software simply costs a lot today. In 1952, the first of the US supercarriers cost $217 million. Today the cost of a single F-35 for Greece costs that much.

In 2016, the US agreed to sell Pakistan 8 F-16C/D for $270 million, subsidizing the rest of the $700 million deal under Foreign Military Sales. US congresspeople were opposed to the deal, wanting Pakistan to pay the full amount. This and the 2022 deal show US did not oppose selling Pakistan more F-16s; they did not want the US taxpayer paying. And the US did lift the embargo on many of the F-16s paid for Pakistan and held up because the nuclear-test in 1998. Of course, the US succeeded in pushing China dragon-clasp.

Pakistan has so far not succeeded in obtaining more second-hand F-16s. The reason is the NATO Europeans like Denmark and Netherlands are giving their excess aircraft to Ukraine. For example, Denmark is sending 19 F-16s to Ukraine and 24 to Argentina; the Netherlands is sending 24; and Romania also needs them. The Netherlands has more F-16s, but right now no one is thinking of Pakistan. Greece recently refused to sell any to

Pakistan because of the latter's close alliance with Turkey and also Greece does not want of offend India. Still, there are hundreds of F-16s becoming available in the next 10 years.

Incidentally, the MLU-20 update brings earlier fighters to Block 50/52 standards.

JF-17

Pakistan produced:

- 50 Block I
- 62 Block II
- 50 Block III (under delivery 2022 to 2024) (treat number with caution)
- 26 dual seats in Block II

That makes a total of 188 delivered.

Block III deliveries started in 2022, with No. 16 Squadron as the first unit.

While a Block IV and even a V is rumoured, at this time this is only speculation. Pakistan will upgrade all Block II to Block III, and then see if it can upgrade the Block I. The Block III is also known as the C version.

The Thunder Block-III, also named C version, is an extensively modified version compared to two previous versions with:

1. A new AESA KLJ-7A airborne fire-control radar (FCR);
2. Adding more firepower in combination with the long-range PL-15 air-to-air missile;
3. A new Missile Approach Warning (MAW) system;
4. An enhanced Electronic Warfare (EW) management system and Radar Warning Receiver (RWR) with external ECM pods;
5. Further, the Block-III is equipped with a new Head-Up Display (HUD) integrated with a Head Mounted Display (HMD);
6. The use of more composite materials for weight reduction;
7. Adding a chin-mounted device, which might house an infrared search and tracking (IRST) system.

Figure 6.8: A PAF JF-17 with (left to right) fuel tank, long-range air-to-surface missile, anti-radar missile, medium-range air-to-air missile, and short-range air-to-air missile. Copyright: Society for Aerospace Studies, New Delhi, on behalf of the estate of Pushpindar Singh Chopra

L-15B

The following account relies on *Bilal Khan Quwa.org*[31]

Initially, the PAF was not in favour of a LIFT because its costs are equal to that of light fighters. But the PAF intent to use the JF-17B as a LIFT did not work; the PAF pilots did not transition well from the K-8P advanced trainer to JF-17B. Earlier, the PAF was using Mirage and F-7 after pilots graduated from the K-8 to give them sufficient experience for the F-16 and JF-17. The declining number of Mirage and F-7 and the fact that the pilots were having trouble transitioning from the K-8P, directly made the PAF change its mind in 2017. That same year, the PAF raised a new LIFT unit, designated 'Shooter Squadron,' at the PAF Base, M. M. Alam, located in Mianwali with the F/FT-7P alongside No. 20 OCU, along with F/FT-7B also at Mianwali. This could be only a temporary solution, and it was to be six more years till the PAF settled on the L-15, which presumably will start arriving in 2024.

Pakistan wanted, in late 2018, an aircraft "with an afterburning engine, multi-mode radar, and tactical data-link (TDL) system"[32] In other words, a trainer that was also a light fighter, thus neatly overcoming the PAF's initial reservations about a LIFT costing as much as a regular fighter squadron. Qatar is paying almost $40 million each. The plane cannot cost more than

$20 million flyaway, and Pakistan has much of the infrastructure needed. With 10 years of spares and weapons, it probably costs, at a guess, around $30 million. China has not, for decades, charged "friendship prices". At the same time selling to Pakistan at a discount cannot be ruled out because it expands Chinese influence and marketing around the world.

The L-15B uses the afterburning variant of the AI-222-25F engine, with about 24,000 lbs thrust and 41,000 on afterburner. Maximum armament load is 3500 kg, and maximum speed is Mach 1.4, probable combat radius is about 600 km without external tanks. Life is claimed as 10,000 hours. Maximum take-off is 11,500 kg. The actual combat radius may be as much as 500 km.

The radar is X-band passive electronically scanned array (PESA) radar with a 75-km range. The aircraft has glass cockpits (it is a two-seater). It has digital flight controls (3-axis) and HOTAS.

Aside from the usual assortment of smart bombs and missiles, it has BVR AAMs and within-visual-range AAMs. It can be outfitted with a targeting pod or an ECM pod.

FC-31

Figure 6.9: Speculated photograph of FC-31. Also called J-3. From: South China Morning Post

Possibly 80 of the stealth fighters are on order. As the aircraft is still under deployment (prototype form) while the research was being conducted, it may be some years before the initial aircraft are inducted. The following parameters are claimed by the manufacturer:[33]

- Payload: 2 tons internal, six tons total
- Combat radius 1200-km
- Maximum take-off weight (MTOW) of F-31: 60,000 pounds
- Dimensions (meters): length 17.5, wingspan 11.5, height 4.8
- Designed to use 2 x Russian RD-93MA engines; engine life 4000-hours (but can drop drastically if afterburner is frequently used. Earlier flying with WS-13, now flying with WS-19 engine, 26,500 lb.s.t each[34], vs the RD-93MA's 20,500 lbs.s.t. The WS-19 likely has supercruise (supersonic flight without used of afterburner).
- Maximum Mach 1.8. The estimated maximum attainable speed is Mach 1.8

Table 6.12: Chinese modern fighter engines

Chinese Fighter Engines[35] (1lb thrust = 4.45 newtons = 0.45 kg)	
WS-10B	20,500 lbs dry; 32,000 lbs afterburner, J-10CE, original J-20
WS-13	9000 kg afterburner, originally used for J-31
WS-15 Emei	Projected max 19,000 kg, new for J-20, supercruise
WS-19	12,000 kg, new for FC-31
By comparison	
Russia RD-93MA	9,300 kg 20,400 lbs (vs 8300kg for RD-93) JF-17 Block III PAF
US F-414	22,000- lbs (Indian Tejas 2)

Take the above as approximations.

The JC-31 was developed 'privately' by Chinese companies (that the JC designation vs PLAAF developed J). There has been confusion about the JC-31 because the PLAAF rejected the aircraft and apparently that was mainly because of the underpowered WS-13 engine.[36] Also, while the first prototype flew in 2012 and the second in 2016, few were paying much attention to it. There is more confusion because the JC-31 is sometimes referred to as the J-35 carrier-based fighter. There appear to be at least three prototypes.

When might the FC-31 arrive in Pakistan? A guess is that it might enter Chinese squadron service in 2026,[37] which also would mark Pakistan service.

KAAN (Turkish TFX)

Figure 6.10: Turkish Aviation Industries KAAN Türkiye TFX on its first flight 2024

Source: https://www.tusas.com/medya-merkezi/haberler/milli-muharip-ucak-kaan-ilk-ucusunu-gerceklestirdi

It would seem Pakistan's order for FC-31 would negate participation in Turkey's KAAN stealth fighter program, but presumably Pakistan will continue with design cooperation to learn new skills.

We nonetheless list our original entry (December 2023). Pakistan had a fifth-generation stealth fighter under its Project AZM, which includes guided weapons and drones. It was then announced that Pakistan would work with Turkey on the latter's TFX 'Kann' project. Pakistani designers and engineers are working with Turkey.[38] The PAF is exceptionally prudent with its money as its resources are limited, so it is unclear why Pakistan started on its own 5-Gen fighter, requiring design and manufacturing capabilities far beyond its abilities. Perhaps PAC bureaucrats overreached.

The 'Kaan' was originally scheduled for a first flight in 2025, but that has been moved forward. In November 2023 it began taxiway trials, with the first flight in February 2024. Introduction in Turkish Air Force; 2030 squadron service. These and all figures are subject to change. As such, only approximate figures are given. 'Kaan' is billed as a low-observable 5-Gen aircraft. It will be paired with a Turkish loyal wingman Anka-3 UAV.

- 3 prototypes Block 0 by 2026
- 10 delivered by 2028 Block I
- Squadron service by 2030 Block I
- Late 2030s Block II
- 24/year rate (may expand given Azerbaijan and possibly PAF requirements)

Length 19m[39]
Width 13.5m
Height 5m
Empty 14,150 kg
Max 27,200 kg
Internal fuel: approximately 8,000-kg
Payload: approximately 5000-kg
Ceiling 20,000 meters
Rate of climb is 15,240m/minute
Range 3000 km
Speed 2400 and 1800 cruise (Mach 1.94 and Mach 1.46)

Four questions arise.

- Will US embargo the engine for Pakistani sale? Or will the US feel tired of losing sales because of its multiple embargoes?
- If the first, can 'Kaan' fly with an advanced Chinese or Russian engine and can the PAF accept a loss of capability?
- The 'Kaans' cost has escalated to an unspecified figure compared to TAI's original $100 million[40] (late 2023 TAI estimate); it is bound to increase due to inflation. Can Pakistan afford more than a few?
- Will China's FC-31 improve to approximate 'Kaans' capabilities by 2030? If so, Pakistan may not need the 'Kaan.'

The problem with Chinese and Russian engines (assuming they can be fitted to the 'Kaan' fighter), is the low MTBO. We can assume 1000 hours for the advanced Chinese engines like the WC-15C and 1000 hours for the Russian AL-41 (though higher claims are made) versus 6000 hours for Western engines such as US F-414 and the GE F-110. Both the Chinese and Russian engines are complicated to maintain compared to US engines. And likely have low reliability. This impacts availability, and significantly increases the life cycle cost.

'Kaan' is an approximately 27,000 kg aircraft, with 2 x 13,000 kg thrust engines (presumably maximum wet thrust) giving a 0.9/1 thrust-to-weight ratio and a maximum Mach 1.9 speed and 20,000-metre maximum altitude ceiling. It will use the GE F-110-1xx series engine, some of which have already been delivered) until a Turkish engine is available. An earlier deal to use the EJ200 engine collapsed but has been revived in the design for an indigenous engine. Joseph Trevithick says the engine's placement indicates a "high asymmetric thrust in engine out scenarios"[41] and has vectored thrust control. So do the new Chinese and Russian engines but that does not tell us how that works in practice.

Combat radius ~450 kilometres. Remember, that combat radius is always less than half of the combat range, which is 1100 km. Presumably, that is the clean radius, without external fuel tanks.

In clean mode, the plane can carry 4 x medium-range AAMs internally. There is speculation if that can be augmented by 2 x short-range AAMs. It has a forward-facing Infra-Red Track and Scan and a multi-purpose Electro-Optical Targeting System. Joseph Trevithick says no other 5-Gen has a similar setup.

TAI has not given the weapons loads, which in any case are exaggerated by any manufacturer. We may assume that in the air defence mode, it will carry 4 medium range AAMs and three external fuel tanks for maximum loiter time. Similar aircraft have about 8,000 kg internal fuel load. Assuming the 4 missiles weigh about 800 kg, that leaves about 4000 kg additional payload. It is probable in maximum air defence role 'Kaan' can carry 1 x 3000-liter external tanks, and two underwing 1000-liter tanks. With full internal fuel the 'Kaan' has an operational radius of 450-km. At a guess the 'Kaan' would have a loiter radius of 750 km or more with 4 AAMs and external fuel.

C-130 Update

In 2022, seven ex-Belgian C-130H were purchased. The Royal Air Force has declared 14 C-130s surpluses, remaining after eight (Bangladesh five, Bahrain two, the US Navy one) were sold as it is like Belgium phasing in A400M. There is no mention of Pakistan interest; possibly price was a constraint – the US Navy paid about $30-million for its single purchase. Both Belgium and UK replaced their C-130s 1-for-1 with A400M. To sum up, the PAF currently has:

- 5 C-130B
- 11 C-130E
- 7 CH-130H
- 1 L-100?

Aircraft have upgraded engines, modernized cockpits, and extended fatigue lives.

Original (includes losses)

- US – 9 B
- Iran – 4 B, then 5 Bs
- Australia – 6 E, 1965-66 build, refurbished for PAF at $56-million
- Belgium - 7

Figure 6.11: C-130H No. 4483 (Ex – Belgium CH-12)

Source: https://www.key.aero/article/first-ex-belgian-hercules-pakistan-flies-melsbroek

Table 6.13: C-130 Serials[42]

PAF Serial	Model	Comments
58-0739	B	MAP
61-2646	B	MAP
61-2648	B	MAP
62-4141	B	MAP
62-4142	B	MAP
64145	L-100	
65-12896	E	Ex-RAAF
65-12900	E	Ex-RAAF
65-12902	E	Ex-RAAF
65-12903	E	Ex-RAAF
65-12904	E	Ex-RAAF
65-12906	E	Ex-RAAF
4467	H	Ex Belgium
4479	H	Ex-Belgium
4455	H	Ex Belgium
4482	H	Ex-Belgium
4470	H	Ex Belgium
4476	H	Ex-Belgium
4483	H	Ex Belgium

Saudi Arabia is getting rid of 42 C-130H/J in favour of 33 Brazil C390; presumably, Pakistan will have a new source of spares and whole aircraft. Not that it's clear if it needs more.

In 2014 US Defense Security Cooperation Agency approved a package of $100 million for Pakistan for a C-130 Fleet Upgrade Program and associated equipment, parts, training, and logistical support for an estimated cost of $100 million. The fleet at that time consisted on 5 B and 11 E; the package would extend their life by 10-15 years.[43]

Written Off

Three aircraft have FLIR for counterinsurgency operations. One other similarly equipped was written off. One was bought from Australia for spares; another came from Iran and is used as an instructional airframe.

Table 6.14: C-130 written off

	#s w/o
C-130B	8
C-130E	1
L-100	1

SAR

By replacing its Alouette III for SAR with A139 and Mi-17, Pakistan can achieve a Combat SAR capability. CSAR, which is rescue in a battle zone and requires two crew, two medics, two door gunners, and at least 2 riflemen for protection of the crew on the ground. An Alouette III cannot do the job, but an AW139 can comfortably carry 10+ and a Mil-17 20+. Pakistan will need CSAR in insurgent and maritime zones but may not be aiming at recovering personnel in Indian zones.

This, of course, is only the start. CSAR requires armoured helicopters in pairs, air cover, a coordinating aircraft, even air refuelling for longer missions.

The PAF uses flights of two per main bases, though some have three helicopters. They are however, numbered as squadrons. And two means only one available at a time for sure. You really require three for every squadron, and the PAF seems to be striving for that goal. Still, one hopes this provides an answer to those Pakistani air enthusiasts who ask why the PAF purchased the AW139 at five times the price of an SA-3160 (a newer version of the SA-316 Alouette III). Some of the Mi-17s carry FLIR, adding to Pakistan's low-level reconnaissance capability.

Mi-17 serials (from *Scramble.nl*)

Table 6.15: Mi-17 Serials

02-010	Mi-171Sh	
02-011	Mi-171Sh	(Nur Khan)
02-012	Mi-171Sh	84(CS)sq
02-013	Mi-171Sh	87(SAR)sq
10-014	Mi-171Sh	
10-015	Mi-171Sh	84(SAR)sq
15-016	Written Off	
15-017	Status Unknown	
16-061		
16-062		
16-063		
17-001		
17-002		88
17-003		82(CS)sq
17-004		88
18-005		

There are additional serials not noted here.

Figure 6.12: PAF Mi-171Sh Serial 02-011. Photo from AirHistory.net; copyright by Stephan D. Bruijn, 2005.

Source: https://www.airliners.net/photo/Pakistan-Army/Mil-Mi-171/7104001

AW-139 (From *Scramble.nl*)

Table 6.16: AW139 Serials

Air Force	Unit	Others	Unit
16-061		050	ERC
16-062		051	ERC
16-063		052	ERC
17-001	88 CS	053	ERC
17-002	88 CS	054	ERC
17-003	82 CS	055	ERC
17-004	88 CS	EYE-73	ISI
18-005			
18-006			
18-007			
18-008	84		
18-009			
18-010			
18-011			
18-012			
18-013			
18-014			
18-064			
18-065			
18-066			

ERC = Emergency Response Cell

ISI = Inter Service Intelligence

Figure 6.13: Photo from Bilal Khan, (2019, October 22). AW139: The Pakistan Air Force's New Mainstay SAR Helicopter. Quwa.org

Source: https://quwa.org/2019/10/22/aw139-the-pakistan-air-forces-new-mainstay-sar-helicopter/

T-37B/C and K-8P

Figure 6.14: A K-8 Sherdil of the PAFs acrobatic team. This one, 814, was flown by S/L Kamran Yaseem. Society for Aerospace Studies, New Delhi, estate of Pushpindar Singh Chopra

Accurate trainer numbers are difficult to obtain.[44] This is a composite using a variety of sources including Wikipedia.

Pakistan Air Force-63 aircraft, including 24 T-37Bs and 39 T-37Cs.

- 2008 20 T-37s were delivered that were ordered from the US.
- 2015 Turkish Air Force gave 34 T-37C on 28 October 2015.[45]

Scramble lists about 30 T-37B and 23 T-37C as active. I say "about" because it's difficult to read off unnumbered columns.

The US also gave 43 T-33 and 6 RT-33A (reconnaissance). 36 T-33A and 4 RT-33A are listed by Scramble. Shabbir and Mazar gave serials for 5 RT-33A (they had access to official records).

Figure 6.15: JF-17 Block I No. 16 Squadron Serial #11-135 (Now with Block III). Society for Aerospace Studies, New Delhi Estate of Pushpindar Singh Chopra. Scramble has this particular aircraft as No. 2 Squadron, but the Panther's logo can be clearly seen on the tail. The port wing load is a duel tank (assumed), C802 anti-ship missile, S-6 extended range guided bomb; SD-10A AAM and (wingtip), PL-5 AAM.

Pakistan Navy

There are no new aircraft or helicopter squadrons.[46] There is probably a new CUAV squadron at Pasni.

Table 6.17: Aircraft with each PN Squadron

27 Squadron	Had F-27, retired its last in 2000. I have no further news.
28 Squadron	Orion P-3
29 Squadron	RAS-72
47 Squadron	UAV, Uqab II (replaced or replacing?)
93 Squadron	Maritime Safety Agency, BN-2
111 Squadron	6+ Sea King/Commando (sensor upgraded); ASW, ASuW, SAR
222 Squadron	6 Z-9C (or more)
333 Squadron	7 SA 316, 319 (Overdue for replacement)

While the Sea Sultan is replacing (three delivered, seven on order), it's not clear to me which squadron or squadrons have/will have them. The internal suite is said to be the same as that on the RAS-72.

Table 6.18: Pakistan Navy (Serials from Scramble.nl)

RAS 72 (MPA)	5 (1 is training, ex-PIA; overhaul facility to come)
Hawker 850 (Recce)	1
P-3C (MPA)	6 Known serials: 80, 81, 82, 85, 86, 88, 89
Sea Sultan (MPA)	3+7 more planned, 1st arrived 2021
Mi-14PG	2 likely not active
SA316/319	7
Sea King	10 known serials: 11, 12, 13, 14, 15, 16, 17, 19
Z-9CE	9? Known serials: 20, 21, 22, 24, 25
CUAV	4 at Pasni, more CUAV arriving
UAV	1 squadron Aqab II

Naval Air Station PNS Mehran, Karachi
Naval Air Station PNS Makran, Pasni
Naval Air Station PNS Siddique, Turbat
Naval Air Station PNS Ahsan, Ormara

Sea Sultan is an Embraer Lineage 1000E twin jet, second-hand airframes, for ASW/MR, total of 10 planned; presumably to replace the Orions.

PAF believes it was successful with Swift Retort, but it has made up for deficiencies in radar coverage. Its J-10C gives it an answer to India's Rafales while its J-31 will give it a counter to India's 5 Gen fighter when that appears. It now has Chinese long-range AAMs and has greatly expanded its long-range strike capability and it has additionally invested in the exact areas that worked in 2019. For the PAF, the success of Swift Retort rested on the following pillars: (a) multi-role fighters with long-range air-to-air missiles; (b) electronic support assets; and (c) long-range air-to-surface strike capability through a variety of SOWs.

New Fighters

Following Swift Retort, the PAF ordered and inducted an entirely new fighter type into its fleet—i.e., the J-10CE with the PL-15E LRAAM (145-km range; PAF has confirmed it is on J-10 and JF-17) and high offset bore sight PL-10E AAM, (20-km range). It is nicknamed 'Firebird' by the PAF.

The acquisition was expedited by PAF deficiencies no longer considered acceptable after Swift Retort. In fact, the PAF seemed to have expedited the induction program as it received the aircraft within a year of inking the contract. In most cases, it would take at least two years to induct a new aircraft from the time of closing a deal.

Nonetheless, the J-10CE was under consideration from 2015 onward, in lieu of the PAF's inability to acquire additional F-16s. From a technical standpoint, it would have been easier to add F-16s, leveraging the existing operating infrastructure. So, while the purchase may seem to have been made in haste, the PAF had over several years carefully evaluated the aircraft.

Stand-Off Range Weapons

Taimur is the newest PAF stand-off missile for JF-17 Block III; 290-km range; 1200 lbs. Anti-ship and land attack. Introduced in 2022.

Raad I and Raad II are ACLMs of 350 km and 600 km range. They are an airborne version of the Haft VIII tactical missile and can carry a 450 kg conventional or a nuclear warhead of 5-12 KT. The yield is pure guesswork, repeated *ad infinitum*. The Raad II, at least, is part of the PAF Strategic Command.

H-2 and H-4 are standoff weapons of 60 km and 120 km. There is speculation that the H-4 may be based on the South African Denel Raptor II, which also has a 120 km range.

REK (Range Extension Kit) uses the Pakistan AZB kit to convert bombs into glide bombs.

- AZB 1: 35-km; 80 kg; for UAV

- AZB II: 50-km; 150 kg; for UAV or aircraft
- AZB V: 190-km; 750 kg
- AZB VI: 90-km; 1100 kg

The claimed accuracy is <10 meters. AZB V and VI can have Imaging Infra-Red guidance with 3-meter accuracy. Please treat these figures with caution as they are claimed by the manufacturer.

The 80–90 kg-class AZB-I was developed for use from unmanned aerial vehicles (UAVs), whereas the 150–175 kg-class AZB-II can be deployed from UAVs and manned aircraft. According to GIDS, these have operational ranges of 35–50 km (AZB-I) and 50–75 km (AZB-II), with a circular error probable (CEP) of less than 10 m.

The 750–800 kg-class AZB–V and 1,100–1,200 kg-class AZB-VI REKs are being developed for use in fixed-wing aircraft. The claimed operational ranges are 190–220 km for AZB-V and 90–100 km for AZB-VI, with a CEP of up to 10 m without the IIR and 3 m when fitted with the optional sensor.

Among the REKs, there are also the Al Takbir glide bomb, 100-km range; Al Battar, a 15-km glide bomb; and the Al-Burq I, with an II version to come. The manufacturer Global Industrial and Defense Solution (GIDS) is a state-owned firm with a heavy emphasis on exports, aside from the domestic market. It does not use the ABZ III and IV designations.

In early 2022, the PAF received its first Bayraktar TB-2 UAVs and, as of April 2022, the PAF had deployed them at Murid Airbase.

The PAF is said to have received at least 20 Bayraktar TB-2s, with a larger number still on order.

Pakistan Navy

Bayraktar TB2 has a maximum take-off weight (MTOW) of 700 kg and a payload of 150 kg. It can carry up to four guided munitions. The TB2 offers a range of under 300 km and an endurance of up to 27 hours. It can fly up to 18,000 ft and 25,000 ft. 20-plus more to come.

Shahpar III—first flight, Faaz I/IIER AAM under development BVR

GIDS Shahpar II (Replace Army Uqab II) 50 kg internal; 190 kg external 20/12 hrs 4 x 45 kg PGM, 8km

SATUMA Jasoos

1 squadron CH-3A Burraq

1 squadron GIDS Uqab II, reconnaissance, tactical. 100 km/6-hours

CH-4 see below

TB-2 Bayraktar

Bayraktar Akıncı 6 tons, 1,500 kg payload, 24 hrs, 10,000 meters

Finally, the PN inducted the CH-4 drone. Sources told Quwa that the CH-4 won the PN's drone requirement in 2021.[47] The Pakistan Army is also a CH-4 operator. 1300 kg weight.

Pakistan Navy

47 UAV Squadron Uqab II (probably reequipped)

?? UAV Squadron Turbat Burraq/CH-4

Note: The Navy's Maritime Reconnaissance aircraft have an EM signal gathering capability.

The PAF has largely kept its plans for additional ISTAR (intelligence, surveillance, target acquisition, and reconnaissance) aircraft under wraps. It is not known if it will enlarge its AEW&C or dedicated EA/ECM fleets, at least in terms of manned aircraft like the Saab 2000 or Dassault Falcon 20.

However, its swelling investment in unmanned aerial vehicles (UAV), including large high-altitude, long-endurance (HALE) designs like the Bayraktar Akıncı, could hint at its plans.

Basically, the PAF could use the Bayraktar Akıncı as its primary ISTAR asset in offensive operations. Doing so would eliminate the risks posed to manned aircraft, like the Erieye AEW&C, in such situations. In fact, given the immediate proximity of India and Pakistan to each other, many potential operations may be too dangerous for manned ISTAR assets. Both sides will have fighters with long-range radars and missiles that can put high-value AEW&C and other ISTAR assets in danger.

HALE UAVs, in contrast, could be acquired for a lower cost and, if lost, would not result in the death of a crewman. If the PAF is aiming to scale its ability to carry out Swift Retort type of operations in succession and simultaneously in different areas, HALE UAVs are the clearest sign. They offer a relatively low cost and scalable way to amass, distribute and deploy ISTAR assets to different mission zones.

Of course, the bottleneck in UAVs would be energy output. Thus, it is not known how much coverage and targeting support something like the Bayraktar Akıncı could realistically provide. But UAV-based AEWs are areas that Turkey and other countries are actively studying.

Overall, the PAF has a clear roadmap of how to modernise its fighter fleet, munitions inventory, and other key assets and capabilities. Through the remainder of the 2020s, the PAF will work to develop its capacity to undertake operations as large as Swift Retort in a more scalable and efficient manner. Showing that it can carry out such complex operations in rapid succession or simultaneously in different locations—can establish a level of credible conventional deterrence.

Pakistan Ground-Based Air Defence

We will consider PAF and Army defence together as the two now work together thanks to the PAF's CLIADS into which the Army is also netted. To what degree this interservice integration has proceeded I cannot say, but it is happening.

Radars

A reminder

In 1971 Pakistan had, according to Kaiser Tufail:[48]

Northern Sector

High Level: FPS-20 with AN-6 height finder at Sakesar

Medium Level: Condor at Chuhr Kana, Mudrike, Tatepur (near Multan)

Low level: Cherat (near Peshawar), Kallar Kahar (near Murid), Kirana (near Sargodha) and Rafiqui

Southern Sector

FPS-20 with AN-6 at Badin

P-35 at Malir, moved during the war to Jacobabad

P-35 moved from Dacca to Malir in October 1971

ASR-4 (civil) Karachi

AR-1 at Pir Patho

Type-21 at Khanpur (in useless condition; presumably British late WW-2 radar)

In East Bengal, there was a single AR-1 low-level radar for Dacca. The P-35 at Dacca was removed because, as Kaiser Tufail says, the Southern Sector in West Pakistan needed additional coverage. It was assumed that attacks in East Pakistan would be low-level, which was the case, so then risk of shifting was not high.

Tufail makes no mention of three AR-15 (a mobile version of AR-1) which are said to be acquired in 1968-69.

In the Northern Sector, PAF had air cover with big gaps; in Southern Sector coverage was laughable, and air defence/ground AAA was nominal.

Figure 6.16: Chief of Air Staff, Air Chief Marshal Zaheer Ahmad Babar Sidhu, NI (M), 16th Air Chief. Thanks to ISPR, Pakistan. His last day of service was March 24, 2024, but at the last minute was granted a 1-year extension.

ADGES in 2024

For this section, I thank Prasun Sengupta of the Trishul-Trident Blogspot, Bilal Khan of Quwa.com, and the Pakistan Defence Forum. A wide range of other sources have also been referred to.

Air Defence SAMs

Most of this section is extracted from Bilal Khan.[49]

Till 2019, PAF had little use for SAMs, which were used to protect installations. The lessons of Balakot, reinforced by the 2022-continuing operations in Ukraine led to Pakistan's decision to implement CLIADS and ground-based air defence. It began adding medium and long-range SAMs for area defence, aiming for SAMs as primary air defence response. In addition, it has implemented Electronic Measures for defence, and will introduce Directed Energy Weapons.

Pakistan Air Force HQ-9BE

Guidance is by an INS assisted by a land-based radar and terminal active radar-homing.

HQ-9BE uses the JSG-400 TDR guidance radar, which is designed for TBM interceptions, and the JPG-600 TDR surveillance radar. Furthermore, the battery utilizes a command-and-control (C2) system and electronic counter-countermeasures (ECCM) system, plus several decoy vehicles.

Figure 6.17: PAF HQ-9BE from Quwa.org

Source: https://twitter.com/PCAAbdullah, 23 March 2024.

I am hesitant to accept any of these claims. Anti-missile/glide bomb defence is a very complex matter on which the US has spent tens of billions of dollars and decades of work. We've seen the US shipboard defences work very well—that's against the crude Iran-origin missiles fired by Houthi rebels against civilian ships entering the Red Sea. We've seen sophisticated western SAMs work well against sophisticated Russian systems, with upwards of 0.8 kill rate. But to claim China has approximated Western systems is a bit of a reach.

Pakistan Army HQ-9P

As far as I know, Pakistan Army has three batteries each of four multiple launchers in one regiment. Possibly more are being acquired. A launcher carries four missiles each with a 160-kg warhead, and a reload vehicle carries four more. It is derived from the Russian SA-300. The Pakistan Army has given a range of 75 km for its version. The paper claims for its performance are:

- Against combat aircraft, 260 km.
- Against AGMs, 50-km.
- Cruise missiles, range from 25 km and from a minimum altitude of 20 metres.
- Tactical Ballistic Missiles, range 25 km.

An HQ-9 battery has:

- 4 launchers x 4 missiles 300 km but can be 3 to 6 launchers. The Pakistan system has 125 km range against aircraft and a fifth that against ballistic missiles. Warhead 180 kg.
- 3 radars:
    * Type 120 low-altitude acquisition radar
    * Type 305A or B 3D acquisition radar
    * H-200 mobile engagement radar

Pakistan Army HQ-16A

Also known as LY-80. For the Army, we have identified four LOMADS regiments.

PAF HQ-16B

Also called the H16FE.

In addition to the HQ-9BE, the PAF also revealed that it acquired the Chinese HQ-16FE, which is also designated as the LY-80B. This is a vastly-improved variant of the LY-80 40-km range which is already in service with the Pakistan Army and the Pakistan Navy. The HQ-16FE seems to form the PAF's medium-to-long-range air defence layer.

The HQ-16FE offers a range of 25 km to 160 km with a minimum/maximum intercept altitude of 15 m to 27 km against fighter-sized targets. It leverages a datalink-aided INS guidance system as well as a dual-mode semi-active and active-radar homing (SARH/ARH) seeker. The HQ-16FE's main guidance radar is a 2D active-scanning phased-array system with a range of 250 km against 'normal' fighter-sized targets, likely in reference to a radar cross-section (RCS) of $5m^2$. It can simultaneously track 12 targets and engage 8 at once.

Like it had with the HQ-9BE, the PAF acquired the HQ-16FE to give itself another area-denial system in addition to its fighter fleet. By acquiring both systems, the PAF is building a layered ground-based air defence system. Though Bilal uses the term "densely-layered" we avoid it as the new missiles systems are still insufficient given the length of the air frontier.

The PAF has, likely, evaluated the impact Ukraine is seeing through its use of SAMs against Russian air power. For the PAF, SAMs may offer a quick-response mechanism against incoming enemy aircraft and, if successful, a means to meet an offensive attack before friendly fighters are in the air.

The Air Force quantity of HQ-9 and HQ-16 is unknown. It has NORINCO-supplied CS-RB1 HGR-106 medium-power 210km-range gap filler radars.

The HQ-9BE is marketed as a limited theatre air defence solution that could intercept fighter aircraft and long-range munitions. China Aerospace Science and Industry Corporation (CASIC) says that the HQ-9BE can intercept TBMs with ranges of up to 1,000 km. The HQ-9BE can respond against TBMs in 10 seconds and non-TBMs within 15 seconds. It is primarily the PAF's most advanced SAM system.

The PAF specifically highlighted counter-TBM and counter-cruise missile capabilities. While this was likely in reference to the HQ-9BE, it may indicate that the PAF is interested in the idea of building anti-ballistic missile (ABM) capabilities in the long-term. The HQ-9BE could be the starting point.

Figure 6.18: Pakistan Army HQ-16A (LY-80) air defence missile system battery unit. From *Army Recognition*[50]

Figure 6.19: The LY-80 tube launcher. From *Army Recognition*[51]

The missile weighs 650 kg, while the warhead ~70 kg. The design is based on the Russian collaboration of the BUK missile. In Chinese service, a regiment has a Command-and-Control vehicle, plus a Target Search and Track Vehicle along with 3 batteries of 4 launchers and one Tracking and

Guidance Vehicle each. The Pakistan Army has four regiments. Each battery of the HQ-16 consists of four launcher vehicles, a command post, two radar vehicles, missile transport and reloading vehicles, power supply vehicles and so on. Most of them are based on the same 6x6 high-mobility chassis.

Spada 2000-Plus and its Conversion to Spada CIWS

The MBDA Spada 2000 Plus will likely soldier on. The PAF operates 10 batteries, which it ordered in 2007 from Italy for $47 million US. The Spada 2000 Plus uses a SARH seeker in conjunction with the Falco-Plus fire control radar (FCR) and RAC-3D radar. The PAF will likely continue using them to defend its air bases and other installations, perhaps as a short-range/point-defence system. In PAF service, a squadron has two flights of two launchers but can take four launchers.

The modernisation has unique Pakistani features. Each of the ten squadrons has two batteries of two 6-round missiles each. The battery has a Detection Centre with a RAC-3D radar with 60 km range. The launcher is backed up with a Rheinmetall GDF-005 Skyguard-3 air-defence cannon, apparently (but not confirmed) the gun is on the same truck as tows the launcher. One Falco-Plus FCR and C2 suite is mounted to a 6×6 truck, and the launcher has an Aspide-2000 missiles launcher mounted to a 6×6 truck, and a rear-mounted Oerlikon GDF 35 mm AAG. The system is complemented with an RAC-3D radar for surveillance and situational awareness. According to Bilal Khan, Pakistan is developing its own electronics.

Interestingly, a Pakistani state-owned entity is working on a LOMADS SAM system with a range of 7 km to 100 km. With the HQ-9BE and HQ-16FE in service, the PAF would be in no rush to acquire such a system. However, if it materialises, this in-house LOMADS joins the Spada 2000-Plus as the PAF's lower-ranged complement to the HQ-16FE in the medium-range layer.

Crotale

The PAF has been a longstanding operator of the Thales Crotale, and it currently fields both legacy variants—the Crotale 2000 and Crotale 4000. Though aged, the PAF considers them effective, hence it intends to upgrade the Crotale 4000. Current reliable data on the status of the five Crotale squadrons is hard to come by. The missiles and radar have been upgraded, the missiles presumably to 4000 standards. A squadron has two flights, each of two 4 x 4 armoured personal carrier types and one radar 4 x 4 vehicle, giving a total of 16 missiles per squadron. Reloads are available.

The Crotales are used for point defence. Surprisingly, the bulk of the Crotales appear to have been deployed to protect Kahuta, and not for air base defence. Since Pakistan sold its enrichment facility to China (according to Prasun Sengupta), are they still deployed there? Army has an HQ-7A version, with 6 x 6 launcher vehicles.

6 balloon Barrage wings collocated with Crotale for VA/VP. Are they still operational? Its upgrade plans for the Crotale 4000 involve two phases: an upgrade of the Crotale's ACU (Acquisition Unit)—i. e., radar—and an upgrade of the FU (Firing Unit) as well as its missiles. Plans for these upgrades were showcased at IDEAS 2022 and NASTP.

The modernized ACU apparently leverages a modern 4×4 Hino truck. The radar is to be mounted to a retractable mast. The electronics will be redesigned and enclosed in a modern cabin. The ACU would use new solid-state receivers, giving the ACU greater range.

SHORADS

The PAF has long relied on its Mistral MANPADS as its last line of defence. Mistral comes in a dual launcher turret but Pakistan may be using the single-tube shoulder-fire launch (6000 meters).

The PAF has acquired the FN-16 MANPADS (6000-meters maximum). The PAF has long relied on its Mistral MANPADS as its last line of defence.

FM-90

In Pakistan Army service, an FM-90 ESHORADS battery has 3 launchers, 1 radar and 10 support vehicles; 15 km range vs FM-80's 8.5 km. It is sometimes called VSHORADS or ESHORDS.

Fifteen batteries have been mentioned. We have identified only one regiment, presumably with three batteries.

Pakistan Army (PA) gun AD assets

The PA's other battlefield AAA assets include 35mm Oerlikon Contraves GDF-005 cannons with Ericsson Giraffe radars (200 distributed among eight Brigades), NORINCO-supplied P793 37mm cannons, RBS-70 Rayrider VSHORADS mounted on M-113 'Mouz' tracked APCs of the Light Air-Defence Self-Propelled Regiments, plus the newer PG-99s supplied by NORINCO.

The latter is a twin-barrel 35mm AD gun. A Chinese regiment with a Combined Army Brigade has 3 companies, each of two batteries, each of two guns and two support vehicles each.

CIWS

In addition to the Spada CIWS concept, the PAF is also interested in procuring one of the Chinese Type 730 30-mm or Type 1130 systems. The Pakistan Navy uses this system. The 730 has an effective range of 3-4000 km and an alleged 5000 rounds per minute.

The land version uses two x 500-round ammunition boxes. The CIWS is particularly useful against missiles or guided bombs that leak through missile defences.

Electronic Warfare

For the PAF, electronic warfare (EW) was traditionally an essential part of its offensive operations but it is now leveraging EW for area denial. In its promotional video, the PAF highlighted at least three new land-based EW systems: HISAR-1, MIGAES, and EADS…HQ-9BE.

The HQ-9BE missile's guidance suite uses an inertial navigation system (INS) aided by a land-based targeting radar via datalink and a terminal-stage active radar-homing (ARH) seeker.

Unlike the older HT-XXX series of guidance radars found on the FD-2000, the HQ-9BE uses the JSG-400 TDR guidance radar, which is designed for TBM interceptions, and the JPG-600 TDR surveillance radar.

Furthermore, the battery utilizes a command-and-control (C2) system and electronic counter-countermeasures (ECCM) system, plus several decoy vehicles.

Though the HQ-16FE is also an area defence weapon like the HQ-9, it gives Pakistan multi-layer protection.

The PAF likely wants to emulate the impact Ukraine is seeing through its use of SAMs against Russian air power. For the PAF, SAMs may offer a quick-response mechanism against incoming enemy aircraft and, if successful, a means to deprecate an offensive attack before friendly fighters are in the air.

An alternative model was also shown at NASTP. This system adopts the same configuration as above but with one major difference with Pakistani sensors in place of the Falco-Plus FCR and RAC-3D.

A Bombardier 6000 equipped for EW has been ordered. While adding it to No. 24 Squadron's three aircraft will be logical, there is no real information on its deployment.

Radars

TPS-77

The PAF's six squadrons with one each L-band Lockheed Martin TPS-77 high-power airspace surveillance radar along with a YLC-2V High Guard 3-D S-Band radar are located at:

- Korangi Creek, which is a suburb of Karachi, about 8 km east.
- Masroor, which is a PAF airbase about 8 km WSW of Karachi.
- Sakesar, which is 38 km east of Mianwali air and at an elevation of about 1300 metres.
- Kirana Hills, which are about 25 km NW of Sargodha Air Base, at a maximum altitude of 300 metres.
- Lower Topa, which is near Murre and overlooks Rawalpindi from an altitude of 2000 metres.
- Rafiqui Air Base, Shorkot Road, which is about 100 km NE of Multan, MSL about 150 metres.

As with current production TPS-77s and other next generation Lockheed Martin radars, the TPS-77 MRR uses Gallium Nitride (GaN) technology in its design. Utilising GaN, the radar's high-power amplifiers consume much less power, ultimately increasing reliability, lowering life-cycle costs and extending the useful life of the radar to 20-40 years.

TPS-77MRR

Pakistan is in the process of installing 13 radars as gap-fillers.[52] But it is not clear if all are US radars or if the 13 include Chinese radars. The TPS-77 Multi-Role Radar is mobile (2 6x6 vehicles) with a 2 to 150 km low-level range and 450 km high-level range. It can detect cruise missiles.

- Badin (known as TPS-77MRR site)
- Naya Chor (known as TPS-77MRR site)

Figure 6.20: MMR radar (leading) and support vehicle in transit

Other gap-fillers:

- Arfiwala
- Kamra
- Malir
- Dera Nawab Khan
- Deosi (near Skardu)
- Mangla
- Pasrur
- Chunian (near Kasur)
- Bholari
- Pano Aqil
- Bhawalpur
- Cherat

YLC-2

Four PAF squadrons. L Band. 330 km

YLC-6M

Four radars, Low-Level S Band 180 km. In service with two MCCs along with MPDRs

YLC-8E

Number unknown. Claimed anti-stealth.

YLC-18A

5 purchased in 2019; an accurate range of 200 km, detection 500 km, claimed anti-stealth.[53]

L Band. 360 degrees. Please note no one says F-22/F-35 are undetectable. It's just by the time you detect them, you're dead. Also, detecting and tracking/ finding a firing solution for a stealth aircraft are two different things. And, not to forget, both US stealth planes are heavily invested in ECM.

JY-27A

- Skardu
- Gujranwala
- Mangla

Prasun Sengupta says the Skardu radar is netted into a Chinese Air Force radar to the north of Skardu. China has a JY-27A installation at Pangong Lake in Ladakh.

The radar uses the TS-504 multi-point troposcatter communications relay.

L-band Northrop Grumman TPS-63s

4 radars.

E/F-band TPS-43G/J

Four radars. This has been repeatedly modernised and it's reasonable to assume also modernized in PAF service. The J version was purchased in 2003.

A reminder: the PAF is not just looking for total coverage of its air frontier. It aims for *multiple* coverages.

To repeat from page 75

VERA Passive Radar

Pakistan Air Force may have six, produced by a Czech firm, now owned by Americans. This is an extremely complex matter and if you are interested in Pakistan radars, best to read 'The History of Downgraded Vera-E Radar Purchase by PAF' which is based on Wikileaks cables. The discussion is too dense for us enthusiasts.

Because of Pakistan's huge radar rapid expansion after 2019 Balakot, this cannot be considered as a complete list but is, nonetheless, a fairly comprehensive one for amateur use.

The ADGES is built around four control centres, one each at its Air Command HQs North: Peshawar West, Quetta Centre, Sargodha South, Karachi, and seven Mission Control Centres (MCC). The MCCs handle the low-level radars and are, of course, netted with the Main Control Centres.

Pakistan laid the foundation of its modern ADGES in 1975 when it purchased six high-level, long-range TPS-43 radars and 45 MPDRs for low-level gap fillers. In 2002, it added six L-88 Aerostat-based radars to watch the western border (4500 metre height and 400 km detection range). In 2005 it added six mobile TPS-77 high-level radars for $83 million.

After Balakot 2019, Pakistan decided on continuous coverage of its eastern front and greatly boosted the number of radars. It acquired about eight TPS-77 Mobile Medium Radar, but used as a gap filler, supplemented by five YLC-18A. Two YLC-6 low-level radars and some YLC-2 and YLC-8 radars were also added. In 2020, at least three J-27A advanced radars were added to help protect the ballistic missile fields.

There are rumours that China is to gift an SLC-18 radar in exchange for the data.[54] The radar is used for upper atmosphere and space surveillance, and can search, detect, and track objects such as ballistic missiles and low Earth orbit (LEO) satellites.

Low-Level

YLC-6 2 mission control centres

YLC-8E.

YLC-18 x 5. One at Gwadar sat to able to track satellites in LEO

MPDRs 7 MCCs

GMCC (Generic Mission Control Centre). SMCC (Sector Mission Control Centre) and ADOC (Air Defence Operational Centre). The main point is that all of Pakistan's radars including Chinese are alleged to be degraded systems. Again, I don't know if this is true in all cases or just in some cases.

Radars are operated by (among other units):

- No. 481 Control & Reporting Centre (CRC) (Lahore)
- No. 482 CRC Rafiqui (Shorkot)
- No. 483 CRC Samungli (Quetta)
- No. 484 CRC Upper Topa (Rawalpindi)
- No. 485 CRC Kirana Hills (Sargodha)
- No. 486 CRC Chaklala (Lahore)

68 Siemens SILLACS L-Band MPDR-45 (45 km-range), MPDR-60 (60km-range), MPDR-90 (90 km-range) low-level gap filler radars for protecting the VAs, VPs and air-corridor approaches to the air base, now being updated by Hensoldt, in a solid-state version.

- No. 242 Sqn
- No. 408 Sqn
- No. 409 Sqn
- No. 410 Sqn
- No. 471 Sqn
- No. 541 Sqn
- No. 904 Sqn

My problem in this section is that all of a sudden, the PAF has expanded its SAM inventory, so now we're dealing with both services. A further complication is that the Chinese SAMs are referred to by several names. Since there is no consistency in nomenclature, it's easy to make mistakes. Additionally, different sources give different numbers of missiles acquired. I will have to request your indulgence for this section.

Army Strategic Missiles

- Ghaznavis with conventional warheads Deosai Plateau, Gujranwala and Mangla.

- Shaheen-1s pre-surveyed launch pads in the Deosai Plateau.
- Haft-9/Nasr Pasrur Cantt.
- Abdali/Ghaznavi/Shaheen-1 Sargodha and Mangla.

Missile Brigade South (Masroor)
 25 Missile Group
 35 Missile Group
 40 Missile Group

Missile Brigade North (Sargodha)
 14 Missile Group
 18 Missile Group
 47 Missile Group

Other Missile groups for which I have identification numbers:

- 1st Strategic Missile Group (Shaheen II/Haft IV)
- 2nd Strategic Missile Group (Haft III/Ghaznavi on 2006) (Sargodha)
- 3rd Strategic Missile Group (Khuzdar)
- 23rd Missile Group (includes Babur battalion, 4 batteries, 24 launchers, reloads)
- 26th Missile Group

 Note: Group = 18 TEL, 54 reloads
 3 × Batteries × 6 and may also have 24 reloads.

All missiles with HE or FAE warheads. Additionally, there is the Babur cruise miles, 700 km, with a quadruple pack per launcher.

Notes to below

- Lt Air Defense Missile: Bofors SAM
- RCS: Radar Control
- LOMAD: Low Altitude Missile: (LY-80)
- HIMAD: High Altitude Missile (HQ-9B)
- ESHORAD: Extremely Short Range Missile (FM-90)

Pakistan Army Ground Based Air Defence

The Pakistan Army Air Defence is not easily identified. The following is our best guess. Since Pakistan air defence is integrated, we are providing Army missile/AD regiments. The confusion between RCG and AD Regiments is unfortunate and may be because of a change in nomenclature.

3 Air Defence Division Sargodha

4 Air Defence Division Malir

Estimated 14 Air Defence Brigades, among them[55]

3 AD Brigade	Sargodha
4 AD Brigade	Lahore
29 AD Brigade	Gujranwala
101 AD Brigade	Mangla
102 AD Brigade	Multan
106 AD Brigade	Gujranwala
105 AD Brigade	Mailsi
107 AD Brigade	Multan
109 AD Brigade	Multan

Pakistan Army Air Defence Regiments

SCR: Surveillance and Control Radar (presumably controlling Bofors)

SP Regiment: Likely with APC mounted SAMs

Two types of gun/missile regiment[56]

Type I: These are equipped with:

4 × 35mm twin Oerlikon guns + Sky Guard radar

8 × RBS-70 + SAMs with Giraffe radar.

Type II: These are equipped with:

6 × 37 mm AA Guns and 6 × 14.5 mm Quad A-A Guns.

8 RBS-70+ with Giraffe radar.

Twelve and 20 units are not really regiment sized units. These units are between 300 and 400 troops. This is wastage of HQ units, but perhaps the Pakistan Army has its own reasons.

I have collected from various sources and from Jaidev Jamwal.[57]

Note on RB-70

The original RB-70 missiles had a life of 15 years. In the period 2017-2021, 931 missiles were re-lifed by Bofors. The Pakistan Army has 160 launchers.

The low-level radars MPDR-45/60/90 (Giraffe mast-mounted Mobile Pulse Doppler Radar) are being replaced by Hensoldt TRML-3D/32 type solid state, mobile and 60 kits in 2019 were ordered. Mobile Pulse Doppler Radar, Bilal Khan says can be set up in less than 10 minutes by a/in a 8x8 cross-country vehicle.

Link-17 is Pakistan's homegrown, indigenous tactical data link system. Tactical Data link system is part of Network Centric System which enable its operators to transmit and share Data.

L-15B Description and Actual vs Brochure Range

The following account is a precis based on Bilal Khan *Quwa.org*[58]

Initially, the PAF was not in favor of a LIFT because its costs are equal to that for light fighters. But the PAF intent to use the JF-17B as a LIFT did not work; the PAF pilots did not transition well from the K-8P advanced trainer to JF-17B. Earlier, the PAF was using Mirage and F-7 after pilots graduated from the K-8 to give them sufficient experience for the F-16 and JF-17. The declining number of Mirage and F-7 and that the pilots were having trouble transitioning from the K-8P directly made the PAF change its mind in 2017. That same year, the PAF raised a new LIFT unit, designated 'Shooter Squadron,' at PAF Base M.M. Alam located in Mianwali with the F/FT-7P alongside No. 20 OCU, also with F/FT-7B also at Mianwali. This could be only a temporary solution, and it was to be six more years till the PAF settled on the L-15, which presumably will start arriving in 2024.

In late 2018, Pakistan wanted an aircraft "with an afterburning engine, multi-mode radar, and tactical data-link (TDL) system" (Bilal Khan). In other words, a trainer that was also a light fighter, thus neatly overcoming the PAF's initial reservations about a LIFT costing as much as a regular fighter squadron. Qatar is paying almost $40 million each. The plane cannot cost more than $20 million flyaway, and Pakistan has much of the infrastructure needed. With 10-years of spares and weapons it probably costs, at a guess, around $30 million. China has not, for decades,.charged 'friendship prices.' At the same time selling to Pakistan at a discount cannot be ruled out because it expands Chinese influence and marketing around the world.

The L-15B improves uses the after burning variant of the Ukraine AI-222-25F engine,[59] with about 5553 lbs. max take-off thrust, maximum 9562 m lbs.

on afterburner. Maximum armament load is 3500 kg, and maximum speed is Mach 1.4. Probable real clean combat radius is about 300 km without external tanks. Life is 4,000 hours as given by Brazil, which has tested the aircraft, engine life 1500 hours, overhaul 700-800 hours[60] claimed as 10,000 hours which seems unlikely but does not matter to our radius calculation. Maximum take-off is 11,500 kg.[61] The radar is X-band passive electronically scanned array (PESA) radar with a 75-km range. The aircraft has glass cockpits (it is a two-seater), digital flight controls (3-axis) and HOTAS.

Aside from the usual assortment of smart bombs and missiles, it has BVR AAMs and within-visual-range AAMs. It can be outfitted with a targeting pod or an ECM pod.

The Chinese have their own version of the -25F engine. The Minshan WS-17. It is said to have greater thrust than than the -25F, but I am sticking to the Russian engine because that is most usual given for the L-15B.[62]

Quwa.com anticipates that the PAF could order an initial 12 to 16 aircraft to first fulfil its LIFT needs, but then acquire additional units over the long term. Total PAF orders could amount to 32-40 units.

Combat radius

Readers might question my low estimates of fighter ranges. First, fighter range is an immensely complex matter well beyond the consideration of amateurs like me. That the brochure and actual rates vary greatly is no secret. Range depends on a wide variety of factors including temperature, gross weight, external weapons configuration, altitude, speed, flight profile, maintenance/age of the engine, and pilot skill. Maximum take-off is 18,964-lb, empty is 9,921-lb, giving a max payload of 9093 lbs.[63]

Let us assume:

- Gunpod: 480-lbs, Gsh-23 (or equivalent) 250 rounds
- 2 x PL-10 AAM: 462 lbs
- 2 x PL-15 AAM: 924 lbs
- ECM pod: None
- 2 x underwing fuel tanks (empty): 400 lbs

(Two underwing tanks or four? That depends on the aircraft's internal tankage, which we don't know at this time.)

That is 2286-lbs, leaving 18964 – 2286 – 9921 = 6547 lbs fuel, or 3223 lbs per engine.

Now, we do not know how much fuel L-15B can carry in reality; we assume 3223 lbs/per engine for the purpose of our crude calculation. Reduce that by 15 per cent for take-off, climb, wind resistance, landing etc., which leaves 4910 lbs. (As seen from the F-15 example below, the US figure would be 25 per cent, but since PAF is operating over own bases, we assume lower.) Specific fuel consumption for the AI-222K engine is 1.46 lbs/hr at military power; we're going to multiply that to 2.2x for after burning, or 3.2 lbs/hr per hour of flight.

We'll arbitrarily assume:

- Take-off/climb at max military power 3 minutes[a]
- Afterburner for 3 minutes[b]
- Rest at .80 military power[c]

(a) Masroor air base (Karachi) has a main runway of 2743 metres. Is this enough for a fully loaded L-15B? I'm going to assume yes. (Karachi IAP has a 3330-meter runway). Why Masroor? Just using it as an example.

(b) For combat use.

(c) This is a guess.

Table 6.19: Estimated fuel consumption for L-15 air-to-air sortie

Max military power 5550-lbs	thrust 1.4lbst/hr	135 lbs/min per engine
At 80 per cent power		108 lbs/min per engine
At afterburner	1.46 x	297 lbs/min per engine

3 minutes TO/Climb = 135 lbs x 3 = 405 lbs; distance toward target assume +20-km
3 minutes afterburner = 297 lbs x 3 minutes = 710 lbs fuel
Total for cruise = 4910-405-710 = 1115, leaving = 3835 lbs fuel
1 engine At 3835lb fuel/108-lbs/min (0.8 full military power for cruise) = 36 min
2 engines = 18 min
Assume 1000-kmh = 9-minute radius say 10 minutes = 111-km, add arbitrary 50-km for long-range missile reach + 20-km gained during take-off = 180 km radius

This is 1/3rd of the brochure's claim! Yet, it is adequate for VA/VP defence. And the aircraft/pilot could probably do three sorties a day. The real stress (except combat) is at take-off/landing.

Radius is obviously going to be half the range, and usually given for clean configuration. The F-4, for example, would use its internal fuel load at military power in one hour. Military power is maximum without using afterburner, which back in the bad old days meant maximum without engaging the afterburner.[64]

Taking the F-15 as an example, at maximum afterburner and sea level, it uses 6.4-lbs second, lasting 6-minutes. No one flies at full after burner: the afterburner is used for specific combat speeds in specific scenarios, two minutes at worst.

This is an F-15s regular non-combat profile while ferry.[65] Notice almost 20 per cent of maximum fuel in reserve. No wind reserve has been provided, which should be around 3-5 per cent. The landing reserve is covered by the 20-minutes landing reserve, which is ample unless airspace above your airbases is contested. The fuel used for take-off is 3 per cent of 700 lbs whereas for a two-engine fighter 2000 lbs is more reasonable.

I doubt that anyone goes to guns mano-e-mano anymore. Given that fighters carry 4, 8, or even more AAMs, it's probably suicidal to get into gunfight range. While the BVRs add range, there will hardly be a pilot willing to trade his gunpod for a few extra km of range.

Table 6.20: L-15 fuel consumption[66]

	F-15 ferry range 3x dropt tanks DI = 12,2+2×5,5 = 22,2											
	TAS/GS		Altitude	Mach	Specific cons.		Fuel	Reserve	Available	Consumption	Distance	
	kt	km/h	ft	–	nm/lb	kg/km	lb	lb	lb	lb	nm	km
takeoff+startup + taxi							26,355			700		
A- Ground ops. Reserve								1,000				
E- 5% wind reserve												
E- 5% reserve								1,500				
E- 20 min max. end reserve								1,467				
Acceleration for before climb										800		
Climb			36,000	0.84					20,888	2,500	32	59
Cruising heavy					0,085	2,88						
Cruising light			43,000	0.87	0,128	1,91						
Cruising average	490	908	39,500	0,855	0,10143	2,41			18,388	18,388	1,865	3,456
Descent											40	74
Total											1,937	3,589

Now, the most a Pakistan fighter will use on afterburner is 3 minutes. That's to help take off fully-loaded and to evade the adversary's AAMs and SAMs. It may well use less, but let's be conservative. An F-15, which has one of the most economical engines, will use 15 per cent of its maximum fuel on take-off, prepare for climb, and climb, and will keep about the same in reserve.

Pakistan Navy Bases

Mehran (HQ and main base)
Gwadar
Turbat
Ormara

Table 6.21: Pakistan Navy Aircraft

RAS 72 (MPA) (ATR) Sea Eagle	5	77(2018), 78, 79, xx and xx unknown
Hawker 850 (Recce) 1	1	
Sea Sultan MPA	3	+ 7 more. Based on Embraer Lineage 1000E
P-3C (MPA)	6	Scramble says 7: Serials #80-81; #85-86; #88-87
Mi-14 2	2	
SA316/319	7	
Sea King 45/HAR3/HC4 19	19	
Z-9C	9	

Table 6.22: Pakistan Navy squadrons

Squadron	
111	6 Sea King, upgraded electronics
222	6 Z-9C, for F-22 frigates
333	7 SA-316/319; PNS Moawin A39 carries 2 + 2 Sea King
27	Former Fokker Friendship, phased out 2020
28	6 P-3, Sea Sultan replacing[67] 1st #91 Embraer E-190. ASuW, ASW, ISR, SAR
29	5 RAS-72 Eagle MPA; 1 Hawker BAe125-850XP IW/EM, 5th serial = 77
47	Uqab II UAV; PN has at least 2 x Luna (Germany), will Uqab II replace?
??	CH-4 UAV Turbat new squadron, also had Burraq UAV

Pakistan Navy also operates Shahpar II and TB series (Turkey) drones.

Figure 6.21: Sea Sultan Pakistan Navy 3D model from Sketchfab. As nearly as I can tell, it is equipped with 2 x short-range and 2 x long-range AAMs, plus one heavy anti-ship missile. It can obviously carry a bigger underwing payload, presumably at the cost of range, but does not need drop tanks as its theoretical maximum range is 8500 km.

Source: https://sketchfab.com/3d-models/embraer-sea-sultan-pakistan-navy-1d24b188b8e743c88b2799bc397b6fff. Embraer E190

CAMM-ER

In addition to equipping its four 2900 on MILGEN corvettes, Pakistan is also buying a truck-mounted land-based version for protection of its bases, as part of Pakistan's layered air defence.[68] Apparently Pakistan was the launch customer for this 45-km+ SAM. At the minimum, Pakistan would want to protect its bases at Karachi, Gwadar, Turbat, and Pasni which implies four units. But there is no indication of what a unit consists of. Views of CAMM-ER in the video referenced above show (a) six missiles in a launcher. (b) two independently moveable launchers, which means 12 missiles; and (c) quadruple launcher, each independently moveable, which implies 24.

Other missiles:

- LY-80 SAM

- Albatross anti-ship (derivative of CAMMER)
- RBS-70 SAM
- ANZA II SAM
- Zarb cruise anti-ship land-based (450-km)
- Harbah cruise anti-ship (350-km)
- Babur III
- C-802A anti-ship
- C-602
- Harpoon anti-ship (124-km)
- Exocet anti-ship (45-km+)

Pakistan Army

- 101 Aviation Group
- 202 Aviation Group
- 303 Aviation Group
- 404 Aviation Group (AH-1F)
- 505 Aviation Group (UAV)
- 606 Aviation Group
- 503 EME Workshop

Electronic & Mechanical Engineer Battalions

199 EME Battalion overhaul Schweizer 300C, MFI-17
299 EME Battalion overhaul SA315B
399 EME Battalion overhaul IAR330/SA330
499 EME Battalion overhaul AH-1F, Bell 206B-2/3
599 EME Battalion overhaul Bell 412, IAR330/SA330

Table 6.23: Pakistan Army Squadrons, bases and aircraft

ISI Squadron		
1 Squadron	Mangla	505 Avn. Gp. MFI-17 SA316B
2 Squadron		5 x MFI-17
3 Squadron	Multan	MFI-17 SA315B

4 Squadron	Quetta	Bell 412EP Mi-17-1V Mi-35M
5 Squadron	Skardu	Mil-17, AS-350
6 Squadron	Islamabad	AW139 (Emergency Response Cell) #Six-050 to 055 Bell 412EP (As above)
7 Squadron	Mehran	
8 Squadron	Rawalpindi	AS350B3 MFI-17 SA315B SA316B
9 Squadron		H125 (AS350B3e) MFI-17 SA315B SA316B
10 Squadron	Quetta	AS350B3 Ce208B EX PAC/MFI-17
11 Squadron		AS350B3 PAC/MFI-17 SA315B
12 Squadron	Mangla	Bell 412EP? MFI-17
13 Squadron		AS350B3 AS550C3 Ce421C Ce550/560 MFI-17 Mi-172 RC690C/Jetprop 840 IAR330L/SA330J 4 x Y-12-II
21 Squadron	Rawalpindi	Quick Reaction 101 AG AS550C3 Mi-17-1V Mi-17V-5
24 Squadron	Multan	IAR330L/SA330J UH-1H

25 Squadron	Multan	Bell 412
28 Squadron	Rawalpindi	SA-30
29 Squadron	Rahwali	Mi-17
31 Squadron	Multan	AH-1F, Bell 206
33 Squadron	Multan	AH-1F, Bell 206
35 Squadron	Multan	AH-1F, Bell 206
50 Squadron MOI	Quetta	ISI Mi-17V-5
56 IRS Squadron	Rawalpindi	Beech 200 Beech 350/350i Ce208B Ce208B EX
60 Special Duty	Rawalpindi	101 AG Bell 412EP
Frontier Works Org.	Peshawar	AS350B3 Beech 350ER H125 (AS350B3e)
Army Aviation School	Rahwali	MF17, Schweizer 300

Army aviation inventory[69]

Please note that much rumour surrounds the attack helicopter acquisition. It appears that the PAF will buy 20 from China. Pakistan tested the Z-10E extensively but found it underpowered for the desert. This is a new version of the same helicopter, with the new WZ-16 engine. This engine has 1667 shp. vs WZ 9's 1300 shp. Personally, I see no need to worry if a helicopter cannot carry a full load of 16 x ATGMs: on today's battlefield, you don't want to be hanging around to get in more shots. Shoot and scoot is the name of today's game. Pakistan's proposal for 30 T-129s from Turkey (which number is the minimum needed for three attack helio squadrons), was stymied by the US refusal to clear engines for Pakistan. The T-129 buy was cancelled in 2022 in favour the Chinese helicopter. Turkey is now buying T-129 engines from Ukraine, and also designing indigenous one, but how far this goes to solve Pakistan's problem is unknown at this time. As far as I know, each attack helicopter squadron has 10 AH-1 and 2 Bell Jet Rangers.

Table 6.24: Pakistan Army Inventory

King Air 350 (Recce) x 3 Cessna 208 x 13	Recon
Citation Bravo x 1 King Air 350 x 6 Turbo Commander x 2 Y-12F x 4	Light transport
Combat helicopter	
AH-1F 50 Z-10 ME x 20 (arriving)	Not correct; more likely 30 operational, rest for spares Earlier rejected for desert operations, new version, attack
AW139 x 7 Bell 412 x 31 H125M/AS550 x 35 Mi-8/17/171 x 48 Mi-35 x 4 SA315 x 17 SA316 x 13 SA330 x 42 T129 x 30 UH-1H x 1	Not correct: fewer US not cleared; 14 engines Ukraine under delivery to Turkey
Training aircraft/helicopters	
Bell 206 18 Enstrom 280 19 Hughes 269 15 MFI-17 214	

Note: helicopters with EYE serials may belong to the ISI, with 73 being one.

Pakistan Army CUAVs

Murid 4 X Bayraktar TB-2, eventually 20, PAF 6-tons, 1500-kg, 24 hours

Akinci-B

Bahawalpur 4 x CH-4 (Cai Hai) 350-kg payload

Turbat 4 x CH-4 (Navy) and Burraq, Aqab out

Wing Loong II 48 being assembled in Pakistan for PAF 480-kg payloads, 32 hours max

Shahpar I/II/III 12 hours armed endurance, 190 kg (locally made) PAF/PA

Main Bases

Pakistan has four types of bases: Main, Forward, Satellite, and Non-Flying.

- Main bases are full-fledged air bases.
- Forward Operating Bases are standby bases fully activated in wartime.
- Satellite bases are used for emergency recovery.
- Non-Flying are used as technical bases.

Main Bases
NAC = Northern Air Command
CAC = Central Air Command
SAC = Southern Air Command

Table 6.25: PAF Main Bases

	Name (location)	Old Name	Runway (metres/feet)
1	PAF Base Mushaf (Sargodha)	Sargodha	10,253/ 3,124 & 7,956/2,424
2	PAF Base Bholari (Bholari)	New Base	3,365 /11,000 (2 runways)
3	PAF Base Masroor (Karachi)	Mauripur	2,628/8,622 & 2,750/9,022
4	PAF Base Rafiqui (Shorkot)	Shorkot Road	3,048 /10,000 + taxiway
5	PAF Base Peshawar (Peshawar)	Peshawar	2,713/8,900
6	PAF Base Murid (Chakwal)	Chakwal	2,724/8,940
7	PAF Base Samungli (Quetta)	Samungli	3,650/12,000, ditto IAP
8	PAF Base M.M. Alam (Mianwali)	Mianwali	3154/10348 & 3097/10161
9	PAF Base Minhas (Kamra)	Kamra	3,033/9,950
10	PAF Base Nur Khan (Rawalpindi)	Rawalpindi	3,295/10,809
11	PAF Base Faisal (Karachi)	Drigh Road	2,450/8,038
12	PAF Base Risalpur (PAF Academy)	Risalpur	2765/9085 & 1780/5846
13	PAF Base Shahbaz (Jacobabad)	Jacobabad	3,074/10,086 & 3,060/10,040
14	PAF Base Qadri (Skardu)	Skardu	3,641/ 11,944, ditto civil

- Skardu was an FOB till 2020; note extra-long runway due to altitude. No assigned squadrons, aircraft come on rotation.
- Bholari, Shahbaz came up due to insufficient Southern Pakistan coverage in 1971 War.
- Masroor is the largest PAF base in terms of area.
- We have omitted satellite bases which are used for wartime dispersal and emergency recovery.

Forward Operating Bases

Many of these bases are located at international airports, some also have co-located PAF bases.

Table 6.26: PAF Forward Operating Bases

Base	Town/City	Command
PAF Base Murid	Chakwal	NAC
PAF Base Sukkur	Sukkur	SAC
PAF Base Farid	Rajanpur	CAC
PAF Base Multan	Multan	CAC
PAF Base Talhar	Badin	SAC
PAF Base Nawabshah	Benazirabad	SAC
PAF Base Risalewala	Faisalabad	CAC
PAF Base Chandhar	Gujranwala	CAC
PAF Base Vehari	Vehari	CAC
PAF Base Rahimyar	Rahimyar Khan	CAC
PAF Base Pasni	Pasni	SAC
PAF Base Gwadar	Gwadar	SAC
PAF Base Lahore	Lahore	CAC
PAF Base Islamabad	Islamabad	NAC
PAF Base Karachi	Karachi	SAC
PAF Base Bahawalpur	Bahawalpur	CAC

Nonflying Bases

Table 6.27: PAF Non-Flying Bases

PAF Base Korangi Creek (Karachi)
PAF Base Malir (Karachi)
PAF Base Lower Topa (Murree)
PAF Base Kallar Kahar (Kallar Kahar)
PAF Base Kohat (Kohat)
PAF Base Lahore (Lahore)
PAF Base Sakesar (Sakesar)
PAF Base Kalabagh (Nathia Gali)

Civil Air Traffic Control system

In 2015, began a modernisation of its civilian Air Traffic Control system. Integrating civil ATC and military systems is common. We do know the ATC is integrated into Pakistan's air defence network.

Pakistan ATC

This is not a complete listing.

The objective is to replace older ATC radars plus add new ones.

- In 2015 Pakistan ordered two INDRA Aircon 2100 radar for Lahore and Karachi. This is an automated traffic management system made by Spain.[70]
- In 2019 Monopulse Secondary Surveillance Radar (MSSR) and Primary Surveillance Radar (PSR) were installed at Karachi, Lahore, and Islamabad, extending the surveillance range to 450 km from 360 km. MSSR was also installed at Rojhan (near Rahim Yar Khan), Pasni (Baluchistan), and Lak Pass (near Quetta).
- Pakistan Meteorological Department has a new weather forecasting system 3-10 days. A VLF/LF system to detect lightning strikes is being installed with Chinese collaboration.

Pakistan Air Traffic Control is divided into the Lahore and Karachi areas with 3 and 4 sectors. Recently North Karachi Sector has been merged in the Lahore area. It is surprisingly difficult to get a clear picture of the sectors, so I don't know if there are still seven sectors. Some reports say there are eight. Other reports say under long-term expansion plans there will be ten. The Lahore sectors are now Upper West, West, East and South.

The Pakistan system is connected to

- North - Urumqi
- East – Delhi
- West – Kabul and Teheran
- South – Muscat and Mumbai

Country of origin of PAF aircraft[71] (in per cent)

Table 6.28: PAF Aircraft Country of Origin

	Total	Legacy attack	Modern attack	ISR, transport	Command & Control	Training	Helicopters
China	45	55	65	4	33	27	0
US	20	0	35	45	0	16	0
Russia	1	0	0	8	0	0	12
France	17	45	0	22	17	0	46
Pakistan	13	0	0	0	0	56	0
Other	5	0	0	20	50	0	42

Squadron Updates

No. 1 Squadron (K-8), the fighter conversion unit which trains fighter pilots straight out of the PAF Academy. It is—as you may have guessed—an air defence squadron in wartime.

No. 2 Squadron (JF-17) Masroor. Raised in 1954 with T-33, included the B-57 for some years. It was number plated 1990 and re-raised in 2015 with JF-17. Pilot Officer Rashid Minhas (under training) was awarded the PAF's sole Nishan-e-Haider (equivalent of Victoria Cross or Medal of Honour) in 1971. He was on a solo when a defecting Bengali-origin pilot stopped Minhas as he taxied, jumped into the instructor seat and tried to force Minhas to take him to India. Minhas deliberately crashed the aircraft short of the Indian border instead of complying.

The words in the red circle are from La Marseillaise, the French National Anthem. The patch was made for the visit to France, and an excellent example of the PAF's public relations effort, but unfortunate in that the figure looks like an incompletely evolved alien being.

No. 3 Squadron used to be the transport training squadron in its previous incarnation, now AEW with Saab 2000. The PAF now calls it program "Horizon-7".

No. 4 Squadron (ZDK-03) PAF is withdrawing the ZDK-03 from service and equipping with three Saab 2000 Mk. 2 as replacements. The squadron used to be a mixed transport and SAR squadron. Then it went to four SA-16 for MR and SAR, then with 2 SA-16 and 2 H-19; number plated in 1969 and reraised with ZDK-03 in 1988.

Pushpindar Singh Chopra, at the 2019 Paris Air Show, Copyright Society For Aerospace Studies, New Delhi, On the left, from Estate of Pushpindar Singh Chopra. On the right, the official squadron insignia for No. 2 Squadron from https://www.heraldry-wiki.com/wiki/No_2_Squadron,_Pakistan_Air_Force.

The first ZDK-03 arrived in 2011. The phase-out after just 12 years of service naturally arouses speculation. The PAF's explanation is that (a) the plane is not compatible with Pakistan's western-origin air defence; and (b) it is maintenance heavy. I hesitate to give credence to the blogosphere, which speculates that Chinese equipment is junk. After all, PAF is buying the J-10CE fighter and L-15B trainer/light fighter and has signed for the J-31. It has a number of Chinese early warning radars.

No. 5 Squadron After flying Mirage 3s for 43 years, in 2010 the squadron began transitioning to the F-16C/D. Raised August 15, 1947, this is one of the PAF's oldest squadrons, with a 65-year history. It was the first Mirage unit, reequipping in 1968.

No. 6 Squadron C-130 Chaklala ('The Antelopes'). It was the PAF's main transport squadron until No. 21 Squadron was raised. Its most well-known loss was when due to sabotage President General Zia was killed in 1988. The squadron was major beneficiary of US assistance after the US's invasion of Afghanistan in 2001. No. 6 is the oldest PAF squadron.

Figure 6.22: Badge from Pakistan Defence Archived at Wayback Machine

Source: https://web.archive.org/web/20081226215736/http://www.pakdef.info/pakmilitary/airforce/squadrons/sqdr6.html

No. 7 Squadron Mirage. Masroor. According to Prasun Sengupta,[72] due for replacement by J-10 along with No. 22 Squadron.

No. 8 Squadron has converted from Mirage to JF-17III on 28 January 2024. This is contrary to earlier reports the squadron would take the J-10. Masroor.

No. 9 Squadron F-16A/B. Mushaf.

No. 10 Squadron Il-78. Nur Khan Islamabad. Used to be the B-57 training unit before being resurrected as the aerial refuelling squadron on the Il-78.

No. 11 Squadron F-16 Sargodha, participated in 2019 "Swift Retort," claimed downing Su-30, which India denies.

Figure 6.23: F-16B of No. 11 Squadron. Serial No. 84606. Drawing © Tom Cooper

No. 12 Squadron Transport, Nur Khan (Islamabad) has shed several aircraft and was down to just three aircraft by 2015. In 2022 acquired an Airbus 319. It flies VIPs. The letter J in aircraft serial numbers stand for Jinnah, the creator and first leader of Pakistan.

Table 6.29: No. 12 Squadron aircraft

A319	1102 A; likely used by President and possibly Prime Minister for international flights	2nd hand; acquired 2022; No J number as yet.
Citation Excel 560XL	J-754; apparently used by COAS for domestic flights	
Gulfstream IVSP	J-755	
Gulfstream 450	J-756	

No. 14 Squadron JF-17. Rafique.

No. 15 Squadron First J-10 squadron; formerly Mirage. Minhas.

No. 16 Squadron Reequipped second time with JF-17, now Block III. Minhas.

Figure 6.24: JF-17 Block II No. 16 Squadron Serial number 17-246 "Black Panthers". Drawing © Tom Cooper. In 2024 the squadron transitioned to Block III

No. 17 Squadron Still F-7PG. Peshawar (Rumored JF-17; this is logical but I cannot consider it confirmed).

No. 18 Squadron LIFT Re-equipped with JF-17B. Bholari.

Figure 6.25: Image from *The Diplomat*

Source: https://thediplomat.com/tag/jf-17b/

No. 19 Squadron with F-16A/B. Bholari.

No. 20 Squadron Still with F-7. Mianwali. The squadron was raised in 1957, number plated 1972-79 and has a fascinating history as a PAF photo-recon unit first with RT-33A, then Mirage 3DP, then F-6, and last with F-7.[73]

No. 21 Squadron C-130E Shera Faisal (Islamabad).

No. 22 Squadron Mirage (Masroor).

No. 23 Squadron CCS Still with F-7.

No. 24 Squadron Mushaf. (Sargodha). Acquired one Falcon 20 J-753 for conversion to EW; now making three aircraft. It is rumoured one more aircraft may be acquired, but this is speculation. This would be the second-hand Bombardier 6000, J-758.

No. 25 Squadron Mirage. Rafiqui.

No. 26 Squadron JF-17. Peshawar.

No. 27 Squadron Mirage. Rafiqui.

No. 28 Squadron JF-17. Quetta.

No. 29 Squadron on F-16. Also performs OCU duties; shot down IAF MiG-21 Balakot 2019.

No. 41 Squadron *VIP Light* Communications Nur Khan (Islamabad). Ce172, EMB500, PA-34, PA-46, Y-12 II, now apparently just 4 Embraer 500 Phenom 100, six-seater light executive jet for VIP transport.

Source: https://babriet. tripod.com/airforce/sqd/no41sqd.htm

No. 50 Squadron Mirage. Rafiqui. took Mirages from No. 15 squadron which reequipped with J-10CE end 2021.

No. 52 Squadron Utility squadron is phasing out its four CN-235M-220; no word on a replacement. Nur Khan, Islamabad. Speculation is that maintaining just four aircraft was expensive; that there were maintenance issues; and that PAF seldom had the need for an aircraft this size.

- 9800-kg empty 16,100-kg full load
- Max 6000-kg payload
- 450km/hr max
- 51 passengers, 35 Para troops, 18 stretchers or four HCU-6/E pallets including one on the ramp.

No. 53 Squadron is a new unit with Saab 2000 AEW in Southern Air Command Bholari AB.

Please note there is a tenth Saab 2000, likely without AEW radar, used as a trainer for the AEW squadrons.

Electronic Warfare

For the PAF, electronic warfare (EW) was traditionally an essential part of its offensive operations; but it is now leveraging EW for area denial. In its promotional video, the PAF highlighted at least three new land-based EW systems: HISAR-1, MIGAES, and EADS.

It is unclear what each of these systems are specifically; however, it seems that MIGAES and EADS represent various EW systems that are coupled together to provide an electronic attack (EA) element against enemy radar and communications use over Pakistani territory. The PAF is also improving its electronic counter-countermeasures (ECCM) capabilities to degrade EA/ECM use against Pakistan.

The PAF EADS is unified under one core framework.

JN-1199 communication It consists of a C2 system, a possible electro-optical and infrared (EO/IR) jamming station, a very-high-frequency (VHF) and ultra-high-frequency (UHF) signals jamming station, an L/S/C-band jamming station, and X/Ku-band jamming station.

CHL-906 radar jamming not confirmed. It can jam radars over wide range of systems but is not confirmed in PAF service.

CEW-035 There are suggestions the PAF has acquired these integrated communications jamming systems.

Integrated Electronic Warfare System (IEWS) It uses a domestically produced system said to consist of seven parts:

- Three ESM systems
- Two systems for communication jamming mainly for counter-UAS jamming, mainly tailored for counter-unmanned aerial system (C-UAS), but also capable of jamming guided weapons and aircraft 10 km against UAVs.
- Two systems not specified by Bilal.

ELINT system

UAV/CUAV

Pakistan claims to be the fourth-largest drone operator in the world. If it was true at some point, drones have rapidly proliferated in Ukraine, Russia and India too. We exclude battlefield drones are they are too numerous in Pakistan.

Scramble.nl gives numbers for six CUA/UAV squadrons. The Navy may have three squadrons, and the Army has at least one, at Bahawalpur. We will have to ignore tactical UAVs because there are just so many of them.

As to why there are so many different types, we will have to tergiversate the question because I simply do not know.

Recall that according to Bilal Khan, Pakistan is working on attack wings that incorporate CUAVs along with fighter aircraft.

Pakistan Air Force operates:

Table 6.30: Pakistan UAV/CUAV

Shahpur I	Murid	No. 60 Squadron
Falco (Pakistan)	Mushaf	No. 61 Squadron
Shahpar-II (Pakistan)	Minhas	No. 62 Squadron
Wing Loong II (China)	Mianwali	No. 63 Squadron
Bayraktar TB2 (Turkey)	Murid	No. 64 Squadron
Akinci (Turkey)	Murid	No. 65 Squadron
Shahpur II	Murid	No. 66 Squadron

Now, here's a conundrum: Farook Bhai[74] posts a picture which he says contains 39 UAVs excluding the Wing Loongs I/2/4 MALE CUAVs at Murid. This implies the term "squadron" is loosely used unless there are other unidentified squadrons at Murid.

Though Pakistan manufactures parts for Turkey's Anka drone, it is not confirmed that Pakistan uses them.

The Navy has No. 47 Squadron with the Uqab II (likely reequipping), and a new one at Turbat, confirmed with the Wing Loong.

The Army is supposed to have Wing Loongs at Bhawalpur, used for strikes against Iran this year in Operation Marg Bar Sarmachar, Persian for "death to insurgents".[75]

Falco Silex[76]

Italian production in Pakistan started in 2009, medium range, 70-kg. Initially, they were only for reconnaissance. This comprised:

Synthetic Aperture Radar

50 produced

Maximum height 6,500 metres

Endurance 8 to 14 hours

This was thereafter upgraded to 750 kg TO weight, 120 kg payload, and endurance 18 hours. Sample payload package of EVO model, successor to Falcon:

- Gabbiano T20 Ultra-Light SAR Radar.
- Ground Moving Target Indication
- EO turret up to 16"
- Laser Marker; Laser designator (LD)
- AIS (Automatic Identification System)
- ESM: COMINT SIGINT
- SATCOM

Figure 6.26: Image from Air Force Technology

Shahpar II Block II[77]

A domestically-made drone in service with PAF and PN, it is going on to version III. Quwa.org says it has a "maximum take-off weight (MTOW) of 1650 kg, payload of 400 kg to 530 kg across six hardpoints, 20 hours of endurance, range of 3000 km, and service ceiling of 35,000 feet." Shahpar II has about half the payload and range of its successor. Pakistan has put considerable effort into developing (along with Turkey) a series of mini-guided weapons and AAMs for its drones. For example, the Barq laser-guided weapon has a weight of 45 kg and a range of 8 km. Said 6 are in service.

Pakistan claims it offers better performance than the CH-4, Baykar, and Bayraktar TB2. A Block III is under development.

Figure 6.27: Shahpar II Block II

Source: https://www.eurasiantimes.com/pakistan-flaunts-indigenous-shahpar-ii-drone/

Bayraktar-1 TBK was developed by Turkey. The Bayraktar-1 TBK had a range of 300 km and could carry a 500 kg payload. It could also perform precision strikes on ground targets with a laser-guided weapon system. Pakistan has since upgraded its Bayraktar-1 TBK with new features such as improved avionics, navigation systems, and weapons. Pakistan has also deployed several UCAVs for combat operations against the Tehrik-i-Taliban Pakistan (TTP) in North Waziristan's Shawal Valley.

TB2 Drone

The Turkish Baykar Bayraktar TB2 is a MALE (Medium Altitude Long Endurance) armed Turkish drone capable of conducting surveillance, intelligence, reconnaissance and armed attack missions. The drone made its maiden flight in August 2014. It is the most successful drone of Turkish origin that performed very well in the Azerbaijan-Armenia 2020 war and gained global attention. Turkey has also used this drone extensively in Syria and Libya. To date, TB2 has completed more than 400,000 flight hours.

TB2 is configured with 6 aerial vehicle platforms, three ground data terminals (GDT), two ground control stations, two remote video terminals (RVT) and ground support equipment. Each aerial platform is equipped with a triply redundant avionics system. It features fully automatic flight control and 3 redundant autopilot systems (Triple Redundant) and is also capable of automatic landing and take-off without dependence on ground systems. It features navigation with Internal Sensor Fusion without dependency on GPS.

The drone carries a payload of a maximum of 150 kg with a maximum take-off weight of 700 kg. The drone has a length of 21 ft. 4 inches and a wingspan of 39 ft. 4 inches. It is powered by a 105-hp Rotax 912-iS internal combustion injection engine and has 2-bladed variable-pitch propellers. It has a fuel capacity of 300 litres. The drone has a maximum speed of 220 km/h, a cruise speed of 130 km/h with a range of 4000 km and a communication range of less than 300 km. It has a flight endurance of 27 hours. The maximum service ceiling is 25,000 ft.

The drone has 4 hardpoints which can carry MAM-C and MAM-L guided bombs, L-UMTAS (Long Range Anti-Tank Missile System), Roketsan Cirit (70 mm Missile System), TUBITAK-SAGE BOZOK Laser Guided Rockets, TUBITAK-SAGE TOGAN [quad rack of GPS/INS guided 81 mm mortars], Advanced Precision Kill Weapon System [70 mm laser-guided rocket] (proposed).

Turkish Bayraktar Akinci[78]

Figure 6.28: Bayraktar Akinci CUAV

Source: Company Brochure; https://baykartech.com/en/uav/bayraktar-akinci/

Bayraktar Akinci is a HALE (High-Altitude Long-Endurance) Unmanned Combat Aerial Vehicle (UCAV)/Drone being manufactured by the Turkish company Baykar. The UCAV is equipped with dual artificial intelligence avionics which supports signal processing, sensor fusion and situational awareness in real-time. According to Baykar, Bayraktar Akinci is capable of conducting operations that are performed with fighter jets. It carries electronic support systems, dual satellite communication systems, air-to-air radar, collision avoidance radar and synthetic aperture radar. It can also be used in air-to-ground and air-to-air attack missions. The drone is equipped with an indigenously manufactured active electronically scanned array (AESA) radar, a SAR/GMTI radar and a surveillance system. It features dual redundant SATCOM plus dual redundant LOS. Furthermore, it features fully automatic flight control and 3 redundant autopilot systems (Triple Redundant). Like TB2 it is also capable of automatic landing and take-off without dependence on ground systems. It features navigation with internal sensor fusion without dependency on GPS.

Its advanced features include:

- Fully Automatic Navigation and Route Tracking Feature
- Precise Auto Take-off and Landing with Built-in Sensor Fusion
- Fully Automatic Taxi and Parking Features
- Semi-Autonomous Flight Modes Support
- Fault Tolerant and 3 Redundant Sensor Fusion Application
- Cross Redundant YKI System
- Unique Redundant Servo Actuator Units
- Unique Redundant Lithium-Based Battery Units

The drone carries a payload of a maximum of 1500kg with a maximum take-off weight of 6000 kg. The drone has a length of 40 ft. and a wingspan of 65 ft. 7 inches and a height of 13 ft. 5 inches. It is powered by 2 Ukrainian turboprop engines, which produce 560 kW (750 hp) each. It features a 5-bladed composite constant-speed propeller. The drone has a maximum speed of 361 km/h and a cruise speed of 240 km/h with a range of 7,500 km. It has a flight endurance of 24 hours. The maximum service ceiling is 45,000 ft. and the drone has an operational altitude of 30,000-40,000 ft. The drone has 8 hardpoints that can carry a wide range of weapons.

Weapons layout

Missiles include:

CIRIT

L-UMTAS ASM

Gökdoğan BVR AAM

Bozdoğan AAM
Akdoğan AAM
Gökhan AAM
SOM ALCM
TUBITAK-SAGE BOZOK Laser Guided Rockets
TUBITAK-SAGE KUZGUN-TJ/KY/ER/EW
AKBABA (AtS) & (ARM)
ROKETSAN ÇAKIR Missile Family
ÇAKIR LIR/SW

Bombs include:
Teber-81 (Mark 81 bomb w/ ROKETSAN Laser Guidance Kit)
HGK-82 (Mark 82 bomb w/ TUBITAK-SAGE Precision Guidance Kit)
KGK-82 (Mark 82 bomb w/ TUBITAK-SAGE Wing Assisted Guidance Kit)
Teber-82 (Mark 82 bomb w/ ROKETSAN Laser Guidance Kit)
HGK-83 (Mark 83 bomb w/ TUBITAK-SAGE Precision Guidance Kit)
KGK-83 (Mark 83 bomb w/ TUBITAK-SAGE Wing Assisted Guidance Kit)
HGK-84 (Mark 84 bomb w/ TUBITAK-SAGE Precision Guidance Kit)
LHGK-84 (Mark 84 bomb w/ TUBITAK-SAGE Laser Sensitive Guidance Kit)
TUBITAK-SAGE TOGAN Rack of four 81 mm mortars (GPS/INS or unguided)
TUBITAK-SAGE KUZGUN-SS Glide bomb
Aselsan Miniature Bomb (MB)
SARB-83 Bunker buster
NEB-84 Bunker buster
MAM-C/L/T

Tactical C/UAVs[79]

This list is dated.

- Ababeel (Pakistan Aeronautical Complex)
- Bazz (Pakistan Aeronautical Complex)
- Burraq (NESCOM/PAF) PAF/Army
- Border Eagle (Integrated Dynamics Pakistan)

- Bravo (Air Weapon Complex)
- Hawk (Integrated Dynamics Pakistan)
- Hawk Mk1 (Integrated Dynamics Pakistan)
- Hornet (Integrated Dynamics Pakistan)
- JASSOS (SATUMA Pakistan)
- LUNA
- Nishan Mk1 (Integrated Dynamics Pakistan)
- Nishan TJ 1000 (Integrated Dynamics Pakistan)
- Shadow (Integrated Dynamics Pakistan)
- Tornado (Integrated Dynamics Pakistan)
- Vector (Integrated Dynamics Pakistan)
- Vision MK1 (Integrated Dynamics Pakistan)
- Vision MK2 (Integrated Dynamics Pakistan)

As to PAF numbers, in January 2021 Bilal Khan estimated "44 Falco UAVs, 35 Burraqs, and 70 Shahpars."[80] He is basing this on serial numbers, but he says the serials could have gaps for attrition aircraft.

PAF Pilot Training

This information is taken from Alan Warnes[81] and the PAF official site (which often does not work for all pages and often is inaccessible as it times out).[82] Warnes has intimate access to the PAF not enjoyed by a journalist from any country and is careful with details. Correspondingly, he cannot write anything critical that the PAF may not like.

PAF has two air colleges, at Lower Topa and Risalpur, that take aspiring youngsters of both sexes starting in Grade 8. Though not all students at the colleges intend a PAF career—they can, for example, opt for a civilian flying career. After graduating from school, they can apply to the PAF Academy, which takes 1000 cadets a year in two batches, approximately 500 each. Relatively few—about 100 annually—go on to become fighter pilots. There are multiple other flying and non-flying opportunities in the PAF, of course.

After 18 months at the Academy, students start their six-month primary flying of 55 hours. Solo flying comes after 10 hours. Though some cadets fail at this stage, the PAF has acted to reduce wastage and therefore training costs.

Forty Super Mushshak aircraft trainers with 20 Qualified Flight Instructors are employed.

Basic flight training comes next on T-37 or K-8. For 13 hours students do spins around the airfield and then go solo. Twenty hours are for instrument flying, 16 for navigation and six for night flying. Of the night flying, two sorties are solo.

The successful students graduate as Pilot Officer and are ready to shift from Risalpur to M.M. Alam for fighter conversion. Here they do 50 hours with the K-8s of 1st Squadron. Warne says PAF rules dictate 60 hours, so some extra hours on the T-37 can result. The fighter trainees do 30 hours of enhanced fighter training. They are then posted to No. 18 Squadron for LIFT on the JF-17; No. 22 Squadron (OCU) on Mirage is presumably phasing down.

Failing the LIFT/OCU course permits the pilot to switch to other aircraft types, such as helicopters or transports.

Unsurprisingly, the PAF flying candidates are required to have 6/6 (American 20/20) vision. Surprisingly, the minimum height requirement is 5' 4" because shorter candidates are more suited for Chinese-origin fighters. Women are aggressively recruited for flying roles which again is surprising because Pakistan is a patriarchal society.

Additional information is reproduced verbatim from Pakistan Air Force Online. This source is 20+ years old and bound to be obsolete in some details. But it is still a useful guide and is well-written. Unfortunately, the site does not seem to be active any more.

Formal training for PAF fighter pilots[83]

1. Primary and basic training at the Pakistan Air Force Academy, Risalpur;
2. Combat training at No. 37 (Combat Training) Wing, Mianwali; and
3. Advanced tactics and weapons training at the Combat Commanders' School (CCS), Sargodha.

Formal training for PAF transport pilots is based on three primary stages:

1. Primary and basic training at the Pakistan Air Force Academy, Risalpur;
2. Combat training at No. 37 Combat Training Wing, Mianwali; and
3. Tactical transport training at the Transport Conversion School (TCS), Chaklala.

Formal training for PAF aeronautical engineers is based on two primary stages:

1. Bachelor of Science (BSc.) qualification in Aeronautical Engineering at the Pakistan Air Force Academy, Risalpur; and
2. Postgraduate qualification (MSc. and/or Ph. D) in a domestic or foreign academic institution.

Combat Commanders' School (CCS), Sargodha:

Once pilots have passed their combat training at No. 37 (Combat Training) Wing, Mianwali, they begin their operational careers with the PAF as Flight Lieutenants. In essence, they have become fighter pilots. However, this is not the end of their formal training. Midway in their career, section leaders of the PAF frontline combat squadrons are chosen for advanced tactical training at the prestigious Combat Commanders' School, Sargodha, where they learn the fineness and art of air combat during an intensive and rigorous course lasting six months.

The Combat Commanders' School (CCS) was set up at Sargodha on 5 May 1976. It is the successor of the Flight Leaders' School (FLS) which was established at Sargodha on 15 June 1958. The CCS is a mid-career advanced fighter tactics and weapons school for PAF pilots. The CCS is at the top end of the PAF training scale and represents the pinnacle of the PAF pilot quality. The CCS was established after it was felt that the skills gained by the PAF elite combat squadrons and crack fighter pilots should be passed on in an institutionalised form to the rest of the PAF squadrons and pilots. It is today ranked as the world's best GCI/pilot training school and is considered by the international military aviation community to be one of the world's best fighter tactics and weapons schools. The CCS is an elite within an elite.

Instructor staff at the CCS are generally acknowledged to be the 'best of the best' and would also have a war role to fulfil in the event of a conflict.

Although the CCS was established to 'further polish the skills of the already polished,' it has transformed into a major and vital organisation within the PAF training establishment—so much so that no PAF pilot can hope to remain with or progress to the PAF's frontline fighter squadrons without passing the gruelling CCS training curriculum.

The training system and curriculum of the CCS is classified and as such the CCS is not open to pilots from even friendly foreign air forces. The CCS trains both combat commanders (fighter pilots) and combat controllers (forward air controllers).

Competition even within the CCS is encouraged. Each year there is a trophy for the 'Best Combat Commander' and the 'Best Combat Controller' which is awarded at a formal annual graduation ceremony. Much has been learnt and improved by observing the US Naval Air Station (USNAS) at Miramar, California. What is certain is that there are no books involved and little reading to do at CCS. The primary emphasis is on training and fighting in the air i.e., on 'practice' rather than 'theory,' the best of the best is pitted against each other in a grueling schedule in which there is no room for second-best. However, even at CCS there is pilot wastage, although very low at around 2-5 per cent i. e., out of every 20 PAF pilots who enter CCS, on average only 2-3 fail to pass. (Please note this is 10-15 per cent, not 2-5 per cent.) This is, however, considered an acceptable student attrition rate at CCS.

OCUs (2024 update)

The CCS has three subordinate units. No 23 Squadron (F-7PG/FT-7PG), No. 28 Squadron JF-17, No. 29 Squadron (F-16). Squadrons Dashings (earlier versions of F-7). Last Skybolts (Mirage) disbanded. Now we have to wait for a J-10 CCS, No. 23 is a logical number.

There used to be five OCUs, now there are two because two OCUs are numbered squadrons; one more became a regular squadron. No. 22 Squadron, the Mirage OCU, may become the J-10 OCU. When the F-7s finally depart, there will be no need for No. 23 Squadron OCU, so presumably it will become a JF-17 or J-10 squadron. On the other hand, given the large number of JF-17s, one of these two squadrons may become a second OCU JF-17. There is precedent for two OCU squadrons on one type of aircraft - see below.

Around 2000, the line-up was:

- No. 7 Squadron - Mirage 5 OCU. Became a regular Mirage squadron
- No. 9 Squadron - F-7MP OCU. Became a regular F-16 squadron
- No. 11 Squadron - F-16 OCU. Remains the F-16 OCU
- No. 22 Squadron - Mirage III OCU. Remains Mirage OCU
- No. 25 Squadron - F-7MP OCU. Became a night attack Mirage squadron and remains

Training for CUAV operators

I have no details for this, except that 44 personnel for the Akinci were trained in Türkiye.[84]

Notes

1. Bilal Khan (2024, March 29). Report on Pakistan's air warfare plans for the decade. *Quwa.org*. https://quwa.org/2024/03/29/report-pakistans-air-warfare-plans-for-the-decade/
2. Ravi Rikhye (2022) *India's Ability to fight a 2-front war.* New Delhi: Kalpana Shukla/KW Publishers Pvt. Ltd.
3. Bilal Khan (January 26, 2024). Pakistan quietly inducts a new AEWC system. Quwa.org. https://quwa.org/2024/01/26/pakistan-quietly-inducts-a-new-erieye-aewc-system/
4. Serials are from Scramble https://www.scramble.nl/database/military/pk*#results*
5. N.a (2023, October 15). 14 nation mega aerial warfare exercises of PAF named Indus Shield 2023 in full swing. https://www.radio.gov.pk/15-10-2023/14-nation-mega-aerial-warfare-exercises-of-paf-named-indus-shield-2023-in-full-swing
6. https://pdf.defence.pk/threads/pakistan-and-chinas-air-forces-commence-large-scale-aerial-warfare-exercises-the-tenth-iteration-of-the-shaheen-exercises.775225/ IX in 2020
7. Pakistan arrives for first Red Flag, https://www.nellis.af.mil/About/Innovation/5G/igphoto/2000342705/
8. David Cenciotti Pakistani, https://theaviationist.com/2016/07/22/pakistani-f-16cd-block-52-jes-enroute-to-green-and-red-flag-in-the-u-s-perform-stopover-at-lajes-field, July 22, 2016, Military Aviation
9. Pakistani F-16s invited to Red Flag, from Asif » 13 Oct 2008, 23:56 https://www.f-16.net/forum/viewtopic.php?t=11200 citing, https://aviationweek.com/aw/generic/story_generic.jsp?channel=aerospacedaily&id=news/PAK091908.xml, but URL returns 404
10. Wikipedia.com
11. ACES Meet is an international air exercise hosted and organised by the Pakistan Air Force, which aims to improve the combat preparedness of air forces by providing them with realistic training in air combat and counterterrorism operations. Participants in the exercise include contingents from several air forces throughout the world, including combat pilots and ground support troops with their fighter aircraft.
12. https://paffalcons.com/news/induction-operationalization-ceremony-at-paf-operational-base/ On this page is a short video on the J-10CE that mentions this fact.

13. BR Web Desk. (2024, January 2). PAF inducts new batch of J-10C fighter jets. *Business Recorder.* https://www.brecorder.com/news/40281711
14. Ritu Sharma. (2023, November 23). After JF-17, J-10C Fighters, Cash-Strapped Pakistan Turns To China For Light Combat Aircraft JL-15. *Eurasian Times.* https://www.eurasiantimes.com/after-jf-17-j-10c-fighters-cash-strapped-pakistan-again-turns/
15. The Military Curiosity (2023). J-10C of Pakistan in New Mirage 5 Camouflage Scheme. https://www.youtube.com/watch?v=3qgmxjZ_pOA
16. The Stratcom Bureau (2023, March 30). https://twitter.com/AliNaumanKT/status/1641716020875341826
17. Robert Hewson. (2008m May 19). Chinese J-10 'benefited from the Lavi project'. *Jane's.* http://www.janes.com/news/defence/jdw/jdw080519_2_n.shtml
18. Deino (2006, January 12). Chengdu Jianjiji-9 / J-9 Fighter & Interceptor. https://www.secretprojects.co.uk/threads/chengdu-jianjiji-9-j-9-fighter-interceptor.40/
19. N.a. Pakistan to acquire L-15 Supersonic Jet Trainer Aircraft. *PAF Falcons* Blog. https://paffalcons.com/news/pakistan-to-acquire-l15-supersonic-jet-trainer-aircraft/
20. Bilal Khan (2023, December 2). Pakistan Reportedly Negotiating for L-15 Trainers from China. *Quwa.org* online magazine.
21. Professor Buzzkill (2000, September 20). Mark Twain: "A Lie Can Travel Halfway Around the World Before the Truth Puts On its Shoes" – Quote or No Quote? Blog. https://professorbuzzkill.com/2020/09/30/twain-lie-travels/
22. https://www.key.aero/article/masters-mirage-maintenance
23. https://pdf.defence.pk/threads/capabilities-of-paf-dassault-mirage-iii-v.44991/page-12 monitor
24. For the story behind the Australian Mirages, see http://www.adf-serials.com.au/3a3-Pakistan.htm 32 were converted to ROSE I with No. 7 Squadron and Combat Commanders School; 4 apparently PR with No. 5 Squadrons, and 7 DA went to No. 5 and No. 22 OCU Squadrons
25. Flight Global. (1998, February 10). Pakistan buys refurbished Mirages from France. https://www.flightglobal.com/pakistan-buys-refurbished-mirages-from-france/19476.article
26. Project Rose (n.d.) Wikipedia. https://en.wikipedia.org/wiki/Project_ROSE. Wikipedia article uses as a source a book by Bernard Chenel, Michael Bernard, and Eric Moreau (2014). Mirage III/5/50 en service à l'étranger. Le Vigen, France: Editions LELA Presse.
27. Zeeman. (2019, September 5). Egyptian Mirage V Horus released after stiff opposition from India. *World-Defense.com* Blog. https://world-defense.com/threads/egyptian-mirage-v-horus-released-after-stiff-opposition-from-india.6998/

28. (n.a.) (2018, April 29).Thrifty at 50: Pakistan keeps ageing Mirages flying. *AFP.* https://www.france24.com/en/20180429-thrifty-50-pakistan-keeps-ageing-mirages-flying
29. Defense Security Cooperation Agency (2022, September 7). Pakistan – F-16 Case for Sustainment. https://www.dsca.mil/press-media/major-arms-sales/pakistan-f-16-case-sustainment.
30. Defense Security Cooperation Agency (2024, February 1). India – MQ-9B Remotely Piloted Aircraft. https://www.dsca.mil/press-media/major-arms-sales/india-mq-9b-remotely-piloted-aircraft.
31. Bilal Khan, (March 29, 2024*). Report: Pakistan's Air Warfare Plans for the Decade.* Quwa.Org. https://quwa.org/quwa-premium-excerpt/report-pakistans-air-warfare-plans-for-the-decade-2/
32. Ibid.
33. https://www.tandfonline.com/doi/full/10.1080/00963402.2023.2245260
34. In 2023 Chinese aviation officials said development problems with the WS-19 had been overcome, Yeo, Mike. (2023, March 27) Supply chain issues impede mass production of new Chinese engine. *Defense News*, https://www.defensenews.com/industry/techwatch/2023/03/27/supply-chain-issues-impede-mass-production-of-new-chinese-engine/ The engine referred to is the WS-10 in use on the PAF J-10 and other aircraft.
35. From Wikipedia and other sources
36. No author or date. *Global Security.* https://www.globalsecurity.org/military/world/china/ws19.htm
37. Salisbury, Daniel. (2022, January). PRC Navy Likely Testing Carrier-Based Stealth Fighters. *China Aerospace Studies Institute.* https://www.airuniversity.af.edu/Portals/10/CASI/documents/Research/CASI%20Articles/2022-02-14%20PLA%20Navy%20Likely%20Testing%20Carrier-Based%20Stealth%20Fighters.pdf. (This is a reputable source from the USAF's Air University at Maxwell Air Force Base.)
38. Pakistan Could Join Turkey's Kaan Fighter Project Tony Osborne August 3, 2023, https://aviationweek.com/defense-space/aircraft-propulsion/pakistan-could-join-turkeys-kaan-fighter-project
39 https://www.militaryfactory.com/aircraft/detail.php?aircraft_id=1085#specifications
40. https://www.defensenews.com/global/europe/2023/05/11/the-cost-of-turkeys-tf-x-fighter-jet-could-rise-manufacturer-says/
41. https://www.thedrive.com/the-war-zone/our-first-full-look-at-turkeys-new-tf-x-stealthy-fighter
42. From Scramble.nl Pakistan Air Force Military Data Base.

43. US DSCA (2014, March 11). Pakistan – C-130 Fleet Upgrade Program. https://www.dsca.mil/sites/default/files/mas/pakistan_13-76.pdf
44. Aviation Safety Network https://aviation-safety.net/wikibase/type/T37
45. 63 aircraft, including 24 T-37Bs and 39 T-37Cs. In 2008 20 T-37s were delivered that were ordered from the U.S.[33] On 28 October 2015, the Turkish Air Force gave the Pakistan Air Force 34 T-37Cs, including spares in an agreement between Turkey and Pakistan.
46. Unfortunately, the Pakistan Navy's air arm section has not been officially updated. Pakistan Navy Website https://www.paknavy.gov.pk/air_arm.html
47. See also Quwa 2023, January 13). Updates to Pakistan's Drone Fleet https://quwa.org/daily-news/updates-to-pakistans-drone-fleet/
48. Kaiser Tufail, Air Commodore (2020). Against All Odds: Pakistan Air Force in the 1971 War. Helion Book, Asia at War Series (Warwick, UK). Pages 23 and 25, plus from my notes and other writings by the author. You can read the book free at https://archive.org/details/against-all-odds-pakistan-airforce-in-1971-by-air-cdre-r-kaiser-tufail
49. Bilal Khan. (2024, March 17). Pakistan Air Force Air Defense Development. *Quwa.org.* https://quwa.org/2024/03/17/pakistan-air-force-air-defence-development-2/
50. Army Recognition. (2023, November 8). Search radar vehicle from HQ-16A (LY-80) air defence missile system battery unit. https://armyrecognition.com/china_chinese_army_missile_systems_vehicles/hq-16a_ly-80_ground_to_air_defence_missile_system_technical_data_sheet_specifications_pictures_video.html
51. Ibid.
52. Chowdhury, S, (2022, April 9). New Pakistan radars, including one being installed now, close to Balakot. *Times of India.* https://www.timesnownews.com/india/new-pakistani-radars-including-one-being-installed-now-close-to-balakot-article-90744616 (This is the one at Cherat, 200-km away, hardly close to Balakot.)
53. PakDefense Blog (2020, March 20). YLC-18A Long Range 3D Low Altitude Acquisition Radar. https://www.pakdefense.com/blog/pakistan-air-force/ylc-18a-long-range-three-dimension-low-altitude-blind-compensation-radar/
54. First Post. 2022, November 15. *China gifts anti-satellite radars to Pakistan, aims to destroy India's space program.* https://www.firstpost.com/world/china-gifts-anti-satellite-radars-to-pakistan-aims-to-destroy-indias-space-program-11626701.html
55. Rohit Vats assisted with this list.

55 Puneet Bhalla. (Spring 2012). Pakistan's Air Defense. *Scholar Warrior.* https://archive.claws.in/images/journals_doc/SW%20J.99-106.pdf While this is an excellent source, it is now dated.

56. Jaidev Jamwal (2022, November 16). Pakistani Armed Forces ORBAT, Part 5: Air Defense. https://jjamwal.in/yayavar/pakistani-armed-forces-orbat-part-5-air-defence/
57. Bilal Khan (2023 December 2). Pakistan reportedly negotiating for L-15 trainers from China. *Quwa.org*. https://quwa.org/2023/12/02/pakistan-reportedly-negotiating-for-l-15-trainers-from-china/
58. Wikipedia (Retrieved 2016, April 10). Ivchenko-Progress AI-222. https://en.wikipedia.org/wiki/Ivchenko-Progress_AI-222; Wiki gives slightly greater thrust than Roboexport.
59. Top War (2020, December 2) "The service life of the AI-222 engine is half as much": the Brazilian press explained the advantages of the M-346FA. https://en.topwar.ru/177686-srok-sluzhby-dvigatelja-ai-222-vdvoe-menshe-brazilskaja-pressa-objasnila-preimuschestva-ubs-m-346fa.html
60. AI-222-25F Turbofan Engine With Afterburner. Rosoboronexport. 2014. Kyiv, Ukraine. http://poe.cc.ua/en/products/aviation/engines/ai-222-25f-turbofan-engine-with-afterburner/ Some of the figures may not match with those used in this book.
61. "The L-15B is thought to use the WS-17 Minshan turbofan with a maximum thrust of 10,362lb (4,700kg) with afterburning". Andreas Rupprecht (November 1, 2018*). Eye on the East: China joins the 'Lift' league.* https://www.key.aero/article/eye-east-china-joins-lift-league. Key Aero magazine.
62. Military Factory (2010, last edited 2023, Febuary 22). Hongdu JL-10/L-15. https://www.militaryfactory.com/aircraft/detail.php?aircraft_id=1119
63. Nathan Meier. (2021, September 3, Military Turbojet/Turbofan Specifications). http://jet-engine.net/miltfspec.htm
64. Balázs Molnár (nd). *How much fuel does a clean F-15 burn*. Quora.com. Victor. (2020). How much fuel does a clean F-15 burn. https://www.quora.com/How-much-fuel-per-hour-does-a-clean-F-15-burn-at-its-best-range-cruise-speed-and-altitude-What-speed-and-altitude-gives-the-best-range. The following quotation is from Victor (2020) at the same URL. "The F-15 is a modern, large fighter with two engines. In the Worst-Case Scenario, (in the dense air at sea level with maximum afterburner selected and at high speed), the total fuel flow can be 385 gallons per minute, or 6.4 gallons per second. At that rate, it would use its entire internal fuel supply in about 6 minutes if the pilot did nothing to change the conditions... such as flying higher, turning off the afterburner, and cruising at a much slower, subsonic speed. There is a VAST difference in fuel burn between altitudes, engine power settings, and engine types."
65. Ibid.
66. Xavier, Vavasseur (2021, September 6). First 'Sea Sultan' Maritime Patrol Aircraft Joins Pakistan Navy. N*aval News*. https://www.navalnews.com/naval-news/2021/09/first-sea-sultan-maritime-patrol-aircraft-joins-pakistan-navy/

67. Twitter (2024, January 14). Pak Navy Buying Ground Base CAMM-ER|Pak Navy's Anti-Ship & Surface to Air Missiles 2024. https://twitter.com/Defence_IDA/status/1746551956347437102. This web magazine is published in Estonia and the video is captioned in Hindi which I am very slow to read.
68. Flight Global (2024). Directory of World Air Forces. https://www.flightglobal.com/download?ac=98881
69. Aircon 2100. (2014, April 21). System Highlights and IOP Capabilities. *www.Indra.es,* https://www.icao.i(nt/NACC/Documents/Meetings/2014/AUTOSWIM/AUTOSWIMP03.PDF
70. Samir Lalwani (March 2023). A Threshold Alliance: The China-Pakistan Military Relationship. Special Report No. 517. United States Institute of Peace. https://www.usip.org/sites/default/files/2023-03/sr-517_threshold-alliance-china-pakistan-military-relationship.pdf
71. Prasun Sengupta (2024, March 20). Making Up For Shortfalls Pakistan Air Force buying up to 60 J-10CE M-MRCA from China. *Force India.* https://forceindia.net/feature-report/making-up-for-shortfalls/
72. No. 20 Squadron. (2000). https://www.geocities.ws/pafwebsite/Squadron20.html.
73. Faroq Bhai. (2024, February 27). Post in X (Twitter). https://twitter.com/FarooqB90714421/status/1762492410720887081/photo/1
74. The Hindu Bureau. (2024 , January 18). Pakistan-Iran attacks updates | Death toll in Pakistan strikes on Iran rises to nine. *Hindu.* https://www.thehindu.com/news/international/pakistan-iran-attacks-live-updates-on-january-18-2024/article67751457.ece
75. Air Force Technology. (2009, September 29). Falco Tactical Unmanned Aerial Vehicle (UAV). https://www.airforce-technology.com/projects/falco-uav/?cf-view and Leonardo Company Brochure (2000) Falco Family of UAS. Falco+Family+(MM09053)_LQ.pdf
76. Ashish Dangwal (2024, March 13). Pakistan Flaunts Indigenous Shahpar II Drone To Military. *Eurasian Times.* https://www.eurasiantimes.com/pakistan-flaunts-indigenous-shahpar-ii-drone/
77. Bayraktar Akinci (2024) https://baykartech.com/en/uav/bayraktar-akinci/
78. The source is Pakistan Defence Forum https://defencepk.com/forums/threads/pakistan-uavs-news-discussions.86/ but the reference is to a 2007 source.
79. Bilal Khan (2021, January 21). Pakistan Takes Delivery of CH-4 Drones from China. *Quwa.* https://quwa.org/quwa-premium/pakistan-takes-delivery-of-ch-4-drones-from-china/
80. Alan Warnes. (2016). Pakistan Air Force: Attaining New Heights. The Army Press Islamabad.
81. Pakistan Air Force. https://paf.gov.pk/

82. Ahmad Adnan Faruqi. (2000). Making of A General Duty (Fighter) Pilot. *Pakistan Airforce Online*. https://pakfizaia.tripod.com/gdpilots.html This source is 20+ years old but is still a useful guide.
83. Akhil Kadidal & Akshara Parakala (2022, October 27) Pakistan Air Force personnel train to operate Akinci UAVs. *Jane's*. https://www.janes.com/defence-news/news-detail/pakistan-air-force-personnel-train-to-operate-akinci-uavs

7
Conclusion

In conclusion, I briefly ponder three factors concerning the Pakistan Air Force.

Where is the money coming from?

Making sense of the Pakistan defence budget is difficult because a sharp deterioration of the PKR has confused everything. I will speak in terms of rounded-off figures and approximation, to make matters easier for the reader.

On June 1, 2022, the rate was PKR 198 = $1[1] so the defence budget approved for 2022-23 was about $8 billion or PKS 1.6 trillion. By June 1, 2023, the PKR was down to Rs 286 = $1, so despite a 13% increase for 2023 (PKR 1.8 trillion), the dollar value was down to $6.3 billion for Fiscal 2023-2024 ending on May 31. Full budgetary documents are perfunctory.[2] As of today, 19 April 2024, the exchange rate is PKR 278=$1.

The defence budget has a heading for physical assets; 2023-24 = PKR 461 billion. Civil construction is additional, we can reasonably assume that the entire PKR 461 billion is available for equipment.

Additionally, not included in defence budget, is the 'Armed Forces Development Plan,' 2022-23 = PKR 340 billion. Increasing it by 21 per cent to match overall increase in defence budget gives in PPP terms = $33.5 billion and India ($59 billion x 100/23 PPP) = $256 billion PPP. Imported equipped costs market price of USD, but I am ignoring that for simplicity. Coincidentally, the market value of the two nation's rupees gives the same ratio as PPP: The 7.6-to-1 in PPP, and 7.8-to-1 in market exchange rate.

Putting the development plan and budgeted purchases, we get a total equipment budget of $2.6 billion. But this is not enough. For example,

20 JF-17 Block III cost $800 million. 25 J-10 cost $1 billion. While PRC has probably given credit, but as far as I know, PRC does not give Pakistan military grants. Annually, 100 tanks, 100 artillery guns, and 100 APCs together may cost $800 million a year.

Saudi Arabia is probably giving some grants, together, with some Gulf nations. I'd be surprised if the total adds up to more than $150 million. Pakistan probably makes some money off the manpower/services it provides friendly nations. In 2022-2024, its earning something from its ammunition supplies to Ukraine. It buys much material second hand. But then pays full price to refit these purchases. Don't forget the radar/anti-aircraft missile Pakistan has built in the last four months. This could easily have cost $2 billion. Then, there's the usual replacements of yearly equipment, spare parts, ordnance and so on.

With no satisfactory answers to explain where the Pakistan military gets its cash for equipment. I see two options: (a) Pakistan has arrangements of which we are unaware; and/or (b) it is adding to its already colossal debts with China and internally.[3] (Also see Keshav Padmanabhan in *The Print.*)[4]

Pakistan 2023-24 Defence Budget[5]

According to the above sources, Pakistan, in 2023-2024, had:

- External Debt (March 2023) = $125 billion
- Revenue = PKR 8.6 trillion in 2023-24.
- Debt service = PKR 7.3 trillion (compared to defence PKR 1.8-trillion)
- 2013-2017 (PM Nawaz Sharif) = $36 billion from China alone.

We could argue these issues until the cows come home, are sent to the glue factory, and reincarnated as cows and not get anywhere because the actual data is unavailable.

Again, please remember:

- I have provided only approximations.
- There is no sophistication in my analysis.
- Much of what Pakistan owes China is for giant infrastructure programs so is not unproductive.
- Pakistan is not about to default. As *The Print* says, China BRI 2.0 aims not so much towards infrastructure as ensuring that debtor countries stay solvent.[6]

Thus, the US can see even if Pakistan is borrowing—say $1-2 billion/year from China—it is a small amount compared to its overall debts. The military sees no dilemmas because it is considering the immediate present. Tomorrow is another day. And with loans, Pakistan can spend $3-3.5 billion/year, to meet its annual equipment budgets.

The China Factor

The importance of China as an arms supplier to Pakistan can be understood by a single figure: In 2019-2023 overall, *SIPRI* reports that Pakistan took 61 per cent of arms exported by China.[7]

But more than that, the new, assertive China will come to the aid of Pakistan if required. This requires a lengthy analysis which I cannot undertake here. Back-of-envelope, China can, now, station 200 fighters on India's northern borders, and it can send up to 90 aircraft and several SAM battalions to Pakistan. I'm not going to explain how I derive these figures: just keep them in mind. An Arab aircraft that could reinforce Pakistan is a problem of many variables. It might be zero, and it might be 100, if deployed defensively. Pakistan has the infrastructure and the joint training to host Arab aircraft. The variables are political, not technical.

Much depends on the US attitude; that in turn is contingent on if India is the aggressor or Pakistan. US will not countenance a Pakistan attack on India and will act to limit Arab deployments to Pakistan. Contra wise, if India attacks Pakistan, US may see things differently. Of course, US can have no influence on Chinese deployment

3. Air Lessons from Ukraine

Lessons from Ukraine are more relevant to land warfare and less to air warfare. And the Second Nagorno-Karabakh War 2020, also called the 44-Day War, prefigured Ukraine 2022-present. Turkey and Israel played an essential part on Azerbaijan's side in the matter of the widespread use of C/UAVs.[8] Pakistan Air Force and Army/Navy defence expeditiously and commendably applied these lessons immediately.

Since 2020, when India encountered new smash-and-grab PLA tactics, and since its alliance with the US (though India does not call it an 'alliance'),

India has been relatively unconcerned with Pakistan. Whether it is right to do is, of course, hardly my place to say.

Figure 7.1: PAF Mirage III DP Serial 612 Drawing © Tom Cooper

Notes

1. Exchange-rates.org (2022, June 6). US Dollar (USD) To Pakistan Rupee (PKR) Exchange Rate History for June 7, 2022. https://www.exchange-rates.org/exchange-rate-history/usd-pkr-2022-06-07
2. Government of Pakistan Finance Division. (2022, June 10). Performance Based Budget FYs 2022-23 to 2024-25. pp. 50-53. https://www.finance.gov.pk/budget/Budget_2022_23/Performance_Based_Budget_FY_2022_23_to_2024_25.pdf
3. Abdul Wahid. (August 30, 2023), Pakistan's Debt Dilemma. *IMF.org* Blog. ghttps://blog-pfm.imf.org/en/pfmblog/2023/08/pakistan-s-debt-dilemma
4. Keshav Padmanabhan. (2023, November 13). How much debt is too much debt? Curious case of Pakistan's $69 billion Chinese debt trap. *The Print.* https://theprint.in/economy/how-much-debt-is-too-much-debt-case-of-pakistan-its-chinese-credit-in-aiddata-report/1842106.
5. Usman Ansari. https://www.defensenews.com/global/asia-pacific/2023/06/22/pakistan-unveils-increased-defense-budget-imf-decries-spending-plan. https://www.dawn.com/news/1758922
6. Keshav Padmanabhan. (2023, November 8). Infra lender to emergency creditor—BRI 2.0 is China's new strategy to ensure its debts are paid. *The Print.* https://theprint.in/world/infra-lender-to-emergency-creditor-bri-2-0-is-chinas-new-strategy-to-ensure-its-debts-are-paid/1837035/
7. SIPRI (2024. March). Trends In International Arms Transfers. Arms Transfers, 2023. https://www.sipri.org/sites/default/files/2024-03/fs_2403_at_2023.pdf
8. For more information, see: Haldun Yalçınkaya (2021, January 21). Turkey's Overlooked Role in the Second Nagorno-Karabakh War. *German Marshall Fund of the United States.* https://www.gmfus.org/news/turkeys-overlooked-role-second-nagorno-karabakh-war; and Isabel Debre. (2023, October 5). Israeli arms quietly helped Azerbaijan retake Nagorno-Karabakh, to the dismay of region's Armenians. *AP News.* https://apnews.com/article/armenia-azerbaijan-nagorno-karabakh-weapons-israel-6814437bcd744acc1c4df0409a74406c

8

Operation Sindoor (May 7 to May 11, 2025)

Outcome

Both sides claimed victory, but it's difficult to see what Pakistan achieved. India validated its air strategy, which got a full workout. Pakistan's claims of victory rest primarily on its claim to have shot down five Indian fighters. Foremost, this was not a game in which the outcome is determined by the number of fighter jets downed. Second, it appears Pakistan also lost at least six aircraft including on the ground. At most, Islamabad provided no conclusive evidence for any of its claims; it was the Indian social media that provided conclusive evidence for IAF losing three, perhaps four fighters.

Strategically, the outcome was ambiguous. If India aimed to inflict punishment,.it succeeded. If it were to establish deterrence against terrorist attacks, this would be impossible. India was correct in dismissing Pakistan's tiresome announcements that it would use its nuclear weapons if attacked. India was not deterred from its limited retaliation. Conversely, India did not enter Pakistan or capture ground. Undeterred by Pakistan's attempts at intimidation, India stopped before causing damage that would threaten Pakistan's existence.

One outcome was farcical: the Pakistan Army chief is now promoted to a field marshal. For what? Another was US President Donald claim he negotiated a ceasefire. He negotiated nothing. Both India and Pakistan wanted to limit the conflict. India never wanted to escalate the conflict, while Pakistan was heavily hit as soon as it attempted to do so. The Pakistan Director General of Military operations called his Indian counterpart and sensibly suggested a ceasefire. India merely agreed to a 'pause', but not to a ceasefire. Moreover,

Pakistan got no chance to discuss New Delhi's termination of the Indus Water Treaty, nor any other conditions.

Background

On April 22, 2025, five Pakistan terrorists dressed in military garb captured 26 Indian civilians at Pahalgam, Kashmir, a popular tourist resort and executed them in cold blood. They were made to recite the Kalima,[1] the fundamental Islamic declaration of faith, to sort the believers from the others. Unfortunately for one man, a Muslim, he was unable to comply. One man was a Christian. Twenty-four were Hindus. The sole "mercy" the terrorists showed was to spare the women and children; nonetheless, those spared were made to witness the execution of their husbands, brothers, and fathers.

The timing of this heinous act was perhaps not coincidental. The US Vice President J.D. Vance was visiting New Delhi with his wife of Indian ancestry and three children. As Pakistan has often done, this attack was to grab the attention of Americans and thus force an internationalization of the Kashmir issue. The US had long ago decided the Indians were determined to keep foreign interlocutors out of the Kashmir dispute, maintaining they were serious about treating Kashmir, divided between Pakistan and India after a 15-month war, 1947-49, as an internal affair. There was nothing for the US to mediate. But that did not stop the terrorists. They wanted to involve the US because (a) it is still widely perceived as the world leader, and (b) till Prime Minister Rajiv Gandhi in 1984, for the first 37 years after independence from Britain, the US was an intermittent ally or friend with Pakistan. However, between 1985 and 2025, the US position had changed. Realizing from 1948 that India was the larger and more powerful, and a democracy to boot, the US wooed India till India became a soft ally and commercial partner. By 2025, India's GDP was 12 times Pakistan's.

Indeed, at the start of the Pahalgam incident, the US President said that it was no concern of America's. That quickly changed: the US President, hungry for publicity as always, was drawn into the affair by Pakistan and announced he had brokered a ceasefire. In reality, he had nothing to do with the cessation of hostilities. The US President even talked of mediation, which India firmly made clear was not welcome. And given that America supposedly leads the world in its war against terrorism, there was seemingly no interest among the American public to involve itself in determining the outcome between a terrorist regime and a friend/partner of the US.

Terrorism

One thing must be made clear from the start. Pakistan says it has nothing to do with terrorism. The Kashmiri's are freedom fighters. Well, the Pakistan military Inter-Service Intelligence controls, runs, recruits, equips, and trains terrorist networks. The aim is to impose disproportionate costs as a part of Pakistan's strategy to keep the much more powerful Indians off-balance. The distant aim is to win Indian Administered Kashmir.

In the case of the Indian strike on Bahawalpur, a US-designated terrorist led the prayers. The funeral was attended by GOC-in-C IV Corps, GOC 11 Division, and the brigade commander of 15 Heavy Mechanized Brigade, all from Lahore. The video clearly shows uniformed soldiers carrying the coffins, draped with the Pakistani flag.[2] The Director General of the Inter Service Intelligence (ISI) announced that the leader of the funeral was a simple family man and a preacher. The very fact of my authoring this book, along with input from the Late Pushpindar Singh Chopra, India's foremost aviation expert, shows my impartiality. To me, an Indian-born American whose entire primary family lives/lived in the US, from my parents down to my grandchildren, were/are living here. I hope Pakistan will indulge me when I say, without moralizing, that via the ISI the Pakistan Army is closely intertwined with terrorist groups, for obvious national security reasons. There seems to be little doubt of this assertion. This fact was confirmed by dozens of assessments prepared by US intelligence. It has been made and proven multiple times over the decades. Is it not time we in the West acknowledged this and moved on?

Distasteful and cruel as a strategy of targeting civilians may seem, actively using or supporting terror is an accepted tool in the world order. One person's terrorist is the adversary's freedom fighter. Pakistan, from its inception in 1947, has used terror in attempting to win Kashmir and to control separatist elements, particularly in Balochistan. India came later to the terror game but used it extensively to weaken and ultimately liberate the former East Pakistan, today's Bangladesh. India used terror in its attempt to impose its control over Sri Lanka in the 1980s. India also supports anti-Pakistan groups, albeit in a limited way. The Arab states support terrorism for many reasons, the Shia-Sunni conflict, for example, and the attempt to spread Islam. The United States's religion is democracy, yet the US efforts to use terrorism are extensive and legendary. The US justifies its actions as seeking the liberation of people living under totalitarianism. The European powers used terrorism in their quest for colonial empires, but fortunately for the last 60-80 years, they have divested themselves of their colonies. The Soviet Union and its successor state, Russia used/use terrorism.

One side talks of liberation, and the adversary speaks of terror. This labelling is useful in fighting the information war, but does not alter the objective reality that using the term terror and liberation depends entirely on which side of the fence you stand on. So, it is with Pakistan and India. For India to moralize about Pakistan terrorism is a legitimate, necessary and part of the toolbox of combating that terrorism. At least for academic purposes we must accept that from Pakistan's view, it is not engaged in terrorism but in liberation.

India, for a millennia has seen itself as a peaceful but passive victim of external powers. The Narendra Modi government has embraced an opposite view of what India should stand for. From 2014, when he first came to power, Modi has defined the need for India to see itself not as a victim, but a strong and muscular Hindu nation emerging as a great power.

Foreigners accustomed to the image of Independence of a non-violent, secular society relying on moral power and acting differently from other countries in a violent, crusading world, may be surprised at this change in the Indian image, but versions of a muscular Hindu nation have existed for over 140-years, from when India first began forming political parties. Jawaharlal Nehru, the father of independent India, strongly believed in a secular India but was also sensitive and alert to challenges to his power. He suppressed the right wing because the right was a threat to his supremacy and to a militant Hindu nation. "Hindustan" of course, means "The land of the Hindus." Indians are largely secular, but what brought Modi to power was that many Hindus, an electoral majority, were fed up with the failures of secular democracy and bought into Modi's Hindu nationalist vision.

A core part of that vision is the firm belief that if Pakistan provokes India with terror, India must respond in kind ten-fold. It is no coincidence that the same belief pervades Israel, and that India has become close to Israel.

The need to fearlessly emulate Israel is often discussed in the Indian media. In 2019, PM Modi got his first chance when a suicide bomber killed 40 Indian paramilitary troops in Pulwama, Kashmir. India responded with a limited, attack on a Pakistani terrorist madrassa (religious school) in Pakistan-controlled part of Kashmir, followed by a Pakistani retaliation on a few Indian military targets in Kashmir. Though militarily insignificant, the attack at least served warning to Pakistan that India would not be passive of a terror attack.

In 2025, however, the Pahalgam terror attack forced India into action again. This is what led to the 4-days long Operation Sindoor. "Sindoor" is red powder that Indian married women wear in the part of their hair, and it signifies many things, mainly the blessings of marriage and fidelity to their husbands. More likely, Op Sindoor harks back to the ancient Rajput custom of a warrior cutting his finger with a sword and smearing blood on his wife's forehead as a statement of "I go to fight for your honor." Modern Indian feminists have multiple objections to this concept, but it is a deeply ingrained symbology in India, and this is not a discussion of Indian feminism.

Nonetheless, we should accept that it is not as if the President of Pakistan orders a terrorist attack, because the generals, and not elected politicians, determine events. The complexity begins here because there are several military factions controlling to a less or greater extent many terrorist groups. These 'jihadi' groups have in many cases accumulated power, and the generals have limited control of them. They often determine their own agendas and force the generals to follow them instead of the other way around, as may be assumed. Their agendas can be exclusive or part of the combined jihadi effort to control Pakistan. And the jihadis claim to be religious warriors, but their motivation is to corner a share of earthly things like money and women. The jihadi influence is like a metastasizing cancer. The Pakistan ruling establishment, military and civil, may have a use for jihadis to fight India, but as their influence grows, so does the hostage effect on the ruling establishment and everyday Pakistani life.

The known knowns are:

1. The jihadis keep pushing for more power, and the Pakistani civilian and military state is increasingly at their mercy;
2. Pakistan is in serious economic trouble;
3. Pakistan is in danger of disintegrating into various states;
4. Internal law and order seem to reach new lows yearly;

5. It may seem a terror attack at such a fraught time as the US VP's visit could not have been conducted without highest orders, but the jihadi groups have many sophisticated members independently acting to exploit the world stage and gain recruits and money. Sort through the academic verbiage above, and we end up with we can't tell why Pakistan staged the Pahalgam attack. Indian intelligence, though good, is also unlikely to know the whole story.

The Nuclear Overhang

As someone who has followed Pakistan's N-program from the mid-1970s, I have repeatedly said that nuclear weapons are irrelevant to any Indo-Pakistan conflict. For my pains, my work was simply ignored. In the 1990s, I was refused a fellowship at the University of Maryland because I was told, "India-Pakistan nuclear weapons are bad; we cannot have anything to do with such a topic". So much for academic freedom: at least read the darn book before turning me away!

India has such a freezing phobia about Pakistan's N-weapons, it came as a total surprise that the government said it was not concerned with Pakistan's N-weapons, and according to Tom Cooper, closed the entrance and exit facilities of the nuclear storage facility near Sargodha Air Base and targeted a similar underground facility. I cannot claim even a tiny bit of credit because I had zero input into India's change of attitude!

Mr. Modi's proclamation that any terrorist attack on India would be hereafter treated as war was counter to India's case because it puts the initiative into the hands of terrorists. Pakistan's consistent invocation of nuclear use every time India attacks is equally stupid. It's taken India decades to realize what I've been saying that the N-factor is irrelevant to a subcontinental conflict. Now India has called Pakistan's nuclear bluff, this is the major outcome of the Operation Sindoor.

Years ago, I wrote a brief for Professor Ashley Tellis of the Carnegie Institute for International Peace (Washington, DC) in which I noted that Pakistan's nuclear options were limited in case India launched an all-out Brasstacks sort of assault. Timely identification of the threat axis and accurate retaliation were in practice exceedingly difficult. And to stop a single armoured regiment, several warheads would be necessary. Considering that at that time India had a hundred tank regiments and mechanized battalions, any meaningful response could not be mounted without several hundred, perhaps even a thousand warheads. Exploding many warheads on its own soil would cause major collateral damage. How about a counter-value attack against Indian cities? Such an attack would be met two-fold retaliation against Pakistan. India would be grievously hurt but live to fight another day, while the sanitation company takes out what remains of Pakistan with the weekly trash.[3]

Operation Sindoor Strategy

On May 7, 2025, India made its retaliatory move by attacking nine terror camps and primly and sanctimoniously announcing it did not attack Pakistan military and civil targets (Subset: "India is *so* pious because it has attacked only jihadis and its attack was so precisely limited"). Thus, playing into Pakistan's standard narrative that it has nothing to do with the jihadis. And signaling that it was finished with the affair.

Since around 2008, Pakistan launched over 12,000 terrorist attacks into Kashmir, and over 120 elsewhere into India. Nevertheless, India has very seldom retaliated. There are reasons for this apart from the usual Indian indifference and lethargy. One is that India's overall strategy is to outlast the terrorists. And India does not want to avoid magnifying the fallout of their attack. Another, equally passive, is to keep outsiders from intervening in Kashmir. Whatever the reasons, Modi reluctantly became the new sheriff in town. India struck back in minor ways on the ground and in the air at Balakot in 2019. And oddly, in the case of Nagaland, Tripura, Manipur, and the Maoist insurgencies, the Indian strategy worked, though it took decades. To me, outwaiting the adversary is a lack of strategy, not a strategy. But no one has asked my opinion. The Indians feel their strategy works. The Pakistanis, having seriously learned the lessons of Balakot 2019 and vastly strengthened their air force (as discussed in this book), were already flying up to 20 aircraft CAPs, and India walked into a trap which resulted in the loss of 4 aircraft and perhaps another due to friendly fire.

Here, India made its biggest blunder. Without understanding that times have changed, especially since the Ukraine-Russia War, and the public demands transparency, India clamped down on all information related to aircraft losses, just as it had imposed a total news blackout on the Balakot incident. India lost all credibility. Even though the Indian Air Force won this big melee and inflicted further damage on Pakistan, who was to believe India?

Tom Cooper, an airpower analyst from Austria, believed India from his analysis of the photographic evidence. He says that India did not realize a far more important battle than the tactical fight that was underway, and that was the perception of the world public. Indeed, but for the Indian aviation expert Shiv Aroor, who had the genius idea of putting Tom on NDTV. In India's media channel with the greatest national visibility, the truth might not have become so well-known so fast.

But what convinced Tom, a neutral observer from far away, and quite sarcastic commentator when he detects humbug, that India had actually won the 'skirmishes'?

It was the Indian Air Force itself. Having learned its PR from the Americans, it did not overplay its hand, avoided drama, and backed up its claims by appending photo-recon pictures to each claim. There were no thundering declamations of Indian greatness and glory, just a quietly understated case giving "Just the facts, Ma'am and Sir." Not as slick as the Americans, but then this was the first time the IAF was playing this game, and it played it well. Notice, for example, India has been cautious in making claims about Pakistan's losses.

Others have said that after its initial retaliation, India need not have done more. Absurd, since Pakistan launched a full-scale counter-retaliation. It also invoked as always, a nuclear threat to scare people–namely the US–into forcing a ceasefire.

The Indian Retaliation for Pahalgam

Indians' retaliation for Pakistan's terror attack took place against nine Pakistan terror training camps manned by the Jaish-e-Mohammed (JeM) and Lashkar-e-Taiba (LeT), two of the main anti Indian groups in Kashmir. Also struck was a camp belonging to Hizbul Mujaheddin (HM), clearly stating the aim was to avoid civilian and military casualties, again India being nice by saying it would not escalate. I suppose this self-limited response made some kind of sense to India, which has yet to realize there is no such thing as a limited war. India can hardly be blamed: the US, the pioneer of finely graded escalation, still has not understood this, despite all its losses in limited wars since Korea in 1950.

A valid point by Colonel John Spencer[4]

Col. John Spencer of the Urban War Institute makes a key point when he says, "Success isn't about the scale of destruction—it's about achieving the desired political effect." He is also extremely critical of the biased Western reporting pushing a pro-Pakistan narrative without fact-checking.

American reporting has, indeed, sunk to a low level, but this is the first time I have seen the matter so baldly stated by a Westerner. I must add, however, that the bias is not intentional. Rather the Western press, in its aim to be first for fast stories (as Col. Spencer says), is sloppily accepting standard memes rather than doing its own thinking. Also, to be noted is the Indian tendency to refuse to explain itself because of a perceived affront to its dignity ("why should we deign to explain ourselves when we are so obviously right"). Pakistan, however, has a first-rate propaganda machine, for which it is to be credited. Remember, in the post-truth age, perception is more important than reality. The Indian military services did a superb job of controlling the information space, only to be undone by the censorship imposed by the government.

The Tactical Operation

Pakistan

Little of what is needed to write a sensible analysis is as yet known. Naturally, much attention has been focused on the J-10CE, since 2022 Pakistan's new acquisition. The PAF has 36 in service or on order and hopes to get 14 more. This will be followed up with the J-35 stealth fighter.

The PAF's PL-15E BVR missile was used, but the use of the J-10CE is unclear because the PAF has managed to fit it to the JF-17III. An aircraft from No. 11 Squadron is credited with the first PAK kill of an IAF Rafale (Number BS001). Regardless of the merits of the J-10 versus the Rafale, the PL-15 at least has shown that China has matched or exceeded the range of US BVRs (beyond-visual range air-to-air missiles).

It also appears probable that the Saab 2000 AEW can take control of a PL-15 fired by a fighter and guide it to longer distances than the aircraft's fire control/radar can cover.

Feature[5]	J-10C	Rafale
Origin	China	France
Radar	AESA radar	RBE2-AA AESA
BVR Missiles	PL-15 (range ~300 km)	Meteor (range ~150–200 km)
Cost per Unit	~$30-40 million	~$100 million
Engine	WS-10B	Snecma M88-2
Combat Roles	Air superiority, Ground strike	Multirole

["While the Rafale may have an edge in stealth and electronics, the J-10C offers excellent long-range missile capabilities with the PL-15. It is also significantly more affordable, enabling without straining its defense budget." Pakistan has no money to pay for anything China is delivering. Qatar is doing that for Pakistan. But, the J-10 and JF-17 are as important because they are cheaper to maintain: that's what Pakistan has to pay for.]

India

The story from India's side is the success of its automated indigenous Integrated Air Defense System, which defeated Pakistan's retaliation to India's act of striking nine Pakistan terror camps. Pakistan unleashed a total of three waves of up to 500 attack-UAVs and artillery rockets to target 20 different military facilities in India—with next to no effect. Unfortunately, this book was set for printing when Operation Sindoor was launched. So will have to wait until we get more information.

From Indian aviation experts Achint Gupta and Shiv Aroor,[6] we learn that India may have used drones to mimic Indian fighters, and the fighter losses claimed by Pakistan may include drones. Pakistan may have lost seven aircraft: I don't know if this includes one C-130 and possibly one Saab AWACS, either lost on the ground or at least severely damaged. India has claimed all its pilots returned safely. Achint, reinforcing Colonel Spencer, notes that the number of aircraft shot down is an irrelevant metric. In 1991, Gulf 1, the US lost more aircraft than Iraq. (Twice as many in air combat, 75 versus 36 Iraqis. Yet to claim Iraq won the air war would be fantastical and mendacious.)

A point of interest: India utilized 10-12 satellites to add transparency to the battlefield. Presumably, Pakistan has access to Chinese reconnaissance data.

Meanwhile, here is Tom Cooper's unique and most informed analysis of the operation. It has been very lightly edited.

Illusions and Realities of 'Cross-Border Incidents'[7]

Tom Cooper (May 11-15, 2025)

To round up the latest, four-days-long...erm war between India and Pakistan (which, actually, was neither declared, nor officially announced as 'really over'), here an overview of most momentous events, plus some analysis—also in regards of lessons that can be drawn in regards of the war in Ukraine.

1. On 22 April 2025, five terrorists of 'The Resistance Front' (TRF)—an offshoot of the UN-designated terrorist group Lashkar-e-Taiba (LeT) from Pakistan—attacked tourists near Pahalgam, in India-administered Jammu & Kashmir. They bunched together a sizeable group of tourists, forced them to recite the Islamic kalima (a Muslim declaration of faith) to identify non-Muslims, then executed 26 (24 were Hindu tourists, one Muslim and one Christian).
2. In the light of this attack, New Delhi decided to launch a punitive reaction, limited to terrorist training bases.

   Considering general circumstances, it seems Islamabad originally did not expect an Indian counter-strike. Correspondingly, the TRF publicly assumed responsibility for this attack. When it became obvious that New Delhi was going to hit back, this came as a surprise for Islamabad, and the TRF promptly retracted its claim of responsibility. By then, it was already too late, because the government in New Delhi had changed its doctrine: from one where it was 'merely' issuing diplomatic protest notes in reaction to Pakistan-instigated terror attacks, to one where it is reacting with punitive military strikes.

   However, because India then took more than two weeks to launch its punitive strikes, the Pakistani armed forces were given ample time to prepare their defenses.

   On the other side, as much as the government in New Delhi officially 'gave free hand' to its armed forces to act, whether on order from above, or because of their own traditional insistence on procedures and etiquette, the Indian Armed Forces limited their reaction to striking terror-related targets. This is an estranging decision considering terror organizations like TRF/LeT are linked to Pakistan's Inter-Services Intelligence (ISI): this is a military intelligence agency of Pakistan. It is responsible to both the government and the Director General of the Pakistan Armed Forces, and controls all the other country's intelligence agencies, but it is exclusively staffed by military officers drawn from all service branches of the Pakistani Armed Forces.

So, what's the point of 'targeting terrorists only', if it's clear these are linked to the 'armed forces' to the level where striking ISI's proxies is near-certain to result in striking the Pakistani Armed Forces, too?

That is one thing about which New Delhi might want to think really hard in the future. Indeed, considering Pakistan has launched over 120 different terrorist attacks into India since 2008 alone, and if New Delhi wants to establish and maintain something like 'deterrent' against similar attacks in the future, India might want to consider the option of establishing something like 'quick intervention capability': a group of forces capable of, in the case of future terrorist attacks, striking on much shorter notice (preferably within 24-48 hours). Why? In order to prevent the Pakistani armed forces from preparing themselves.

This is even more important considering that not only the Pakistan's terror attack into India- administered Jammu and Kashmir, but also what was to follow – made it obvious that we're living in the times where there are no 'superpowers' left that would be curious and powerful enough to prevent the outbreak of one or another war, and where the United Nations (the very body established with the aim of preventing wars) are useless. That principles of conflict avoidance and the mechanism of maintaining peace—defined already in the Atlantic Charter of 1941—are null and void, and nobody needs to expect any kind of international mediation, nor any kind of serious repercussions if instigating (yet another) armed conflict.

3. Designated the Operation Sindoor, India's punitive retaliation strike was aiming to hit nine 'terror camps': essentially, nine out of 30+ Madrassas used

by proxies of Pakistan's Inter-Service Intelligence (ISI) to indoctrinate, organize, and train jihadists for terror attacks into India.

Primary targets were facilities used by the LeT and another major ISI-run terror group, the Jaysh-e-Mohammed (JeM).

4. Involving at least 30-40 combat aircraft of the Indian Air Force (IAF)—including one or two of its A-50I and/or Netra AWACS aircraft – but also a number of UCAVs, the punitive strike was run between 01.15 and 01.28 hrs local time, on 7 May 2025. As far as can be assessed from official Indian releases, the aircraft in question deployed SCALP-EG, Crystal Maze, and AGM-250 HAMMER guided weapons. Other terror camps were targeted by attack UAVs, including some of Warmates acquired from Poland, and indigenous types armed with UL-PGMs.

   While India claims to have hit all nine terror camps, and at least some of India's social media presences have provided some of the related satellite imagery, independent reports from the Pakistani social media have confirmed multiple hits on six such facilities. At least five top terrorists have been killed, together with–according to a New Delhi official–over 140 other militants. Official Islamabad is zip-lip about this topic: stressing only civilian casualties. As if in that country, it's only young women and children who arc sleeping inside Madrassas by night (where, actually, they're usually not left anywhere nearby). Unofficial Pakistan—i.e., its social media—is anywhere between flat denial of the existence of terror-training camps and cheering killed jihadists as 'martyrs'. The latter went so far, numerous killed terrorists were buried with military honors sponsored by the Pakistan Army (PA), and in attendance of dozens of PA officers.

   Considering there is at least circumstantial evidence that the JeM suffered serious casualties in this strike, it is surprising there were still so many Pakistani terrorists around their main bases at the time of the Indian counter-strike. 'Normal procedure' would have been for the ISI to order them all out and keep them out until the crisis is over. Was it complacency, ignorance, or accident? No idea.

   Another thing to keep in mind at this point is: Pakistan's deterrent—the strategy of, 'if you hit our terrorists, we're going to hit back at you, your armed forces, civilians, religious sites, even try to instigate sectarian-motivated unrest', 'and we have nukes', 'and are ready to escalate, too'—failed. It did not deter India from striking back. Indeed, Pakistan's deterrence failed also in regard to preventing New Delhi from continuing to escalate in reaction to Islamabad's subsequent 'escalatory retaliations.

This is going so far that, until this very day, and despite the 'quasi cease-fire', the government in Islamabad failed to act even against the government in New Delhi's decision to (in reaction to the terror attack on Pahalgam) suspend the Indus Water Treaty (IWT). Signed in 1960, the IWT grants India control over the Indus River and its tributaries: Pakistan's primary source of water. Means: India has turned off the water tap for Pakistan, and Pakistan found no means to force it to revert that decision–although its top brass has lately declared this issue a 'red line': one of four or five principal reasons for Pakistan striking India with nuclear weapons.

Arguably, with the early onset of this year's monsoon season, this might not be 'particularly urgent'.. unless somebody manages to convince New Delhi to change its stance, it's going to be felt in Pakistan 'only' in some 6-9 months from now.

5. Because they were given ample time to prepare for India's punitive counter-strike, the Pakistani armed forces—and especially the Pakistan Air Force (PAF)—were ready. At least one Saab 2000 AWACS was on station (apparently, somewhere in the Peshawar area), and about 20 fighters airborne at the time the IAF air strike. Indeed, the PAF proved capable of setting up an 'ambush' for several incoming IAF formations. As a result, it definitely shot down a Rafale EH fighter-bomber, and (gauging by different photographs and videos of the resulting wreckage), most likely also shot down:

   1 MiG-29UPG
   1 Mirage 2000H
   1 Su-30MKI

   The Indian military etiquette might demand different procedures, but a matter of fact is that giving an opponent enough time to prepare for defense is never a clever idea. Also, the fact that the Indians were sticking to the unwritten (or written) rule of 'don't shoot (air-to-air missiles) over the international border', does not 'automatically' mean that the Pakistanis 'must' do the same.

This resulted in a situation where the PAF was able to ready a nasty surprise for the IAF – in the form of obtaining the capability to deploy Chinese-made PL-15 long-range air-to-air missiles from Chinese-made JF-17C fighter-bombers underway still inside the Pakistani airspace.

Mind: The radar of the JF-17C has only a maximum detection range of about 150km. With the PL-15 having a maximum engagement range of over 200km, the JF-17C was not supposed to be capable of deploying this weapon to its full capability. Moreover, both Beijing and Islamabad took care to claim the PL-15s delivered to Pakistan are 'PL-15Es', an export version with a maximum range of 'only' 150km–and New Delhi fell for it. That was a major blunder on the part of the Indian intelligence services.

This even more so because the Erieye radar of the Saab 2000 has a maximum detection range of about 450km, and it turned out to be capable of cooperative targeting: means, JF-17Cs were capable of launching PL-15s at incoming IAF fighter-bombers while still well inside Pakistan and while the Indians were still well inside their own airspace—or on the best way of withdrawing into its depth. And the Indian intelligence appears not to have been aware of this fact.

As a result, several of IAF's formations either flew into numerous PL-15s fired at them or were hit by these while withdrawing back into India's airspace. Moreover, nearly all of the IAF aircraft known to have been shot down and crashed to the ground between 80 and 120km deep inside India.

That said:

a. Pakistan's claim for 'shooting down five IAF fighters', including '3 Rafales,' is exaggerated. There is simply no evidence that the IAF lost '3 Rafales'. At most, available evidence is 'confirming' four IAF losses (as listed above). Of course, it is possible that additional aircraft suffered different degrees of combat damage. Moreover,
b. Western claims about PAF deploying J-10Cs armed with PL-15s are *de facto* denied by Pakistani media reports crediting JF-17C pilots for 'downing Rafale'.

Squadron Leader Afridi from No. 14 Squadron – the pilot credited with a 'Rafale kill' on 7 May 2025 – as interviewed by the Pakistani media. Whether he was the one who actually shot down the Rafale EH serial number BS001 remains unknown. However, as is obvious from his 'wing' patch (his right shoulder), and his squadron patch (his right chest, showing the crest of No. 11 Squadron), he flies JF-17. No J-10C.

6. Of particular interest in regards of the IAF air strike on terror camps in Pakistan was the first 'confirmed deployment' of the Russo-Indian Brahmos land-attack missile. However, whether any of Brahmos was really deployed—in terms of any of Brahmos actually being fired at their targets—remains unclear.

Brahmos is a big and heavy weapon, deployed exclusively by Su-30MKIs of the Indian Air Force. It can reach speeds above Mach 3 and its India-modified, air-launched version has a range of 450-500km. The deployment of Brahmos in the IAF air strike became obvious through photographs of their booster stages that were found about 100-120km inside India. Got no problem to shamelessly admit, the photos confused me mightily: original, Soviet/Russian-designed booster-stages for the air-launched Brahmos were relatively short (1-1.5m). Photographs surfacing on 7 May were showing pipe-like structures some 6 or more meters long. Thanks to help from a contact in India, I have figured out why: because the Defense Research and Development Organization (DRDO) of India has designed and pressed into production (and service with the IAF) a much longer version of the booster stage for the Brahmos: this is now some 6m long.

The DRDO-designed booster stage for the Brahmos. Gauging by its size, it is likely to stretch that weapon's range well beyond the usually claimed '450-500km.'

Gauging by its grey color, this booster was not 'fired'. This missile was jettisoned by one of the Su-30MKIs involved in the air strikes of 7 May 2025. (both from Indian social media)

Considering the protective cap which was found nearby. Had the missile been released as planned, it would have crashed to the ground 'kilometers away' from the booster stage.

That said, the presence of intake-covers (or 'caps') on the crash sites of several of Brahmos' boosters, as well as the original, light grey color of boosters' bodies, is indicative of some missiles not being released, but jettisoned. That is ... released without activation, probably by Su-30MKIs, the crews of which were surprised by Pakistani PL-15s, and forced into evasive maneuvering. (Sure, intake- covers/caps are released at the same time the booster stage is released, but they are extremely unlikely to come down to the ground at exactly the same spot.)

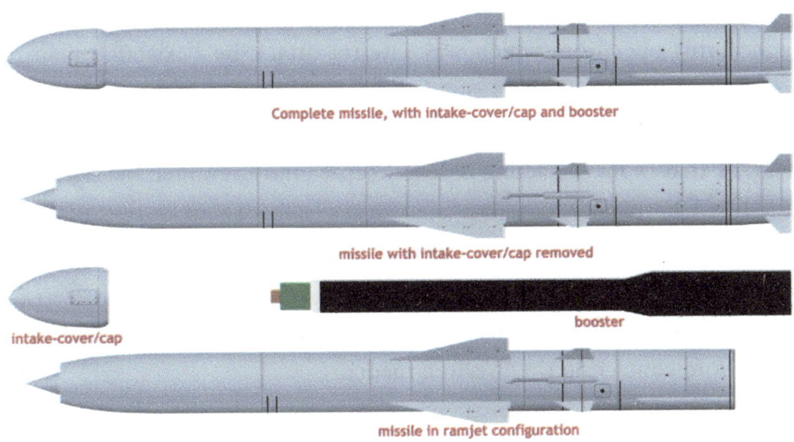

A simplified diagram of an air-launched Brahmos. At the top, the complete missile, with its intake cover/cap, and the booster still in its place. In the center, the missile without its intake cover/cap. Below it, the intake cover/cap and the new DRDO-developed booster. At the bottom, Brahmos the way it looks once its intake cover/cap and booster are away, and the ramjet is activated. (Courtesy: Diagram by Tom Cooper)

While this might appear as 'going off topic', one should keep in mind that after the Indian experiences from clashes with Pakistan in February 2019, there were rumors that the DRDO is working on an 'anti-AWACS-version' of the Brahmos: a version that would enable the targeting of PAF's Saab 2000.

This is prompting the question: could it be that the IAF actually planned to start the Operation Sindoor by deploying one or another of its modified Brahmos to shoot down the PAF Saab 2000 AWACS that was airborne and on station, but this part of the mission was spoiled by timely reaction of PAF interceptors and their deployment of PL-15s?

Arguably, chances of the IAF top brass planning something 'as daring' as this are (extremely) slim (for why: see 'traditions & procedures'). But still: they might have thought in this direction. While we're unlikely to know for sure, any time soon, this possibility should be kept in mind for the future–especially considering the fact that the government in India has adapted its strategy for this kind of crisis with Pakistan.

With the punitive counterstrike on terror camps in Pakistan resulting in the loss of up to four fighter-bombers of the IAF, New Delhi began losing control over the public narrative. Instead of everybody talking about why India launched this operation, which was a terror attack by Pakistan, organized, financed, and trained jihadists on civilians in India-administered Jammu & Kashmir, everybody began talking about IAF's losses. Not only that it became 'irrelevant' that India was acting in self-defense (and as granted the right to do, by the UN Charter), or that even Islamabad's claims about 'dozens of civilian victims' were largely ignored, but the only thing that mattered was how many fighter-bombers has the IAF lost.

Offended by such reactions, official New Delhi reacted by prohibiting its officials from contacting the Western media.

What a mistake... The chauvinists in New Delhi should've swallowed their pride, admitted losses, and emphasize the reasons and achievements of their operation. Nothing can beat the Pakistani, Chinese, and Western double standards and cynicism as the truth. Another mistake were 'too long to watch' press briefings: sure, it was 'demonstrative' these were run by two female officers, but if the two are reading boring statements for the press, 'minutes long', instead of providing 'easy to memorize', illustrative 'facts', easy to re-post in the social media... the entire effort was in vain.

Lesson: New Delhi should've staged compact, easy-to-memorize presentations of FACTS. In this regard, India has degenerated since 2019.

What's more, the IAF was then withdrawn from battle: 'to lick wounds' and think about what had happened to which of its jets, and how to make itself useful again. That took most of the following two days.

Question: what's the point of having a super-turbo-equipped branch of armed forces, the very nature of which is offensive, if, due to a mix of major intelligence failures and conservative, definitely 'obsolete' planning style of the top political- and military brass, this is easily knocked out of action (by, for all practical purposes: a 'single blow')?

Be sure: this is going to be a major 'lesson learned' for a number of other air forces. Definitely so for the PAF. One is left to hope both the Research and Analysis Wing (RAW; India's top intel service) and the IAF might have learned their own lesson, too.

And the Pakistani side? Nobody there learned anything at all. The chauvinistic hysteria went so far, they didn't even figure out that their deterrence has failed. That India dared striking back, regardless of all the possible Pakistani threats.

Unsurprisingly, Pakistan then started setting up its 'retaliation' – designed rather to score additional PR-points in the social media, and impress its own and Western public, rather than India.

What can be concluded about all this?

Well, whatever one likes. Indeed, if you like, join the Pakistanis (and instances like the CNN), and celebrate a 'victory', as their Prime Minister has announced. No doubt, many Indians are feeling angry because their impression is that their government 'did not finish the job'—even if it could.

But mind: New Delhi has switched its strategy in a matter of 'hours', and its armed forces proved capable of following in fashion. Henceforth, Pakistan must expect similar– military–response to any kind of additional terror attacks against India. Pakistan's deterrent has failed: actually, now it's non-existent (especially if the Indians continue improving their stocks of air defense ammunition). The fighting also stopped without Islamabad at least trying to address the issue of New Delhi's suspension of the Indus Water Treaty. Whether Beijing might 'rush' to replace Pakistani losses and the expenditure of ammunition is also questionable: I don't think this is likely to happen—except 'somebody' (read: Qatar) pays.

In regard of military affairs: Contrary to the war in Ukraine, this war was still fought primarily with technologies from the 1990s, with some upgrades to the 2000s. Sure, both India and Pakistan have 'decent' integrated air defense systems (IADS) and have deployed attack UAVs in large numbers.

However, and despite significant upgrades over the last 20 years (and especially the last 10 years), what they have deployed are heavy, expensive systems based on technologies from the late 20th Century. Except for self-imposed constraints (on the Indian side), the mindsets of generals in both countries are also still some 10-15 years 'behind.' That's why both are yet to fully adjust to the latest developments. Indeed, it's likely that precisely this 'detail' contributed to Pakistan's decision not only not to escalate any further, but to stop due to insufficient stocks: insufficiently supplied due to the lack of necessary funding, its armed forces were about to run out of only types of ammunition that have proven as being of any use, like attack UAVs, 'even' in such a short conflict like this one.

Yes, Pakistan used the last few years better than India, and not only obtained 'platforms' (foremost: aircraft). However, the PAF—just like the rest of the Pakistani Armed Forces – is sorely lacking long-range land-attack weapons, and its integrated air defence system consisting of a hodge-podge of C3 systems developed in cooperation with Turkey, US-radars, and Chinese-made radars and SAMs, proved anything else than integrated. Despite all the claims and boasting, they either have none, or far too few, missiles that can hit with pinpoint precision over a range of 300-400km, and the air defence system turned out to be full of gaps.

Unless Pakistan finds a way to manufacture something in the style of Iran's Shahed attack-UAVs, and then in vast numbers, that's unlikely to change soon. In this regard, Pakistani generals have 'missed the train'.

At least the PAF can nowadays fight 'network centric warfare': it is perfectly possible (even likely) that the Pakistani Navy can do the same; only the Pakistani Army is an uncertain factor in this regards.

However, at the second look, India turned out to have vastly outmatched Pakistan in this regards. Working in silence since the late 1990s, the IAF has developed a highly successful, tightly integrated air defence system (IACCS), enabling excellent coordination of not only air force's, but also operations by army air defence.

Once the Indians did a 'reset' of their command and control, and 'started from scratch'—by knocking out the Pakistani air defenses—their conduct of operations became near flawless. Foremost: it became professional and remained focused on what matters. Like knocking out the PAF air defenses and the PA's artillery. When one is running such an operation in a well-organized fashion, positive results are unavoidable. In comparison, the Pakistani conduct began degenerating into targeting religious sites (like Amritsar, with holy sites of the Sikh), and pointless claims about 'destruction of S-400 in Adampur–as if destroying one S-400 SAM-system could've completely turned the outcome of this round.

Above all, intelligence services of Pakistan have failed (and miserably at that) to find out about and report major developments in India, while generals in Islamabad have displayed their amazing lack of imagination and conservatism in overall planning and conduct of operations. Nobody in Pakistan, and nobody in India dares undertake anything risky—because that could become a mistake. Unsurprisingly, one thing remains the same, that's certain already now: in the vocabulary of the Indian Armed Forces, all of this was a 'cross-border incident'. No 'war'...

Last but not least: not only India, but 'the West' might want to–finally–start taking PR Chinese-made weapons systems much more seriously than they are still usually doing.

ADD-ON in reaction to a number of related queries: frankly (as always), can't care less about PR- efforts by CNN & Co KG GesmbH AG, about New Delhi's insistence on 'we're a responsible democracy and thus can't declare military victories', and even less so about Western 'military Experts'.

When one side is bombing nuclear weapons storage facilities of the other, and the other has no ability to retaliate, then that's a clear-cut victory in my books.

In this case: a clear-cut victory for India.

No surprise Islamabad 'sounded' for a 'cease-fire'.

Here, Tom Cooper amplifies his analysis of Op Sindoor, adding more detail.

Because this obviously remains so important to the Pakistanis (and 'fans' abroad), even if official New Delhi denies it, visual evidence became available for the Indian Air Force (IAF) losing a total of 3-4 fighters. Definitely confirmed is only one: a Rafale EH (single-seater), serial number BS001. This came down outside Bathinda (Punjab), 90km from the border to Pakistan, killing one and wounding nine civilians on the ground. Also confirmed are a

Mirage 2000I (an upgraded Mirage 2000H; see pylon with a MICA air-to-air missile), and an MiG-29UPG (see K-36 ejection seat).

...and at least one PAF JF-17C:

Inserted in this photo is a still from a video showing the wreckage of a jet 'with dark radome and IFR-probe' (plus divert less intake), taken early on 7 May. There's only one type in service with both air forces having all such elements: a JF-17C of the Pakistan Air Force. The jet crashed outside Wayun (Pulwama area, Kashmir, in India): the whereabouts of its pilot are unclear. (both from Indian social media)

Q: *Why is official New Delhi not confirming these losses? Isn't this damaging India's credibility?*

A: How about a counter-question: why is official Islamabad not confirming its own losses? Isn't that damaging Pakistan's credibility?

But OK, let's discuss this.

At first glance, yes, this is damaging India's credibility. Apparently, at least, India has started this affair (it didn't, but Pakistan and most of the Western public think that way). Moreover, in a conflict as hotly debated, as loaded as this one, it is always the wrong decision to hide the truth. However, the full consequences of this decision can be understood only when one takes the 'big picture' into account. India's aim was to strike at nine terror camps. This – the Pakistan-instigated terror – is the actual topic of this affair, and not how many jets the IAF has lost in the process. On the contrary, and exactly like in February 2019, Pakistan (and allies, foremost the PR China, but also in the 'Arab World', and then some of 'the West') attempted to lift the public narrative, draw all attention away from these terror camps (and Pakistan's complicity in regards of state-sponsored terrorism), and re-focus on these 3-4 downed IAF fighters.

Official New Delhi decided not to fall into this trap, but to impose its own public narrative.

Moreover, one should keep in mind that the Operation Sindoor is–at least officially–still going on (yes, until this very day). Nobody is revealing tactical details to the opponent as long as a military operation is going on. Why? Because the Indians do not want to let the Pakistanis figure out what of their defensive actions were 'working' and what not.

This was the right decision on the part of New Delhi.

Shield

On 7 May, Pakistan launched its 'retaliation' strikes within frame of the Operation Bunyan Marsoos (Arabic for 'a structure made of lead'). Principal weapons released were 'hundreds' of attack UAVs and artillery rockets (primarily Fateh-1).

This is where I've experienced my first surprise in this affair. I knew about the IAF's Integrated Air Command and Control System (IACCS)—the integrated air defense system (IADS) protecting India—since the 1990s. I knew it was 'advanced' and operational since (at least) the 1990s, covering the country's entire airspace (which, in the case of a country of this size, is a major success on its own). However, whether due to being preoccupied with other issues, or because of underreporting—and although outlining it in my earlier reports—I was not aware just how sophisticated the IACCS meanwhile became. Moreover, I was not aware of how well the air defenses of the Indian Army are integrated into the IACCS, nor all the advances India made in regards of combating UAVs (not even about such of latest short-range air defense systems like Samar, essentially utilising disused R-27 and R-73 air-to-air missiles coupled with fire-control - and surveillance radars). And so, 'boom', literally: turned out, Indians not only have highly sophisticated anti-UAV defense, but also have these available in sufficient numbers to cover all their major military installations, their ground units deployed in the field, and all the major urban centers.

Except for hundreds of smaller attack UAVs (see earlier reporting), Indian air defenses - reportedly - shot down 'several Bayraktar' (Turkish-made UAVs, 'famous' from clashes in Libya and Syria, for example), and 'one Anca' reconnaissance UAV (also of Turkish origin).

Of course, well-known Indian SAM-systems, like IAF's Akash, Barak-8, and Spyder, Indian Army's ZSU-23-4s, Osa-AKMs, Igla, Strelas and other weaponry, as well as electronic countermeasures bore the brunt of Indian defense operations: RUMINT has it, combined, all of them, plus what I've listed above, were shooting down over 90% of incoming Pakistani UAVs and artillery rockets. No doubt, some of the Pakistani weapons did come through and have caused damage and casualties. However, that was not enough: the fact that Pakistan has failed to cause any kind of severe damage is what neutralized much of that country's deterrence.

The 'peak' of the Operation Bunyan Marsoos and the IACCS' defensive operations took place at 02.00hrs of 10 May, when Pakistan launched two ballistic missiles (reportedly: Fateh-2). While many in India have claimed that this targeted New Delhi, both were intercepted by S-400s (including one over Sirsa Air Base, which remained undamaged).

The rarely seen (in public), Indian S-400s were, reportedly, deployed for two primary purposes: anti-ballistic missile defence and 'free hunt' for high-value PAF aircraft. (see 'assault mode'). Presently, the IAF is operating four squadrons equipped with this system, each including four flights (each with four launchers). This still gives India 64 tubes and reloads, a substantial SAM capability. (Indian social media)

Sword

Meanwhile, New Delhi made fundamental–and crucially important–switch in its strategy. Instead of 'just targeting terror camps, it did what is logical (and I think, should have been done right from the start in cases of this kind): it went 'all out'.

When I say, 'all out', I do not mean that India began wildly shooting all over Pakistan, but: the Indian armed forces began methodically and systematically disabling Pakistan's ability to defend.

For cases of this kind, modern-day military strategy envisages something like 'seven or nine circles of targeting'. I'll keep it short and simple: India first sought to disable Pakistan's IADS, then degrade the PAF's ability to operate closer to the international border (and the Line of Control/LoC in Kashmir) and then sought to hit carefully selected points on carefully selected military facilities in Pakistan.

This is where the highly praised, widely reported IADS of the Pakistan Air Force should have played a decisive role. But it didn't. Instead, this was rapidly degraded. I'm cautious and intentionally saying 'degraded' instead of 'destroyed' because the exact level of destruction remains unclear. Moreover, experience from my studies of earlier conflicts is that destroying such systems is, usually impossible. They are so much hardened, have so many assets, so much built-in redundancy, that one can disturb the work of different elements of their system, or knock out some of these – sometimes on a temporary basis, other times for longer periods of time – but: not all of them at once. (Alternatively, one can cause their software to crash, like this regularly happened to the Russians in Syria, because the software of their IADS tended to crash if one or another element of the system was 'suddenly disconnected'). But, completely destroying them for a longer period of time… that's extremely hard.

It appears that the PAF was slow—or at least experiencing significant problems—with the integration of all of its US-made radars with Chinese-made radars and SAMs, and other components. This is a massive task, requiring extensive work on related software, and that's taking years to complete. So much so, the majority of bigger air forces around the world have experienced (often: is still experiencing) endless problems with their modern, computer-supported IADS'. Especially when, like the PAF, they have to buy all of such systems from abroad. (The worst example coming to my mind was a US-designed IADS for Saudi Arabia of the 1980s… this wasn't fully operational even as of the mid-1990s.)

Moreover, several of PAF airmen serving in air defense units (especially those deployed in the Karachi area) have 'excelled' in revealing their (well-concealed) firing positions by posting photos of these in the social media, and then photos that enabled geo-location. Whether the Indians have used this OSINT is unclear, but sorry, such behavior alone is not indicative of a professional armed service. Unsurprisingly, the Indian strikes have knocked out most of two battalions of HQ-9 and one battalion of HQ-16 (the latter was the one in Walton, Lahore, which I've misidentified as 'HQ-9'), at least three AN/TPS-77 radars, and… well, nobody knows how many other Pakistani air defense systems.

Another example: the IAF is known to have knocked out an NG-MMCC trailer-based command center of the PAF, developed in cooperation with Turkey, which served as a backup for the HQ of the Pakistani IADS. This was smashed by a single Indian air-to-ground missile hitting a selected spot between the two trailers at Nur Khan AB.

In other words: the Indians did not 'blow away' or 'destroy' the Pakistani IADS all at once, with a single blow, nor did they destroy it completely. Instead, they've degraded it methodically and systematically, bit-by-bit, and piece-by-piece, by a mix of UAV- and air strikes with lots of electronic warfare, and consequently and patiently. That operation surely took some time to complete, probably the evening of 7 May, the following night, and much of 8 May.

For this purpose, and among others, India not only deployed the mass of its 160 Israeli-made Harop attack-UAVs, but also its own variant of the same, designated Agnikaa. In other words: they have enough re-loads for such operations—now and in the future, too. Once again: indigenous weapons are of crucial importance.

With the PAF IADS (largely) out of the way, the PAF was also forced to withdraw deeper into its own airspace; to withdraw its fighter jets from the international border. This is what, through the night from 9 to 10 May, and then early on 10 May, enabled the IAF to deliver its blows on selected major air bases.

Mind: a typical Indian or Pakistani air base stretches over some 5 by 2-3 kilometers (of course, there are much bigger air bases too, but this is something like 'average'). It's a heavily fortified facility, with underground command posts, underground fuel depots, fortified ammunition depots, and dozens of hardened aircraft shelters, often concealed by vegetation. To really 'destroy' one, depending on the size of the facility in question, it would take 30, 50, even 100 precise hits. The IAF was not after that. It was after targeting carefully selected points at selected major PAF air bases. As far as can be assessed from available satellite photos and videos, that list looked something like this:

- Skardu (Baltistan): forward operating base, runway and POL-dump hit;
- Murid AB: UAV-based, command facilities hit;
- Nur Khan AB (Chaklala): NG-MMCC command center destroyed, hangar destroyed, one C-130 set fire;
- Musaf AB (Sargodha): radars, runway, and hardened aircraft shelters hit;
- Rafiqui AB (Shorkot): fighter-base, several aircraft shelters and support buildings hit;
- Sukkur AB: hangar hit;
- Pasur AB: forward operating base; radar and munition depot hit;
- Shahbaz AB (Jacobabad): hangar and runway hit, 1 Saab 2000 damaged or destroyed;
- Bholari AB: command center, hangar, radar hit, 1 F-16 damaged or destroyed (meanwhile, it is known that this was attacked by two Brahmos, one of which was claimed as shot down by the Pakistanis).

It seems that most of the Indian analysts are assessing these strikes as flown by Rafales deploying SCALP missiles and Hammer PGMs. However, at least one, possibly two strikes by IAF Jaguars armed with Rampage missiles are known, and meanwhile, it's officially confirmed, the IAF did fire (at least) 15 Brahmos missiles (the two that hit the underground facility in the Kirana Hills were Brahmos). As far as is known, the Pakistani air defenses have shot down one SCALP, and—perhaps—one Brahmos.

As mentioned above, the latter should have been shot down while approaching Bholari AB early on 10 May.

Now for your questions:

Q: *I saw the interview on Times TV. Not a single mention of the Rafale downing. Why not? This major incident is not important in the context of the war. Or was it edited out by India's terrible media channels?*

A: I've explained this in regard to the 'public narrative' at the start of this feature. Let me add an even more important aspect.

I find it is impossible to emphasize strongly enough – especially for those still insistent on 'but Pakistan shot down 5, 15, 50 Indian jets: Pakistan won'— that in the case of this war, no matter how short and intensive or not, one must keep in mind: one nuclear power (named India) disabled the nuclear deterrent of another nuclear power (named Pakistan). If you like, name them San Marino and Brunei, or switch names, if it's going to make you feel better. But this is a matter of fact.

Another matter of fact that's of ultimate importance is, is that the former did this to the latter by using conventional weapons only.

I know, this is something entirely new: a concept that never happened before. And perhaps my formulation is not good enough or whatever, but: I'm finding no words to put this to paper in any clearer, more comprehensive fashion.

Nuclear warfare—with or without deployment of nuclear warheads—is the ultimate method of warfare. Presently, humanity has no other, more powerful weapons. Thus, if a nuclear power is prevented from deploying nuclear warheads, it is de facto disarmed. This is what has happened to Pakistan.

Sure, the country has retained its nukes, but it can't use them, it can't deploy them, and even if it would try, it knows (and India knows, too) it can't do so effectively: it can't expect its nukes to survive being assembled and installed on a jet or a ballistic missile, and it can't expect that jet or the ballistic missile carrying such a warhead to actually reach its target.

There is no way to overemphasize this fact.

Compared to achieving this, the IAF could've lost 50, or even 500 Rafales—and that would 'not matter' (except for families and friends of their pilots/crews): it would still be 'worth the result'. This is what everybody interested in this war, but especially those insistent on one or another version of its outcome, and those insistent on 'impossible' (even offended with my conclusions), need to comprehend.

Related to the importance of the above-mentioned issue, is the following (indeed, it's explaining why this affair is with striking Kirana Hills so important):

Q: *Did India have the capability after first hits on airbases to finish PAF on the ground just like Israel did in the June 1967 Arab-Israeli War (the 'Six Days War')?*

A: Of course, it did. Once India has suppressed or disabled at least a better part of the Pakistani IADS, and once it has forced the PAF further away from the border, and then hit its air bases, India would be—theoretically—free to strike at Pakistan Army positions along the LoC and the border. It could pound and pummel them almost at will. New Delhi decided not to do so: obviously, it concluded it 'unnecessary'.

Q: *You, being a credible war historian, surprised me by declaring India as victorious in the recent Indian and Pakistani conflict. How can someone be victorious if there was a ceasefire with no accomplished objectives for either side?*

A: Well, call me a RAW-agent and Islamophobic (you wouldn't be the first; similarly, there are enough Indians calling me names), and continue ignoring what I wrote, but, when one country is targeting the other country's nuclear weapons storage site (here you have it: from a Pakistani source), then that is a clear-cut victory. Because it means that the former does not fear retaliation from the latter. This is a precedent, so I can't say/write 'usually', but henceforth it is going to be so that 'usually this is happening' because the former has disabled the ability of the latter to exercise retaliation.

If that's making it any easier, think of a game of chess in which one of players manages to defeat the other in a matter of 10-12 moves: the majority of figures are still going to be on the board, perhaps the losing player even still has the queen and other influential figures. But his king is checkmated. Game over.

Pakistan's own generals have defined a number of 'red lines'. For example, India abrogating the Indus Water Treaty; India targeting Pakistan's nuclear weapons storage facilities (or other nuclear facilities); the Indian Army driving deep into Pakistan. If India is—obviously—crossing successive of Pakistan's 'red lines' and then blasts carefully selected spots at carefully selected number of military facilities in Pakistan, plus (at least) one of nuclear weapons storage facilities, and Pakistan can't do anything even distantly similar to India, nor stop such strikes, then India won, and Pakistan lost.

That is a simple deduction based on visually confirmed matters of fact, and I would make myself 'incredible' if ignoring it, no matter what reason.

Q: How did India know what was there in the Kirana Hills?

A: Nominally, every country is obliged to declare its nuclear facilities to the International Atomic Energy Agency (IAEA). Moreover, India and Pakistan have an additional agreement to report such facilities to each other. It so happened that Pakistan has constructed a large radar site (operated by No. 4091 Squadron, PAF), and a massive weapons complex and ammunition storage facility at the Kirana Hills - and then did not declare any kind of a nuclear facility there.

However, satellite photographs are confirming the presence of so-called 'TELs' in this facility, making the Kirana Hills also a 'missile garrison' (no idea what Pakistani unit is operating these or based there)—TEL stands for transporter-erector-launcher: that's a truck used to haul, erect and fire a ballistic missile (or similar weapon).

Must be an 'accident', but 'Kirana-I' was also the designation for 24 subcritical experiments on nuclear weapons designs run by Pakistan in the period 1983-1995. What a surprise, then, at least since around 2017, the site is assessed as including a (undeclared) nuclear weapons storage facility, too.

Now, rather unexpectedly, the Indians have hit turned out they've actually targeted and hit the facility itself the underground part in the northwestern corner of this facility. Read: they didn't directly strike this underground part of the facility, but entrances to it, blocking the entry and exit from them (this strike was flown after the Pakistanis deployed a ballistic missile that was shot down over Sirsa, at around 02.00hrs of 10 May).

Of course, one is free to believe that the PAF—which is in control of Pakistan's nuclear weapons, and the Kirana Hills base, too—is growing vegetables in such a place. Here in Austria, just for example, we have lots of underground facilities left over from the Second World War, and several are used exactly for such a purpose: to grow delicious button mushrooms...

Q: Are '4th Generation fighters completely obsolete in a high-density IADS environment? We've seen tactical airpower marginalized in Russia-Ukraine and that first Indian raid, but also Azerbaijan-Armenia a few years ago. Are these jets now only useful as long-range standoff missile launchers?

A: Methinks not. Or at least: it depends on their weaponry and electronic warfare support. For example: a Su-25 or F-16 armed with freefall/iron/ dumb bombs, and lacking EW support are 'toast'. It doesn't matter if US- or Vanuatu-made, they're not going to survive flying into a dense IADS. But, if armed with long-range land-attack weapons—weapons they can release from outside, or from the fringes of the IADS' reach—then they remain very much useful. Between others, the IAF flew some of the air strikes on PAF bases with (35-40 years old) Jaguars deploying Israel-made Rampage air-launched ballistic missiles. MiG-29s of the Indian Navy were armed with these and ready to launch from the aircraft carrier INS Vikrant for another strike, too: this operation was cancelled for unknown reasons.

Q: Has aerial warfare now purely developed into attrition warfare, i.e., forcing the enemy to expend SAM magazines, by deploying hundreds of drones, rockets, missiles, and decoys?

A: SAM stands for surface-to-air missile. Yes. Though, I would say: this kind of warfare was originally developed already in the 1960s-1970s (see the 'theoretical match' between US Navy's carrier battle groups, and Soviet 'carrier-killers', like Tupolev Tu-22s and submarines equipped with heavy anti-ship missiles; back then, the question was that of how many Kh-22 anti-ship missiles could the Tu-22s deploy, and how many surface-to- air missiles could the ships protecting an aircraft carrier deploy). It's just so that no such war was fought back then, and thus, this did not become obvious.

Nowadays, it is a 'pure' battle of attrition. Who can deploy more UAVs, rockets, and missiles so as to overpower the enemy IADS, or the other way around? This is why it would be so important for the Europeans to – finally – start manufacturing their SAMs in VAST numbers, and start delivering these to Ukraine in necessary numbers, too.

Q: Obviously, SEAD/EW plays a role, but my impression is that in none of the recent big wars has SEAD/EW gained any great advantage.

A: SEAD stands for suppression of enemy air defenses; DEAD stands for destruction of enemy air defenses. Ever since it is played (since around

1966 over North Vietnam; since 1969 in the Middle East), SEAD/DEAD is a 'game' that never has 'permanent' effects, never offering some sort of definite- or infinite advantage, and is also a battle of attrition. One knocks out an enemy radar today, it's repaired in the afternoon, or the next morning. One bombs a SAM-site knocks out three launchers, damages the other three, but the fire-control radar and these three other launchers are still operational. One finds out and knocks out one or another SAM launcher, but the rest of the unit remains operational... and so on. Nowadays, one is trying to target both the fire-control vehicle and launchers... and is sometimes successful, other times not, and sometimes partially successful... And then, even if one is super-effective, the next morning the SAM-site is 'back online', because the enemy had enough replacement equipment and has managed to bring this into position.

However, it's kind of 'doesn't matter' if the SEAD/DEAD game has no lasting consequences. What does matter is for the SEAD/DEAD to have consequences lasting long enough for own air power to complete its mission. If this is 20 minutes, and the mission in question was completed: fine. Other times, the results might last 12-24 hours, enabling its own air power to complete its mission even better. And, sometimes, SEAD/DEAD is not effective at all...

That is the nature of the game, and—as perfectly obvious from both Ukraine and India—a lot is depending on whether both the IADS and the SEAD/DEAD efforts are supported by the native arms industry or not. For example: Ukraine is dependent on supplies of Western arms, which are not available in sufficient numbers, and thus its air defenses are, meanwhile, 'nothing but trouble'. India has a strong (and growing) own defense sector and has no problem with replenishing its IADS from its own production. It's the same with aircraft involved in SEAD/DEAD: the party manufacturing their own modern fighter jets (especially those with 'stealth' characteristics) and associated weapons is certain to establish itself in the position of advantage. position of advantage.

Q: Is it better to invest heavily in surface-to-surface missiles (including quasi-tactical ballistic missiles, like Iskander or LORA) and an IADS, instead of fighter jets like Rafales, F-15s, or Su-30s?

A: Depends on threat perceptions of the country in question; on what kind of wars it expects to fight, and against whom. For example: for the last few decades, threat perceptions of the majority of smaller NATO air forces were 'expeditionary operations outside Europe, usually in cooperation with the US Air Force, US Navy, US Marines'. Thus, they were custom-tailored for this kind of operation and could rarely do anything else. Other countries need entirely different air forces, and nothing is wrong with either approach.

Smaller nations, or nations like India, Pakistan, which are facing 'peer' enemies, are well-advised to have 'all of this' (air power, IADS, TBM etc.), because, for example (and as 'perfectly demonstrated' by the Russian Air-Space Force over Ukraine), lacking air power that can survive operating deep within the enemy airspace is greatly limiting offensive capabilities. As long as well-supported by reconnaissance systems – i.e., if integrated into a 'reconnaissance-strike complex' like, theoretically, there should be one in the Russian armed forces – tactical ballistic missiles can do a lot but never replace air power. Similar in regards of an IADS: because aviation is always going to move faster than ground-based armed forces, an IADS is, if nothing else, 'easy to outmaneuver', to literally 'outflank'.

Q: How do you think the Americans would operate air power in any of these environments given their large fleets of 5th generation stealth aircraft, robust SEAD, extensive networking, substantial number of stand-off weapons and ISTAR? Would say the Americans still be able to punch through IADS in say Ukraine circa 2022 scenario or even say Russia as easily as they did in Iraq 1991 or Serbia 1999 (I understand Serb IADS were competent but they did not play a role in stopping allied dominance in the air).

A: To start with, there's something like a running gag that the USA has (at least since 1945) never fought countries with a population larger than 20 million. Thus, at least the last 30-40 years, the likelihood of such a conflict was minimal – even if, yes, the Pentagon was always preparing the US armed forces for a conflict with peer opponents. As for the ability of, for example, the US armed forces to punch through the Ukrainian or Russian IADS… this is a 'what if', and I do not like what ifs, because I don't have lots of imagination. But I'll give it a try. I would say: the USA and NATO have learned a lot from fighting Serbia in 1999. They would not come just with air power but combine lots of different assets (see: 'thousands' of ballistic and cruise missiles, followed by decoys, followed by stealth bombers, stealth fighters, immense volumes of electronic warfare). I would say: they would be largely successful, early on, alone because of their capabilities in regards of the reconnaissance-strike combination. However, they would then experience lots of frustrations – simply because both the Ukrainians and the Russians would continue fighting, no matter what, and regardless of how much their IADS would be damaged or even disabled. They're stubborn and good at improvisations and innovations. Just like the Houthis. And, well, the US politics, its 'modelling of the outcome', and the 'USA and fighting wars longer than a few weeks'...

Q: *Would like to hear your take on the Indo-Pakistani conflict of 2019.*

A: I'm writing and publishing a lot but can't do 'everything'. There are other excellent researchers, with even better insights, better contacts, and better connections. A few years ago, I commissioned Dr. Sanjay Badri-Maharaj (co-author of India's Nuclear Strategy) and Everton Pedroza (researcher from Brazil), to author the book *Terror and Response*. Currently, this is the sole military history book in English on this topic. The same book provides a detailed account of events in February 2019, as one can get through OSINT – but also the full backgrounds, context, and scope of the Indo-Pakistan conflict from 2008 until today.

Q: *Pakistan can be used (by the USA) as an intelligence outpost against Iran, or even the ISI (Inter Service Intelligence of Pakistan) can provide some intel to the CIA in return for something?*

A: Yes and no. As absurd as it might sound, there is close (even if not 'cordial') cooperation between the US and Pakistani intelligence services. They are meeting, they are talking, they often have diametrically different opinions, but are exchanging information – as far as either side is ready to do so (which, usually, depends on quite different interests of the involved people). Shouldn't mean the USA might ever get any permanent bases in Pakistan (beyond what they used to have: whether Peshawar as an airfield from which to launch overflights of the USSR by Lockheed U-2s, back in the late 1950s and early 1960s; or few other, minor facilities, for all sorts of operations in Afghanistan, 2001-2021). Besides, the USA have numerous other bases in Kuwait, Bahrain, Qatar, and more on the other – western (and 'more interesting')—side of Iran (eastern Iran consists largely of mountains and deserts, with sparse population: urban centers are in the north/north-west and along the Persian Gulf).

Q: *There were some articles about an aborted Indo-Israeli attack on Kahuta (note: center of Pakistan's nuclear research) in the 1980s...*

A: Yes, I can recall such features from the 1990s. Probably have one or two still stored somewhere in my home library (thinking of it, I'm actually in touch with one of the authors, too). That said, I do not recall that any has ever mentioned any other specifics—like date and place, for example—beyond that, an Israeli F-15 Eagle was modified for reconnaissance purposes, deployed to India, and sent to fly a reconnaissance mission over Pakistan. I'm not sure what to think of such rumors. Can only add that the IAF was operating its own MiG-25RB reconnaissance jets at the time (and these could fly faster and higher than F-15s).

Q: *You mention General Zia-ul-Haq, military dictator of Pakistan from 1977 to 1988. Who do you think killed Zia? (There are lots of conspiracy theories.)*

A: AFAIK, Zia was killed in a crash of a C-130 Hercules transport aircraft of the Pakistan Air Force, and it was an accident: quite a few of Pakistan's C-130s have crashed over the years.

Q: *Do you think the Meteor missiles had any effect, and did they achieve any kills in the conflict?*

A: I do expect that, yes, they have been deployed in combat and have scored kills. Exactly which and how many: sorry, currently... no confirmation (even if I do have two-three 'clues').

Q: *Should India have used its Navy for a two-pronged attack or as a diversion?*

A: India did so. AFAIK, an air strike from the aircraft carrier INS Vikrant (by MiG-29s equipped with Israeli-made Rampage missiles) was cancelled. No idea why. That said, operations of the carrier battle group centered on INS Vikrant have certainly kept at least a part of the PAF on its toes: as V. Ganesh has posted in reaction to Part 2 of my summary of events from 7 to 10 May:

'Based on what I read on the web yesterday, the Indian Navy wanted to participate in Operation Sindoor and accordingly presented plans for the same, but in the Director-General of Military Operations

[DGMO] press conference of Monday, May 12, 2025, Vice-Admiral A. N. Pramod, the Director-General of Naval Operations [DGNO] of the Indian Navy [IN] said the Indian Navy maintained a deterrent posture.'

Additionally, I've heard theories that the Pakistani air defenses in Karachi were hit so badly precisely because they were expecting an attack from the south (i.e., from the carrier), not from the east.

Q: *How would you have conducted the terror strikes and prepared for Pakistani retaliation if you were the Indians?*

A: As mentioned above, I would do what India did from 8 to 10 May, but right away: no 'limited retaliation strike on terror camps', but '(nuclear) disarmament of Pakistan'.

Q: *Do you think that the Indian Navy [IN]'s Boeing P-8I Neptune Maritime Patrol and Reconnaissance Aircraft [MRPA] was used?*

A: I not only think so: I'm 100% sure. The P-8 Poseidon is an extremely advanced platform: not only a 'maritime patrol aircraft' (MPA), but packed full of communications/signals and electronic intelligence-gathering equipment. AFAIK, the Pakistanis have reported their operations along their coast for days before 7 May, and I'm sure the IN's P-8s have collected plenty of intelligence about both the Pakistani Navy and the PAF IADS.

They also certainly flew anti-submarine patrols in between the *Vikrant* carrier battle group, and the Pakistani coast, just for example.

Notes

1. Goraya, Azhar. (May 16, 2020.) The First Pillar of Islam: Declaration of Faith (Kalima) https://www.reviewofreligions.org/22408/the-first-pillar-of-islam-declaration-of-faith-kalima/
2. https://www.youtube.com/watch?v=YTjM5UvVyCY
3. I'm assuming Indian n-weapons work. So far, many don't. As for Pakistan, there is no incontrovertible evidence that any work. Thanks to its advanced supercomputing facilities, India can reduce the degree of uncertainty, but there is nothing like a minimum of five separate tests.
4. https://x.com/SpencerGuard/status/1922492011526996012
5. How Pak Blog (April 8, 2025). J-10C: A Game-Changer for Pakistan's Air Force. https://howpak.com/j-10c- pakistan-air-force-game-change

6. https://www.youtube.com/watch?v=UfFYkmvfVwE
7. https://xxtomcooperxx.substack.com/p/illusions-and-realities-of-cross

Appendix

From Sameer Patel and Rahul. Observer Research Foundation, New Delhi, May 9, 2025, *Operation Sindoor: Understanding Context and Consequences.* https://www.orfonline.org/expert-speak/operation-sindoor-understanding-context-and-consequences.

Please read this informative article on the Indian Air Force in Operation Sindoor. It will give you a good idea of the Indian Air Force until we get our own write-up in a subsequent edition of this book.

Below from *The Hindu* https://www.thehindu.com/news/national/operation-sindoor-full-list-of-terrorist-camps-in-pakistan-pojk-targeted-by-indian-strikes/article69547986.ece

Operation Sindoor

Special Acknowledgement
to
TOM COOPER

Co-editor of Asia@War Series (Helion, UK)
and has authored / co-authored over
50 books

Appendix I

Pakistan Civil Airfields

Pakistan has over 100 airports, some which are already designated as FOBs, and many capable of wartime emergency use. The PAF also practices using roads, but how much is part of its strategy and how much is public relations it difficult to tell. The large numbers of civil bases complicate an adversary's counter-base operations.

Table A.1: List of civil airports[1]

#1 Islamabad International airport OPIS ISB
#2 Quetta International airport OPQT UET
#3 Skardu airport Skardu OPSD KDU
#4 Sialkot airport Sialkot OPST SKT
#5 Jinnah International airport (Drigh Road) Karachi OPKC KHI
#6 Allama Iqbal International airport Lahore OPLA LHE
#7 Okara airport Okara OPOK
#8 Benazir Bhutto International airport (Chaklala Airbase) Islamabad OPRN
#9 Mianwali airport Mianwali OPMI MWD
#10 Vehari airport Vehari OP21
#11 Jacobabad airport Jacobabad OPJA JAG
#12 Rajanpur airport Rajanpur OP22
#13 Minhas Air Base airport Kamra OPMS G
#14 Shaikh Zaid airport Rahim Yar Khan OPRK RYK
#15 Bahawalpur airport Bahawalpur OPBW BHV
#16 Faisalabad International airport Faisalabad OPFA LYP
#17 Risalpur Air Base airport Risalpur OPRS

#18 Multan International airport Multan OPMT MUX
#19 Masroor Air Base airport Karachi OPMR
#20 Chandhar airport Hafizabad OP1Y
#21 Shaheed Benazirabad airport Nawabshah OPNH WNS
#22 Pasni airport Pasni OPPI PSI
#23 Peshawar International airport Peshawar OPPS PEW
#24 Sukkur airport Mirpur Khas OPSK SKZ
#25 Bhaganwala airport Bhaganwala OPBG BHW
#26 Talhar airport Badin OPTH BDN
#27 Dhingar airport Dhingar OP28
#28 Faisal Air Base airport Karachi OPSF
#29 Mad Jamu airport Mad Jamu Kholelan OP13
#30 Qasim airport Qasim OPQS
#31 Moenjodaro airport Moenjodaro OPMJ MJD
#32 Dera Ghazi Khan airport Dera Ghazi Khan OPDG DEA
#33 Rahwali airport Rahwali OP27
#34 Pano Aqil Southeast airport Pano Aqil OP37
#35 Bannu airport Bannu OPBN BNP
#36 Khuzdar airport Khuzdar OPKH KDD
#37 Sui airport Sui OPSU SUL
#38 Turb airport Turb OPTU TUK
#39 Zhob airport Fort Sandeman OPZB PZH
#40 Jiwani airport Jiwani OPJI JIW
#41 Saidu Sharif airport Saidu Sharif OPSS SDT
#42 Chitral airport Chitral OPCH CJL
#43 Jam Nida Northwest airport Jam Nida OP1A
#44 Gilgit airport Gilgit OPGT GIL
#45 Juzzak airport Juzzak OP35
#46 Dera Ismail Khan airport Dera Ismail Khan OPDI DSK
#47 Mangla airport Mangla OPMA XJM
#48 Ormara airport Ormara Raik OPOR ORW
#49 Panjgur airport Panjgur OPPG PJG
#50 Gwadar Internional airport Gwadar OPGD GWD
#51 Robray airport Kech OP36
#52 Belab airport Belab OP14

#53 Thar airport Chuchra OP10
#54 Thal airport Thal OP23
#55 Walton airport Walton OPLH
#56 Parachinar airport Parachinar OPPC PAJ
#57 UEPL Khaskheli Airstrip airport Badin OP16
#58 Kashmor airport Kashmor OP31
#59 Kandhkot airport Kandhkot OP33
#60 Nok Kundi airport Nok Kundi OP34
#61 Khewra airport Khewra OP26
#62 Chashma airport Kundian OP19
#63 Kot Addu airport Kot Addu OP18
#64 Gurha Salim airport Gurha Salim OP25
#65 Khairpur airport Khairpur OP32
#66 Wana airport Wana OPWN WAF
#67 Muzaffarabad airport Muzaffarabad OPMF MFG
#68 Rawalakot airport Rawalakot OPRT RAZ
#69 Ouzkani airport Khandor OP15
#70 Mir Baz airport Mir Baz OP11
#71 Shamsi airport Washuk OP12
#72 Mandi Bahauddin Air Base airport Mandi Bahauddin OP24
#73 Bela airport Khan Bela OPBL
#74 Bahawalnagar airport Bahawalnagar OPBR WGB
#75 Chilas airport Chilas OPCL CHB
#76 Chir airport Nowshera OPCT
#77 Dalbandin airport Dalbandin OPDB DBA
#78 Dadu airport Dadu OPDD DDU
#79 Daharki airport Daharki OPDK
#80 Cape Monz airport Cape Monz OPKA
#81 Hyderabad airport Hyderabad OPKD HDD
#82 Chore airport Chore OPKE
#83 Gharo airport Gharo OPKF
#84 Koh airport Koh OPKT OHT
#85 Loralai airport Loralai OPLL LRG
#86 Mirpur Khas airport Mirpur Khas OPMK
#87 Miram Shah airport Miram Shah OPMN

#88 Sindhri Tharparkar airport Sindhri OPMP MPD
#89 Pishin airport Pishin OPPN
#90 Rafiqui Air Base airport Shorkot OPRQ
#91 Sibi airport Sibi OPSB SBQ
#92 Sehwan Sharif airport Sehwan Sharif OPSN SYW
#93 Mushaf Air Base airport Sargodha OPSR SGI
#94 Sawan airport Sawan OPSW RZS
#95 Tarbela Dam airport Tarbela OPTA TLB
#96 Taftan airport Taftan OPTT TFT
#97 Basal airport Basal PK-0002
#98 Kharan East airport Kharan PK-0006
#99 PAF Murid Air Base airport Murid PK-0009
#100 Sialkot Cantonment airport Sialkot PK-0013
#101 Khanpur airport Khanpur PK-0014
#102 Larkana airport Larkana PK-0015
#103 Petaro airport Cadet College Petaro PK-0016
#104 Jungshahi Airstrip airport Jungshahi PK-0017
#105 Sujawal airport Sujawal PK-0020
#106 Jamal Din Wali airport Rahim Yar Khan PK-0045
#107 Al Ghaba Airstrip airport Rahim Yar Khan PK-0046
#108 Qadirpur airport Ghotki PK-0047
#109 PAF Khalid Air Base airport Quetta PK-0049
#110 SUPARCO Beach airport Gaddani PK-0062
#111 PAF Bholari airport PK-0070
#112 Campbellpore airport Campbellpore CWP PK-CWP
#113 Gujr airport Gujr GRT PK-GRT
#114 Kadanwari airport Kadanwari KCF PK-KCF
#115 Reko Diq airport Chagai REQ PK-REQ

Note

1. "Airports with the longest runways in Pakistan". Downloaded March 14, 2024. https://www.bigorre.org/aero/meteo/op1a/en

Appendix II

PAF aircraft losses

Sources include PAFFalcons.com, Aviation Safety Data, Scramble (from 15 June 1995), https://babriet.tripod.com/airforce/attrition/pattrition00.htm, and a variety of others, including Pakistan newspapers. It has only an estimated 85 per cent accuracy because of omissions and transcription errors on my part due to lack of clarity in some Pakistan media.

Interestingly, the US in the 1950s experienced horrendous accident rates. For example, 383 per 100,000 hours for the air defence fighter F-89 Scorpion over its 18-year service life. By comparison, today's F-15 has about 0.5! The 1948 accident rate per 100,000 hours was 156 for the F-80, 174 for the F-84, and 145 for the F-86. Of course, this is when the USAF was transitioning from props to 1 Gen jets. The aircraft themselves were faulty, the engines unreliable, and training inadequate. Also, World War II propeller pilots had a cocky attitude about their jet capabilities whereas the jet is an entirely different beast.

Scramble lists 200 F7 and 60 A-5C aircraft, but there are many aircraft of there is little information. The listing of about A-5C 14 losses in our table seems too low. Whereas the IAF has managed to bring down its accident rate to 7 per 100,000 hours, the PAF's rate has soared to an estimated 18 per 100,000 hours.[1]

The primary reason appears to be Pakistan's efforts to keep obsolete aircraft flying. Regarding the F-16, for example, the PAF has a very low accident rate, four aircraft in 30 years. And the US in the 1950s went through horrendous accident rates – 383 per 100,000 hours.[2]

For the air defence fighter F-89 Scorpion, for example, over its 18-year service life. By comparison, today's -15 has about 0.5! The 1948 accident rate per 100,000 hours ran to 156 for the F-80, 174 for the F-84, and 145 for the F-86.[3]

If an aircraft crashes, it can be assumed to be a loss. But if it is written off, it does not necessarily mean a crash, but "The aircraft has been extensively damaged and the cost of repairs would be more than the aircraft is worth."[4] This could be on the ground, nonetheless, written off is a total loss. We don't include aircraft sent to museums or used at gate guards because those are not losses.

One source, Global Defence,[5] seems to imply that in 2020 up to 5 October Pakistan lost six JF-17s but so far, I have not found any supporting evidence. Just an example of the small problem of compiling PAF losses.

In the 2010 decade, whereas the IAF managed to bring down its accident rate to 7 per 100,000 hours, the PAF's rate soared to an estimated 18 per 100,000 hours according to Strategy Page,[6] 10-times Western rates, but this is not an academically reliable source.

For 1947-64 I relied primarily on the Aviation Safety Network. While Pakistan has been coy about its crashes in that period, India has been more open.[7]

For example, in 1951 India admitted to 7 military crashes but Pakistan reported none. In 1959 Pakistan admitted to one crash, India to six. In 1960 India admitted to nine military crashes but Pakistan to only one. The IAF is, of course, much larger than Pakistan, but still: just one crash in one year seems improbable.

Included are Army and Navy crashes, as far as I am aware of them.

1947			
No military crashed reported in 1947 after Pakistan Independence Day 14 August 1947			
1948			
Nov 04	C-47, escaped	1 killed	Intercepted and shot at by RIAF 65-km south of Gilgit
1949			
Aug 09	Tempest II	safe	Sind desert

1950			
Apr 08	Bristol 170 Freighter 21	16 killed	Crashed on the mountain between Gilgit and Peshawar, Pakistan in poor weather conditions.
Aug 05	Sea Fury	1 killed	Karachi
1952			
Aug 26	Bristol 170 Freighter 21P	18 killed	#G-783 near Khewra
Sep 25	Bristol 170 Freighter 21P	2 killed	#G-799 near Lahore
1953			
May 11	Attacker (jet)	1 killed	Karachi; routine flight
June 04	?	1 killed	Peshawar
Nov 11	Bristol 170 Freighter 21P	2 killed	#G-809 Karachi
1954			
Mar 14	?	1 killed	Near Karachi
Oct 12	AT-16	2 killed	Trainer, crash at Lowari Pass
1958			
1959			
	Bristol 170 31M	7 killed	#S4426 near Chaklala
1960			
March 2	B-57C		#53-3834 ?Zhob. Took off Peshawar?
1961			
Mar 16	Light aircraft		
1962			
Jun 26	Bristol 170 Freighter 31M	3 killed	near Rawalpindi #S4414
1963			
Nov 13[8]	F-104A	1 safe	F/O Asghar Khan survived high-speed ejection #56-802
1964			
Sep 03	F-104A	1 killed	F/L Tariq Masood, ground attack practice #56-803
1965			
Apr 19	F-86		
Aug 18	C-130B		#12648, skidded off runway, destroyed, 3 years old aircraft

Sep 04	F-86F	EOT	F/O Nasir M Butt - 18 Sqn - 4716 - Shot down by F/L V S Pathania
Sep 04	F-86F	EOT	F/L Hasan Akhtar - 14 Sqn - 3832 - Bird Hit Accident
Sep 06	F-86F	1 KIA	S/L Sarfaraz A Rafiqui - 5 Sqn - F-86F - 5248 - Shot down by F/L D N Rathore
Sep 06	F-86F	1 KIA	F/L Yunus Hussain - 5 Sqn - 1173 - Shot down by F/O V K Neb
Sep 06	B-57	2 KIA	S/L S Alam Siddiqui and S/L Aslam Qureshi (Navigator) - 8 Sqn - 3941 - Shot down by AAA
Sep 07	F-86F	1 KIA	F/O M Afzal Khan - 14 Sqn - 4027 - Shot down by F/L Alfred T Cooke
Sep 07	F-86F	1 KIA	F/L A T M Aziz - 14 Sqn - 4028 - Combat Related Accident
Sep 07	F-86F	Fatal	F/O Sikander Azam - 18 Sqn - 4849 - Engine flamed out after take-off (Non-Combat Related Accident)
Sep 07	F-86F	-	3843 - Destroyed on ground - 1 Sqn raid (Mystéres)
Sep 07[9]	F-104A	EOT	F/L Amjad Hussain - 9 Sqn - 877 - Combat Related Accident - Mid-air debris collision with Mystére following close-range shooting
Sep 08	F-86F	EOT	F/L Sadruddin - 15 Sqn - 3427 - Shot down by own AAA
Sep 11	F-86F	1 KIA	S/L Muniruddin Ahmed - 1180 - Shot down by AAA
Sep 11	RB-57	2 KIA	S/L Muhammad Iqbal and F/L Saifullah Lodhi (Navigator) - 24 Sqn - 3961 - Shot down by own AAA
Sep 12	OH-13	2 KIA	Phillora
Sep 13	F-86F	1 KIA	S/L Alauddin Ahmad - 18 Sqn - 5160 - Combat Related Accident
Sep 14	B-57	2 POW	F/L Shaikh A Rehman and F/L B A Chaudhri (Navigator) - 7 Sqn - 3891 - Shot down by AAA
Sep 16	F-86F	1 POW	F/O Shaukat-ul-Islam - 11 Sqn - F-86F - 5232 - Shot down by F/O P S Pingale

Sep 16	L-19	1 safe	Sargodha
Sep 16	F-104A	1 safe	F/L Gulam Abbasi - 9 Sqn - #56-807 Crashed disoriented while landing in dust storm
Sep 17	B-57	fatal	F/L M A Butt of 7 Sqn and F/L Khalid-uz-Zaman (Navigator) of 8 Sqn - 3942 - Non Combat Related Accident - Crashed during night landing; possible disorientation
Sep 19	F-86F	1 safe	F/L S M Ahmed - 17 Sqn - 1199 - Hit by F/L V Kapila. crashed on landing due to damage
Sep 20	F-86F	1 safe	F/L A H Malik - 5 Sqn - 1174 - Shot down in combat by F/L A K Mazumdar
Nov 18	0-1E		Ground fire, Sialkot
1966			
April 7	O-1E		Written off
Jul 15	C-130B	10 killed	#3768 Crashed into mountain (3-yrs old)
Dec 26	F-86	-	Flt. Lt. Abbas
?	O-1		
1967			
Jan 21	F-6		
May 24	B-57	1 killed	Air Cdre Masroor Hussain the Base Commander died in bird-hit while landing
Jun 16	F-86		
Jun 16	F-86		Scramble.nl lists two a/c lost on 16 June
1968			
Apr 30	L-100	22 killed	Enroute to Chaklala #64145 (Hercules)
Jun 15	F-86		F/O Medhi
Jun 15	F-86		S/L Rehman
Apr 15	F-104A	1 killed	F/L Ghulam Abbasi, fire on ground #56-807
July 15	F-104A	1 safe	S/L Arif Iqbal, fire on ground #56-806
1969			
Apr 23	F-86		
Jul 08	C-130B		Destroyed in fire while refuel, Islamabad #23490
	CL-13B		#1594

Nov 20	F-86		F/L A. Irfan
1970			
Mar 4	C-130B		Write off #23489
	CL-13B		Written off #1616
Jul 9	F-86		S/L. M.Akbar
1971			
Jun 18	F-86		
Aug 20	T-33	2 killed	#2 Sqn. #1622. Hijacked by F/L Matur-Rehman aiming to defect to India. Resisted in flight by pilot F/L Minhas. Is awarded Nishan-i-Haider, highest award
Nov 22	CL-13B		Shot down Boyra, East Pakistan No. 14 Sqn
Nov 22	CL-13B		Shot down Boyra, East Pakistan No. 14 Sqn
Dec 04	CL-13B	1 died	W/C S.M. Ahmed, Garibpur. No. 14 Sqn. ejected believed killed ground by mob
Dec 04	CL-13B	1 died	F/O Sajjad Noor – No. 14 Sqn Garibpur, ejected safely, believed killed on ground by mob
Dec 04		1 died	F/L Nayyar Iqbal No. 17 Sqn Flame out after TO from Shorkot
Dec 05	F-104A	POW	S/L Amjad Hussain - 9 Sqn - 804 - shot down by AAA, Hav T C Ramaswamy, 27 AD Regt
Dec 06	B-57	2 KIA	F/L Javed Iqbal and F/L G M Malik (Navigator) - 7 Sqn - 3948 - shot down by AAA Hav Gopala Krishnan, 27 AD Regt
Dec 06	B-57	2 KIA	S/L Ishfaq Hameed and S/L Zulfiqar Ahmed - 7 Sqn - 3943 - Failed to return, presumed shot down by AAA
Dec 06	B-57	2 KIA	S/L Khusro and S/L Peter Christy (Navigator) - 7 Sqn - 3939 - Failed to return, presumed shot down by AAA
Dec 06	RB-57	-	3934 - Destroyed on ground by Canberra raid
Dec 06	O-1E		Written off
Dec 07	F-86F	EOT	F/O Hamid A Khawaja - 15 Sqn - 4030 - Flamed-out while chasing Hunter
Dec 07	O-1E		Written off

Dec 07	F-6	POW	F/L Wajid Ali Khan - 11 Sqn - 4110 - shot down by Naik Bal Bahadur, AAA 29 AD Regt
Dec 07	CL-13B	1 safe	S/L Cecil Choudhry 18 Sqn #1657
Dec 08	B-57	-	3945 - Caught fire during servicing (Non-Combat Related Accident)
Dec 08	F-86F	0	#1095 Destroyed on ground by IAF 20 Sqn
Dec 08	F-86F	0	#3839 Destroyed on ground by IAF 20 Sqn
Dec 08	F-86F	0	#3848 Destroyed on ground by IAF 20 Sqn
Dec 08	F-86F	0	#3851 Destroyed on ground by IAF 20 Sqn
Dec 08	F-86F	0	#4018 Destroyed on ground by IAF 20 Sqn
Dec 08	F-6	KIA	F/L Afzal J Siddiqui - 23 Sqn - 1508 - Possible fratricide by Leader; own AAA also not ruled out (Combat Related Accident)
Dec 08	F-86F	KIA	F/L Fazal Elahi - 26 Sqn - 4019 - Shot down by Hav Uttam Jawalge, AAA 501 AD Gp
Dec 08	F-86		#3848 written off
Dec 10	F-86F	KIA	S/L Aslam Choudhry - 26 Sqn - 3856 - Shot down by S/L R N Bharadwaj
Dec 12	F-104A	KIA	W/C M L Middlecoat - 9 Sqn - 773 - Shot down by F/L Bharat B Soni
Dec 12	F-6	EOT	F/L Ejazuddin - 23 Sqn - 1703 - Shot down by F/L S S Malhotra
Dec 13	F-86E	KIA	F/O N N A Baig - 19 Sqn - 1718 - Shot down by F/L Farokh J Mehta
Dec 16	T-33A		Sabotaged by PAF in East Pakistan
Dec 16	RT-33A		Sabotaged by PAF in East Pakistan
Dec 16	CL-13B		Sabotaged by PAF in East Pakistan #1506
Dec 16	CL-13B		Sabotaged by PAF in East Pakistan #1608
Dec 16	CL-13B		Sabotaged by PAF in East Pakistan #1617
Dec 16	CL-13B		Sabotaged by PAF in East Pakistan #1663
Dec 16	CL-13B		Sabotaged by PAF in East Pakistan #1735
Dec 16	CL-13B		Sabotaged by PAF in East Pakistan #1763
Dec 16	CL-13B		Sabotaged by PAF in East Pakistan
Dec 16	CL-13B		Sabotaged by PAF in East Pakistan
Dec 16	CL-13B		Sabotaged by PAF in East Pakistan

Dec 16	CL-13B		Sabotaged by PAF in East Pakistan
Dec 16	CL-13B		Sabotaged by PAF in East Pakistan
Dec 17	F-104A	KIA	F/L Samad Changezi - 9 Sqn - 787 - Shot down by F/L Aruna K Datta; ex-RJAF F-104
Dec 17	F-6	KIA	F/L Shahid Raza - 25 Sqn - 4108 - Shot down by Hav M Kycharala, 45 AD Regt
1972			
Apr 20	Unknown		Written off
??	CL-13B		Written off, no details
1973			
Mar 12	F-86		A/Com A. R. Yousefzai
Apr 07	F-86		S/L J. A. Carrapeitt
1974			
May 07	F-86		F/O Sikandar
Jul 27	Mirage		G/C W. Azim
Dec 21	Mirage		Flt. Lt. S.Arshad
1975	Unknown		Written off
1976			
Mar 12	F-6		Flg. Off. Z. H. Malik
Apr 03	Mirage		
Oct 03	F-6		Flg. Off. Hifazat
Dec 23	F-6		Flt. Lt. S. H. Ashfaq
1977			
May 16	F-6		Sqn. Ldr. Maqsood
May 24	F-6		Flg. Off. Masroor
Oct 11	Mirage		
Oct 27	F-6		P/O M. M. Ayub
1978			
Jan 04	F-6		P.O S. Ashraf
Apr 10	Mirage		
Mar 07	F-6		Flg. Off. Obaid
Jun 08	F-6		Sqn. Ldr. Farooq
Jun 12	F-6		Flg. Off. Naeem
Jul 11	F-6		P.O. Arshad
Dec 16	F-6		Flg. Off. Javed

1979			
Feb 01	F-6		Flg. Off. Younas
Feb 01	C-130B	0	Night engine test Chaklala, jumped chocks, collided with C-130E, writeoff #23488
Feb 01	C-130E	0	Collided with above C-130B, writeoff #10687
Sep 08	F-6		Sqn. Ldr. H. A. Khawaja
Jul 18	F-6		P.O Shahid
Aug 18	F-6		Flt. Lt. Rizvi
Dec 03	F-6		Sqn. Ldr. Nazar
1980			
Jan 06	F-6		F/O A. Mazhar
Mar 16	F-6		F/O Z. I. Haider
May 11	F-6	1 safe	F/O A. Najamul
Aug 18	F-6		F/O S. Raza
Nov 12	A-5		
Dec 10	A-5		
Oct 08	T-37	1 killed	During a practice session, Sherdils team leader Flt. Lt. Alamdar Hussain went down in a mid-air collision involving his slot man posthumous Sitara-i-Basalat.
1981			
Jan 12	F-6	1 OK	F/O Marawat
Mar 25	F-6	1 OK	F/L T. Mujaher
Aug 10	Mirage	1 OK	
Aug 24	F-6	1 OK	F/L P. Tanassam
Sep 14	Mirage	1 OK	
1982			
Mar 16	F-6		P/O FH Sikander
Apr 7	F-6		P/O Bilal
May 15	Mirage	1 OK	
May 20	F-6		P/O Z. Malik
Jun 21	F-6		F/L A. Bashir
Sep 7	Mirage		

Oct 11	F-6		S/L Chaudharay
1983			
Jan 11	F-6	1 safe	F/O Abbasi
Jun 04	F-6		F/L Humanyun
Jun 13	F-6	1 safe	P/O Fauz-il-Haq
Nov 10	Mirage 3RP	1 safe	#67-201
Nov 29	Mirage		
1984			
Mar 13	Mirage		
Apr 08	F-6		F/L S. Yar
Aug 30	F-6		P/O Fazal
Oct 26	F-6		F/L Shaukat
1985			
Jan 25	Mirage		
Aug 14	F-6		
Dec 27	F-6		F/L Khizar
1986			
Mar 04	F-6		F/O A. Zaheer
Jul 10	F-6	1 safe	F/L Ejaz Ahmed
Aug 10	F-6		F/L Muqtadar
Nov 21	F-6	1 safe	F/L Ejaz Ahmed
Dec 18	F-16B	-	#81-1504 Hit wild boar while taking off from Sargodha, one pilot was S/L Faaiz Amir.
1987			
Mar 23	Mirage 5	1 killed	Mirage jet crashed due to a bird strike just 50 seconds before it was to dip in salute to President Mohammad Zia ul-Haq at the National Day military parade in Rawalpindi. Pilot Mohammad Saeed Iqbal was killed.
Apr 29	F-16A	1 survived	#85-720 No. 14 Sdn fell victim to a missile fired by W/C Amjad Javed - mistakenly shooting down his wingman during an engagement with 6 MiG-23s of Afghan Air Force. F/L Shahid Sikandar Khan safe.
Jun 03	F-16A	1 OK	F-16A hit wild boar on runway during takeoff from Sargodha AB

1988			
Jan 12	MFI-17	2 dead	-
Jul 07	Mirage-3DP	15 killed, 25 injured	Mirage trainer crashed into a factory after an in-flight fire killing both pilots and 13 others on ground while injuring 25 others.
Aug 17	C-130	37 dead	C-130 with Chief Executive of Pakistan Zia-ul-Haq and other generals and diplomats exploded mid-air shortly after take-off. Sabotage suspected.
Aug 28	F-6		S/L Abid
Sep 14	F-6		F/L Arshad
Sep 23	A-5C	-	Aircraft crashed during a routine flight near Pindi Gheb in Attock District, 90km south-west of Islamabad.
1989	Unknown		No details
	Unknown		No details
1990			
Feb 06	F-6		S/L Imran
Feb 15	F-6		F/O Aziz
Mar 05	SA-315B	4 killed	Engine fire
1991			
Jun 16	F-16A	1 safe	No. 9 Sqn, # 85-723, engine failed S/L S.H. Raza
Oct 28	F-16A	1 safe	No. Sqn #85-725, engine failed (due non-standard part) during dogfight maneuver, S/L Anjum Nadeem
Dec 20	-	1 killed	The pilot died while trying to steer the aircraft away from populated areas and was not able to eject
1992			
Apr 22	MFI-17	2 killed	The pilot bailed out of the trainer which crashed killing two on ground.
Mar 15	A-5		S/L K.F. Lodhi
Apr 22	F-7P[10]	1 safe	F/L Akmal bailed
Apr 24	F-7P	1 safe	The plane crashed after engine failure
May 18	Mirage		
Aug 01	SA-315B	3 killed	Crashed in a snowstorm caused a white-out.
Sep 02	MFI-17	2 killed	The plane crashed possibly a bird strike.

Oct 17	A-5		F/L F.A. Baig
Nov 01	Mirage		
Nov 07	Mirage		F/L Taimuri
Aug 01	SA-315B	3 killed	Crashed in a snowstorm
Sep 02	MFI-17	2 killed	The plane crashed possibly after a bird strike
1993			
May 04	Mirage	2 safe	F/L S.M. Ali; both pilots injured
Aug 23	Mirage 3DP		
Sep 27	Mirage		
Oct 14	A-5	1 safe	
Sep 06	Fighter	-	-
Sep 28	SA-319	All survived	Navy's ASW Alouette III rolled over on landing at the Naval Air Station.
Nov 10	F-16B	2 safe	S/L Khawaja Abdul Majeed, S/L Nawaz
1994			
Mar 17	F-16A	-	Aircraft serial no. 85-721 crashed under unknown circumstances and written off.
Apr 26	F-16A	1 killed	Crashed on approach Sargodha Air Base.
Jun 07	PA Heli	1 killed?	-
Jun 15	Mirage-3DP	-	-
Aug 30	A-5C	1 killed	Crashed after notifying a technical problem.
Aug 31	F-7P	1 killed	Flying Officer Imran Yousaf, crashed while trying to land an F-7P aircraft after it lost its canopy. He was fatally injured. No. 19 OCU.
Sep 01	Trainer	1 killed	The trainer aircraft crashed killing the pilot.
Oct 22	F-16A	-	Aircraft serial no. 82-701 of No. 11 Squadron.
1995			
Mar 22	Fighter	1 injury	The fighter aircraft crashed while the pilot received serious injuries.
Mar 25	Fighter	1 killed	F/L Tariq Javed, routine training, crashed in northeast Punjab
Mar 28	Trainer	2 safe	Trainer aircraft crashed, yet both pilots managed to escape.
Sep 06	F-16A	-	Aircraft crashed after an in-flight fire.
Mar 19	Mirage IIIEP	1 safe	Flame-out during a sortie from its base at Rafiqui, crashed into an open field in Punjab area

Mar 22	Fighter	1 hurt	The fighter crashed while the pilot received serious injuries.
Mar 25	F-7P	1 killed	F/L Tariq Javed. Routine training, technical problems, northeast of Punjab province.
Mar 28	Trainer	2 safe	The trainer aircraft crashed, yet both pilots managed to escape.
May 28	F-6	1 safe	Aircraft crashed while taking-off.
Sep 06	F-16A	1 killed	Aircraft crashed after an in-flight fire.
Oct 09	Fighter	1 hurt	A fighter aircraft crashed, seriously injuring the pilot.
Oct 31	SA-315B Lama	-	Shot down by India
1996			
Feb 06	Fighter	1 survived	Aircraft while on a routine training mission crashed near Manser Camp in district Attock in Northwestern Pakistan. The pilot ejected safely.
Mar 22	F-7P		Midair collision
May 08	Fighter	1 dead, 1 safe	F/O Tanveer-ur-Rehman safe; F/L Muhammad Zubair Khan killed, near Isa Khel
Aug 13	F-6	1 safe	F-6 crashed in a camp in the outskirts of Quetta. The pilot ejected but was seriously injured
Aug 27	F-6	1 safe	F-6 crashed Paind Khan village near Samungli Air Base.
Sep 15	Fighter	1 safe	Aircraft crashed while pilot ejected safely. The plane was on a routine training flight.
Sept 20	Trainer	1 killed	
1997			
Jan 20	Fighter	1 killed	Aircraft crashed near Chakwal, South of the Islamabad. Flying Officer Syed Ahmar Tamkee
Feb 14	Fighter	1 safe	Aircraft crashed after a bird strike. The pilot ejected safely.
Mar 25	Fighter	1 safe	
Sept 07	F-7	1 safe	Bird strike, Bhakkar near Lahore
Oct 03	F-7P	1 safe	F-7P crashed near Lahore due to a bird strike injuring a farmer on the ground.

Nov 21	F-6	1 killed	F-6 crashed near Saranan, about 30 km South of Quetta on a routine flight with two other aircraft. Flt. Lt. Zarrar Rahman Niazi, ejected but parachute failed
Dec 13	Mirage	1 killed	Crashed routine training near Karachi. The aircraft caught fire while landing at Masroor AB. Pilot Flt. Lt. Rashid Khan.
1998			
Jul 30	F-7P	1 killed	No 2 Squadron #98-540 Technical malfunction, aircraft took off from Masroor Air Base.
Sep 10	2 x C-130B	5 killed	Two C-130Bs serial No. 23491 & 24143 of No. 6 Squadron collided with another parked C-130B after brake failure due to a fire. Killed S/L. Nadeem Qasim (Pilot), F/L. Amir Rana (Co-pilot), S/L. Sohail, F/O. Bilal, W/O Khalid.
1999			
Feb ?	F-6		
Feb 09	F-7P	1 killed	Chakwal
Mar 04	A-5C	1 OK	Nr. Quetta
Mar 11	A-5C	1 OK	Nr Quetta
Mar 25	MFI-17	1 killed	Nr. Risalpur
May 05	Fighter	2 OK	Aircraft crashed near Mianwali AB training
Jun 10	SA-330J	11 killed	Army, Skardu
Jun 30	MF-17	2 killed	Army, 20 km from Multan
Aug 10	Atlantic	17 killed	Pakistan Navy ASW Atlantic c/n 33 29 Sqn. shot down by two Indian MiG-21s that violated Pakistani airspace
Oct 26	Mirage-IIIE	1 OK	Routine flight when it crashed north of its base near Karachi.
Oct 29	P-3CII5	21 killed	Navy #83/28 Sqn; exercises off Pasni
Oct 30	MFI-17	2 killed	Army. Near Rahwali
2000			
Jan 07	FT-7	2	Mianwali
Apr 05	F-7P	1 OK	F-7P, routine training, near Pindi Gheb
Apr 07	A-5C	1 killed	Flt. Lt. Zia-ul-Hasan killed, take off Peshawar

Jun 05	Mirage	1 OK	Mirage took off from Masroor AB a routine mission.
Jul 05	Mirage-5	1 OK	Mirage-5 crashed 40 miles north of Masroor AB
Jul 20	F-7	1 OK	Routine flight Hyderabad to Mianwali, crash landing.
Jul 27	Unknown		
Sept 12	Mirage		
Oct 04	Mushshak	2 OK	Rawalkot, Army
Nov 10	Mirage-5EF	-	Being upgraded in France; crashed
2001			
Jan 25	F-7P	I OK	Pilot was Fazzi, training sorties from Mianwali
Mar 20	Mar 20		Fighter. Crashed at Kushab
Apr 18	F-6	1 OK	Landing accident at Samungli
Apr 26	Mirage 5F	1 OK	S/L Ihtesham. #752 Bhakwal Village after take-off Minhas AB.
May 30	Mirage	1 OK	Near Mianwali
June 18	F-7P	1 OK	Near Peshawar
Jul 26	Mirage 3OA	1 killed	G/C Ali Asad crashed near Hub River
Aug 12	Fighter	1 OK	Crashed near Quetta
Aug 27	F-7P		
Sep 27	F-7P	1 killed	F/O Shahid, Mochko Hills
Aug 27	Unknown		

2002			
Jan 17	A-5C	1 killed	No. 26 Sqn. took off from Murid AB, crashed near Chakwal
Jan 24	Mirage-5PA3	1 killed	Mirage 5PA3 from No. 7 Squadron crashed somewhere in the Arabian Sea during a solo training mission. The pilot, Wg. Cdr. Nazar is still missing and presumed dead.
Feb 06	F-7P	1 survived	F-7P crashed south part of Sind near Mirpurkhas.
Mar 18	F-6	1 survived	The F-6 crashed during a training flight near Quetta. The pilot ejected safely.

Mar 26	F-7P	1 survived	F-7P crashed 16 km south of Multan during a training mission Flt. Lt. Naveed Ahmed.
Apr 20	F-6	1 survived	Last crash of the F-6 in PAF service. The pilot ejected safely.
Apr 25	Mirage-5F	-	Aircraft from No. 25 Squadron.
May ?	A-5C	1 killed	Aircraft from No. 16 Squadron.
May ?	F-7P	-	-
Jul 17	Fighter	-	40km short of Masroor.
Aug ?	Mirage	1 killed	Gp. Cpt. martyred.
Aug 18	F-7P	1 OK	Makhad
Oct 2	Bell 206B	All survived	Army, landed hard in mountainous.
Nov 15	Mirage-5PA	1 killed	Mirage-5PA serial no. No. 405 of PAF Base Rafiqui, Shorkot crashed. Sqn. Ldr. Hasnat Ikram died from injuries.
Dec 10	2 x F-7PG	2 survived	Two F-7PGs collided mid-air during air combat training in Mastung district, 60km south of Quetta. The fighters belonging to the No. 23 Wg. Cdr. Tariq and Flt. Lt. Mohsin were able to eject safely.
2003			
Feb 10	A-5C	1 killed	F/L Nadeem Bhatti near Chakwal. Failed to eject.
Feb 20	Fokker F-27	17 killed	Fokker F27, serial no. J-10254, crashed into the Cherat mountain range
Apr 12		1 killed, 1 survived	Training killing F/L Tausif Ahmed, injuring Cadet Naveed.
Apr 12	A-5C	1 survived	A-5C Fantan crashed near Pindi Gheb in central Punjab province, the pilot managed to eject safely.
Apr 24	Mi-171	-	Serial no. 58614
Jul 12	Mirage	1 killed	Mirage aircraft crashed near Shorkot routine training. Pilot Sq. Ldr. Shahab Nawaz.
Aug 18	F-7P	1 survived	F-7P crashed near Makhad, 44 miles north-west of Islamabad. The pilot managed to eject safely.

Sep 30	Mirage-5	1 survived	Masroor Air Base crashed at Hub, Baluchistan
Oct 16	Mirage-5	2 survived	A Mirage-5 aircraft of PAF which was on a routine training flight, crashed two miles east of Quaid-e-Azam International airport and inside Malir cantonment this morning. Both the instructor & pilot ejected safely.
Dec 10	F-7P	1 survived	F-7 aircraft of PAF crashed near Tamman (Talagang), District Chakwal.
2004			
Mar 19	F-7P	1 survived	F-7 fighter aircraft, while on a routine operational training mission, crashed 20 miles west of Jhang.
Apr 08	F-7P	1 killed	Routine operational training mission, crashed 20 miles west of Jhang (Punjab Province). Flt. Lt. Imran Tariq died
Aug 05	Mil-17	13 killed	Army, north west Pakistan
2005			
Jul 27	Mirage	1 survived	Crashed, 80 km south-west of Islamabad, The pilot managed to eject in time
Aug 05	Mirage	1 survived	Mirage aircraft, while on a routine operational training mission, crashed 28 miles north-east of Quetta
Aug 25	Mirage	1 survived	Mirage aircraft crashed, near 350 km from Karachi technical malfunction.
Sep 11	Mirage	1 killed	Mirage crashed during a training mission in Punjab. Payee Khel, about 200 km south-west Islamabad.
Dec 08	Mirage	1 killed	Mirage was crashed in the hilly terrain near Mianwali due to bad weather.
2006			
Apr 20	Mirage		W/O
May 20	Mirage	1 ejected	
Jul 05	A-5	1 ejected	Technical malfunction training flight near Peshawar capital of North West Frontier Province. F/L Iltifat safe
Jul 05	Mirage 5		W/O
Aug 31	F-7	1 killed	Technical malfunction S/L Faisal Bashir

Sep 14	Mirage		W/O
Oct 19	Mirage 5		W/O
Nov 20	Mirage IIIEA ROSE I	1 ejected	Wing Commander Faisal Mumtaz Rao ejected safely
Dec 20	Mirage 5	1 ejected	Large bird ingested by engine, outskirts of Karachi
2007			
Feb 01		1 ejected	Ex-Shorkot, crashed near Jhang
Feb 07	Mirage 5	1 ejected	Crashed near Jhang.
Feb 15	F-7	1 ejected	Crashed within perimeter of Masroor, bird hit
Mar 13	FT-7PG		No. 17 Squadron
2008			
Jan 22	T-37	1 killed	Caught fire, hit Ghulam Ishaq Khan Institute of Engineering Sciences and Technology, Topi, some 100 km from Islamabad.
Feb 08	UAV (Jasoos II)	-	Crashed in the outskirts of Peshawar.
Feb 15	Mirage	1 killed	Mirage crashed while on a routine operational training mission, 30km south east of Sargodha. Wing Commander Azhar Ismael was martyred in the accident.
Apr 17	FT-7	1 ejected	
Jun 21	FT-7	2 ejected	
Oct 09	F-7	1 ejected	
2009			
July 03	Mi-17	41 killed	Khyber Agency
July 17	F-16	1 killed	#92- 0405. S/L Saud, crashed Khopshab, near Sargodha
Aug 05	F-7	1 killed	Crashed near Attock in Punjab; F/L Shahryar Nisar
Aug 07	FT-7	2 killed	Near Mianwali S/L Haris bin Khalid, F/O Ibaad ur Rehman
2010			
Feb 24	Heli		Army

2011			
May 03	Mirage 5	safe	
Aug 15	F-7P	1 safe	#90-609 near to Kalur Kot Khakkar (Mianwali training area) F/O Nida Tahir (lady pilot)
Oct 11	Mirage 5		W/O
Oct 19	Mirage		No. 8 Sdn
Nov 11	Mirage		No. 7 Sqn
Nov 25	Mirage 5		No. 7 Sqn
Nov 15	JF-17	1 killed	S/L Leader Muhammad Hussain, was killed - parachute did not open on bail out.
2012			
Jan 17	?	1 PAF, 1 Turkish AF killed	S/L Masood Hussain was piloting the aircraft; reports mention Turkish "trainees"
Jan 25	FT-7	2 safe	No. 19 Squadron 1 pilot was lady trainee
Jan 25	Mirage 5PA3		No. 7 Squadron
Feb 08	F-7PG	pilot killed	Routine training mission, at Pishin near Quetta
Apr 03	Helio		
Apr 25	Mirage 5F		No. 25 Squadron
May 01	Mirage 5	safe	
May 17	2 x MFI-17	4 pilots killed	S/L Syed Masood Rizvi, S/L Zaigham Abbas plus trainees F/L Mustafa, S/L Moazzam,
May 19			
May 20	UAV Falco		
May 23	300C helio	2 killed	Army, Chenab River
May 29	FT-7	2 safe	
Jun 12	Mirage 5DD	1 safe	No. 7 Squadron
July 12	Mi-17	6 killed	Army, Skardu
Aug 06	MFI-17	none	Charsadda #78-6055
Aug 15	Mirage 5	pilot ejected	Thal, "technical reasons"

Aug 28	UAV	no casualties	
Nov 22	Mirage 5EF	killed	S/L Bilal Babri, near Jhang, on a night sortie; No. 25 Sqn
Aug 16	Saab AEWC	none	Terror attack #10049 writeoff Minhas AB
?	Mi-17	1 killed	
2013			
May 13	F-7	pilot survived	Near Mianwali during training
Nov 21	Mirage III	pilot killed	Punjab
2014			
Jan 16	Mirage 3D		
Apr 16	Mirage		
June 04	Mirage 5DD	2 killed	#04-003 Karachi. W/C Khurram Sammad, S/L Umair Elahi
Dec 01	Mirage 5	1 safe	w/o Punjab Province
2015			
May 18	Mi-17	8 killed, 12 injured	Gilgit
Apr 16	Mirage	1 safe	Baluchistan
Mar 03	Mirage	2 killed	At Dera Ismail Khan
May 25	K-8	2 safe	Swabi District, Khyber Pakthoonwala
Nov 24	F-7PG	1 dead	#03-689 F/O Mariam Mukhtiar, 1st female pilot loss, S/L Muhammad Hussain survived; pilots saved plane from crashing into populated area; Kundian, Punjab
2016			
Sep 27	JF-17	written off	Possibly 15-209
Oct 18	Mirage 3EL		00-910 No. 22 Squadron
2017			
May 02			00-904 No. 22 Squadron
2018			
Jul 14	Mirage	1 killed	Near Masroor AB
Sep		1 killed	PAF, Khyber Agency

Nov 09	C-130E 65-12905		Chaklala tyre burst landing; hit wall. W/O 6 Sqdn
2019			
July 30	Army		5 crew reportedly killed + civilians on ground
2020			
Jan 07	FT-7P	2 killed	# 90-611 S/L Haris bin Khalid, F/O Ibaadur No. 18 Squadron Rehman near Mianwali
Feb 07	Mirage 5		W/O
Feb 12	MFI 395	2 safe	Takhat Bhai, Mardan, Army
Feb 15	Mirage 3/5		Shorkot Road
Mar 11	F-16	1 killed	#92- 0406 Shakarparin, Islamabad Wing Com Nauman Akram rehearsing for parade
Sept 15	JF-17	1 safe	#17-241 Pindi Gheb Near Attock No. 14 Sqn
Oct 07	JF-17	1 safe	Attock
	3 x JF-17	3 killed	https://www.globaldefensecorp.com/2020/10/05/pakistan-air-force-jf-17-jet-crashes/ says a total of 5 F-17 crashes have taken place since January 2020 3 killed, two safe
2021			
Apr 13	Mushshak	2 killed	Army. Major Umer, Lt. Faizan; near Gujarat
Aug 06	JF-17B	both safe	#20-614 Near Attock while training
2022			
Mar 22	?	2 killed	Trg a/c, Peshawar
May 17	2 x Mushshak	4 killed	Risalpur, formation flying. S/L Syed Masood Rizvi & S/L and Zaigham Abbas instructors; F/L Mustafa & S/Lr Moazzam were trainees
May 25	FT-7P	pilot safe	Near Mianwali, flying solo
Aug 01	Heli AS 350	6 killed	Flood relief, Las Bela Baluchistan, GOC XII Corps killed
Sep 26	Heli 412EP	6 killed	Army, near Khost
Nov 22	Mirage	1 killed	S/L Tanvir Ahmed, near Karachi

2023			
Feb 08	MFI-395	2 safe	Mardan, Khyber
Mar 23	?	2 killed	Peshawar
Sep 23	Helio	3 killed	Navy, Gwadar
2024			
Feb 12	MFI-395	2 safe	Nowshera

Notes

1. See for example Strategy World.com (2013, January 9). "Pakistan Air Force crumbling away". Strategypage.com Downloaded July 6, 2013. http://www.strategypage.com/htmw/htatrit/20121227.aspx. The figures given in the article are higher than the estimate made here.
2. Duggy The F-89 Scorpion. https://axis-and-allies-paintworks.com/e107_plugins/forum/forum_viewtopic.php?id=18745?last=1. I have seen a 389 accident rate but don't still have the reference.
3. Those Were the Days: Flying Safety during the Transition to Jets, 1944-53 Kenneth P. Werrell Air Power History, Vol. 52, No. 4 (Winter 2005), pp. 38-53 (16 pages). https://www.jstor.org/stable/26274695?read-now=1&seq=12#page_scan_tab_contents
4. Nicholas Cummins. (2019, August 9). When Does An Aircraft Get Written Off? https://simpleflying.com/when-aircraft-written-off
5. https://www.globaldefensecorp.com/2020/10/05/pakistan-air-force-jf-17-jet-crashes/
6. See for example Strategy World.com (2013, January 9, article dated December 12, 2012). "Pakistan Air Force crumbling away". Strategypage.com http://www.strategypage.com/htmw/htatrit/20121227.aspx. The accident rate given is too high; nonetheless, the reasons given for the high accident rate are correct.
7. Aviation Safety Network. (Updated to 12 March 2024. https//aviation-safety.net
8. All F-104A data from Hubert Peitzmeier (2022, June 19) http://www.916-starfighter.de/F-104_PAF_web.htm has details on nine RJAF F-104 sent to Masroor, December 13 1971, too late to be of much use. See also Shabbar and Mazhar, op.cit. page 7 for 104A/B delivery dates.
9. Paffalcons.com gives the aircraft as an MFI-17 trainer. As far as we know the plane does not have ejection seats.

10. According to CIA report 6 AM EDT 8 September 1965, Pakistan admitted loss of six aircraft during war so far, (India admitted 8). US CIA (1965, September 8). Redacted report No. OCI 1989/65 Office of Current Intelligence Report #19 "The India-Pakistan situation". Released 2006. We have 9 aircraft lost in the war as of September 7.

Appendix III

A note on Pakistan's acquisition of Canadair Mk.6 Sabre from Iran in 1965

Though this subject is outside the scope of this book, it's worth relating that Iran says PAF received 60, not 90 Sabre Mk. 6 (ex-Luftwaffe) from Iran. The story is related in Duncan Curtis's book on the F-86.[1]

Still there are so many twists and turns to this story that I would not dispute that, as said in the book, 80 were delivered to Iran. Curtis further says that according to the Iranians, sixty went to Pakistan of which 40 were retained. The problem with research is that one cannot rest on satisficing, the first 'good enough' answer. And here we have Usman Shabbir & Yawar Mazhar's history of the PAF,[2] which tells us in 1971 the PAF had 74 F-86Es, which is what it called the Sabre 6. It was more advanced than the F model and equipped four squadrons. Allowing for losses over five years, it does seem that a number equal to or greater than 80 aircraft must have been delivered. Then *Scramble*[3] gives 96 serials for the CL-13-1B as the Sabre 6 was technically known; of which 4 are listed as FAKE, but of these, three are then listed as 'preserved.' So, we're now at 95 aircraft!

Notes

1. Duncan Curtis (2000). North American F-86 Sabre, pp. 166-168. Crowood Press, UK. 202 pages. You can read the book free online at Scribd https://www.scribd.com/document/195586267/North-American-F-86-Sabre with a guest login.
2. Usman Shabbir & Yawar Mazhar. (2003.) Eagles of Destiny: Volume 2 - Growth and Wars of the Pakistani Air Force 1956-1971 Asia@War series by Helion, UK.

3. https://www.scramble.nl/database/military/pk#results. By the way, to see more than 30 listings for a specific type you have to pay for a modest subscription. Be sure to type in the Canadian name CL-13-1B in this particular case.

Index

139
RESCUE
1. PUSH BUTTON TO OPEN DOOR
2. PULL HANDLE OUT 15 FEET TO
SHATTER CANOPY
JF-17 Fighter